HOW TO GENERATE RETIREMENT INCOME

A Practical Guide to Paying Yourself

in Your Golden Years

Mark Sharp, CFP®

Acknowledgments

To my incredibly supportive mother, who always believed in me and encouraged me to follow my dreams. Thank you for your love and support, which have meant everything to me. I am so grateful to have you as my mother and closest friend.

To my steadfast father, who always nurtured my relentless curiosity. Thank you for your wisdom, your friendship, and your love. I am so lucky to have had you as my father and friend.

To the two of you, who have given me so much. I am privileged to have shared this journey with you.

A heartfelt tribute goes to my friend and mentor, Justamona, whose courage, drive, and vision inspired me to always strive for success.

I dedicate this book to all of you.

Preface

Growing up in a small family in the Midwest, I saw how grandparents and friends of the family approached and went through retirement. Because their employers largely paid for retirement, they did not face the challenges confronting retirees today, who must not only figure out how much to save and where to invest those savings but must also find a way to generate income to live comfortably in retirement without running out of money.

Skills, such as saving diligently and investing wisely, that had served them well before retirement proved less useful in retirement, where finding effective strategies to transform savings into lifelong income grew in importance. As I began my career, I realized people retiring today need guidance on creating steady income with their accumulated wealth. Therefore, I decided to dedicate my focus to helping them find viable pathways to transition from saving and investing to spending in retirement.

After nearly a decade of working in financial services as a certified financial planner and retirement income strategist, I started gathering my most valuable insights and advice into what would eventually become this book. I hope to provide readers with the tools and knowledge they need to make informed decisions about using their financial resources to create dependable income in retirement.

Contents

Introduction

As members of the baby boomer generation continue to cross the retirement threshold—many without a traditional pension plan—they must now address the other side of the retirement equation: turning their accumulated savings into an income stream. The overriding question for many is, "How can I bridge the gap between my financial resources and a comfortable retirement?". Now the emphasis gradually shifts from the accumulation phase to the drawdown phase, as it's no longer just about obtaining a paycheck to pay for living expenses. The transition from saving to spending in retirement is challenging because the aptitude for saving is more developed than that for spending. It will be essential for retirement households to find solutions to generate steady cash flow from assets accumulated while working to pay for retirement expenses.

Saving for retirement is a skill many people have strived for over the years. Some have done this more effectively than others. Knowing how to use these savings once retired requires skill as well. The key to a successful retirement is saving enough money *and* creating lasting income from that money. The retirement journey is best visualized as someone climbing a mountain to reach the summit and return safely.

An ascent corresponds to saving, while a descent corresponds to spending. No matter how you look at it, the journey is perilous. Spending too much in retirement or saving too little before retirement can spell trouble.

If you have reached the summit, you have saved money wisely. But don't take a victory lap yet. Your work is halfway done. Now comes the tough part: deciding how to descend the mountain safely--or how to spend down assets as long as retirement lasts.

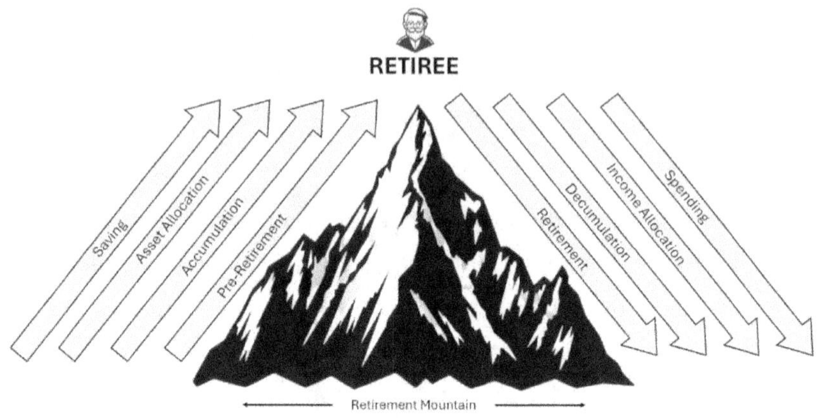

Experienced climbers know that the descent of a mountain is often more treacherous than the ascent. From fatigue to gravity to human biology to accidents, many factors contribute to this. A British Medical Journal study found that 73 percent of Mt. Everest's climbers died after ascending higher than 8,000 meters, 56 percent died on their descent, and 17 percent died after turning back. Similarly, retirement is riddled with obstacles, such as unknown time horizons, unpredictable market returns, rising inflation, fluctuating taxes, and other risks not encountered while working that could prove disastrous for an otherwise well-thought-out retirement.

Planning for retirement is difficult because no one knows how long it will last. How many years are we talking about? 20, 30, 40 or longer? It is impossible to know.

People often get tripped up here since the skills they developed when saving for retirement are less useful when spending. It is now important to create income to live comfortably in retirement without running out of money.

What must the soon-to-retire and newly retired do if they lack these skills to descend the mountain successfully?

Here, well-thought-out income planning serves as a guide for descending the mountain and plays an important role. This area of financial planning focuses on managing spending and risks to meet income needs for as long as possible to maintain a desired standard of living, preserve liquidity for unexpected expenses, and leave a legacy – all you'll need to do to get back down the mountain.

It will be essential for retirees to find ways to bridge the gulf between their resources and a comfortable lifestyle. This starts with an income strategy that optimizes the use of various assets to balance the spending goals with minimal risks.

For example, Sam, a 65-year-old married male with a pension, savings, Social Security, and modest spending goals, has concerns about running out of money, rising inflation, and unpredictability in healthcare costs. He wants to find an income strategy to meet his spending goals for as long as necessary while reducing inflation and protecting against unknown healthcare costs at the same time.

In Sam's case, what is the best course of action?

Sam should learn the four main spending goals in retirement. These are longevity (the income to cover day-to-day expenses), liquidity (the income to meet life's unexpected expenses), lifestyle (the income to fund the things that make life fun, like hobbies, travel, education, and philanthropy), and legacy (the income to pass along to future generations).

He should know that moving from saving for retirement to spending that savings will require him to navigate the practical challenges and overcome the psychological barriers involved in retirement finances.

He must find ways to fund the various spending goals and manage the risks to those goals. Retirement brings with it both familiar and new risks.

He should consider the risks associated with life expectancy. Having a long life is wonderful, but it does come at a price, including higher living expenses, increased healthcare-related costs, and increased exposure to other risks.

He should consider some facts: When relying on unpredictable market returns, it can be difficult to create reliable income since market volatility can cause income fluctuations that disrupt spending plans. To maintain his standard of living, he must increase his income over time due to inflation.

A solution must be found for him to deal with spending shocks such as health emergencies, an unexpected need for long-term care, housing and housing-related costs, the loss of a spouse, or other events that create higher-than-anticipated spending needs that can undermine financial security as assets are diverted to meet the expenses.

For these reasons, and many more we'll discuss here, retirement income planning, not retirement saving planning, is arguably the more important aspect of retirement.

Why retirement income planning is important:

> *Planning equals success.* Those who plan are more successful, worry less, and report more life satisfaction.

> *Insufficient income streams.* Most people today don't have enough Social Security or company pension income to meet their needs alone, placing added importance on transforming other assets into additional income streams.

> *It's complex.* There are income needs, other financial goals, and retirement risks to consider in an ever-changing environment demanding quick and effective responses.

> *Stakes are high.* Failure means running out of money at an older age when it is too late to do anything about it. Financial security is much more achievable earlier in retirement than later.

> ➤ ***Income matters, not wealth.*** Retirement planning has been centered around growing assets rather than spending assets, leaving many ill-prepared to navigate how to turn these assets into income.

You may be wondering how to generate steady cash flow from savings, what plans you must make to transition from saving to spending, or how you will pay yourself when you retire. This book offers a unique approach to finding answers to these questions and more using retirement income planning to support a successful transition to retirement. You will gain insight, motivation, and creative inspiration to apply to your retirement.

My goal in writing this book isn't to alarm you, only to give you a healthy appreciation of the challenge ahead of achieving your spending goals while protecting those goals from harm. It's doable but not easy. A successful transition from work to retirement will require additional knowledge, new skills, and a different mindset than while working.

Retirement saving is a top concern for most people, and that's good. However, retirement is not so much about how much you have accumulated but how you intend to spend it. Many people only focus on growing assets to secure a comfortable retirement, and little attention is given to how to spend those assets wisely. As the title suggests, this book outlines a detailed process for determining how to generate retirement income if you are not sure how.

What are the Learning Goals?

After reading this book, you will gain knowledge of the following:

> ➤ Learn effective ways to turn your assets into income.
>
> ➤ Learn when retirement will be a reality by quantifying your assets and liabilities.
>
> ➤ Learn risk management techniques to protect assets and achieve spending goals.

> ➢ Learn best practices for managing taxes to reduce costs, extend asset life, and maximize spending.

> ➢ Learn strategies to optimize efficiencies to boost spending and increase wealth.

How to Use the Material

This book provides a structured learning path for those deciding how to use their retirement funds. It takes a building-block approach where individual components or "blocks" are developed or addressed separately and then combined to create a larger structure and solution. Imagine building a LEGO set, where each brick represents a stand-alone component. When pieced together in the right order and configuration, they form a larger structure that is greater than the individual parts.

In a similar fashion, each chapter in this book builds upon the previous and sets the stage for the next. A good way to make sure you get the most from the material is to read it through from beginning to end. Depending on your knowledge level and where you are on your retirement income planning journey, you may wish to focus on the material most relevant to your situation and skim the less relevant content.

Chapter 1 is foundational material important to subsequent chapters, and it's one chapter you don't want to skip. We'll review the role income biases play on income preferences, and how they influence your income style, which is indicative of how you intend to use your assets to fund retirement. We next establish the all-important connection between income style and income strategy in Chapter 2.

Here, we compare and contrast the four major retirement income strategies used to source income during retirement. You'll learn new ways to generate income during retirement, tailored to your income preferences and aligned to your income style.

You cannot plan effectively for retirement unless you know how much you have available and can spend in retirement. Chapter 3 contains pivotal material to learn how to assess these amounts. Chapter 4 focuses on the risks that affect spending goals, the taxes that can erode purchasing power, and the efficiencies that can boost spending and legacy amounts. We'll review strategies to mitigate risk, manage taxes, and maximize efficiencies.

Creating income in retirement is the major theme of this book, and Chapter 5 discusses how to go about it. This chapter examines why you shouldn't count on traditional income strategies to turn your assets into income, and why profiling your income preferences is the best way to identify an income strategy to create income.

Chapter 6 brings all the key material from the previous chapters into a coherent and comprehensive retirement income plan to serve as a blueprint for how to approach, transition into, and navigate your way to live your best retirement.

How We'll Cover it

The material will be presented through the eyes of a fictitious couple, David and Dawn Banner, who are at the end of their careers and in the home stretch to retirement. They have accumulated savings and invested well and are seeking guidance on creating secure, stable, and sustainable income.

This case study will give you a greater appreciation and understanding of retirement income planning, its practical applications, how to use it in retirement, and what to consider when seeking outside assistance.

Planning for a rewarding retirement is hard work. You should not look for shortcuts here. If you want something sugar-coated, grab a donut. However, if you'd like to learn a real-world, systematic approach to draw income from your assets efficiently and with the least amount of risk, you're in the right place. And maybe grab that donut to enjoy while you read.

Whatever stage you're at in planning your retirement, one thing remains true: you must figure out how to generate steady cash flow from your financial resources to support your lifestyle over your remaining lifetime. Hopefully, this book will be useful as a roadmap in your endeavor.

CHAPTER 1

Income Preferences Matter

"To crave the result, but not the process is to guarantee disappointment."

— JAMES CLEAR

Learning Objectives

➤ What Got You Here Won't Get You Much Farther

➤ Examine Your Income Beliefs to Learn Your Income Preferences

➤ What are Income Preferences?

➤ Preferences, Styles, and Strategies Matter

➤ What Income Preferences Mean for Spending

➤ Assess Your Income Beliefs to Determine Your Preferences

➤ Case Study: How the Banners Identify Their Income Preferences, Style, and Strategy

The path to success in retirement is neither straight nor clear. Many believe retiring depends largely on the savings rate, retirement date, planning horizon, and when to take Social Security. Though these things must be carefully considered, they pale compared to the decision one must make about how to draw income from the assets accumulated while working to fund retirement. This starts with choosing an income strategy.

Choosing the best strategy for you is not an easy task. It is most effective to first identify your preferences on how to receive income and let those guide you to an appropriate strategy. You'll also need to examine your beliefs about income and potentially reconsider them.

What Got You Here Won't Get You Much Farther

The transition to retirement presents several challenges. You must formulate a strategy to transform your financial resources into income that may span multiple decades. Furthermore, you must contend with issues like market volatility, spending shocks, and longevity-issues that were once irrelevant or easier to solve.

Aside from this, you may also experience a shift in priorities during retirement. Your focus might shift from growing the nest egg to preserving it, with the goal of maintaining sufficient cash flow to meet spending needs. You may think more about your legacy while maintaining your living standard and sufficient liquidity in case of unexpected expenses. Perhaps it's something else completely. Being in retirement can feel different from expectations you had beforehand.

You may need to abandon investment strategies that worked well before retirement but could be detrimental in retirement. This might mean investing with a mindset that aims to fund spending goals with the highest net return for the level of risk rather than simply getting the highest returns to accumulate assets.

The defined-benefit pension, once one of the most common sources of retirement income, is less common today. A greater burden of spending is placed on other assets.

Retirement costs increase as retirement lengthens. The longer we live, the more years we need income to remain comfortable.

It may be necessary to rethink taxes since strategies that were effective while working may not be available or as effective.

As you transition from pre-retirement to post-retirement, you'll need to be flexible and open to exploring new ideas that may not be familiar to you but will be invaluable to your retirement.

Retirement is not the end of a journey but a new beginning. We tend to undervalue the importance of effectively drawing down assets in retirement. However, it will be crucial to maintain a desirable lifestyle and financial security. The approach determines success. You can have either an income or a withdrawal mindset. There is a difference, and it can have a significant impact.

Someone with a withdrawal mindset will likely view the 4% rule, which is designed to provide retirees with a way to determine how much they can safely withdraw from their retirement savings each year without risk of depletion, as the only viable means of sourcing income from invested assets. The 4% Rule is an example of a withdrawal strategy that seeks to balance financial needs with the longevity of an investment portfolio. The strategy focuses on preserving the value of the portfolio while providing income. Several risks are associated with this view of how to spend down assets, and the singular focus on meeting spending goals without considering other factors might threaten the ability to reach those goals.

By contrast, an income mindset emphasizes income strategies designed to balance goals and protect against risks. The first mindset ignores and downplays risks, while this one incorporates them as a key component of retirement planning.

The most important thing you can take away from this book is the need for a comprehensive income solution to generate income to fund retirement while protecting that income from risks. To expand the possibilities to solutions for achieving better retirement planning outcomes, entrenched ideas about how you do this must be dislodged. This starts by identifying and leaning into your income preferences to reveal an income style resulting in the income solution that is right for you.

Examine Your Income Beliefs to Learn Your Income Preferences

Any discussion about income strategies must begin with income preferences. But we must start with our income beliefs to determine our income preferences. These beliefs are rooted in our financial biases affecting our decision-making.

What are biases, why do biases exist, and how do they work? Biases are cognitive or emotional tendencies that predispose us to take certain actions over others. We use them to cope with the everyday stress of decision-making. Education, experience, and upbringing shaped them. They include guidelines, best practices, and rules of thumb that we use as shortcuts to solve minor problems or to narrow options down when there are many. Although these biases can be quite effective in simple, day-to-day decision-making, they can be counterproductive to our ability to make effective decisions for more complex retirement decisions.

Let's look at common financial biases:

1. *Confirmation Bias*: the tendency to seek out and interpret information to confirm existing attitudes and beliefs. **Indicative of someone who avoids information contrary to their beliefs.**

2. *Loss Aversion*: the tendency to feel the pain of losses more strongly than the pleasure of gains, leading to action that avoids losses, often at the expense of potential gains. **Indicative of someone who is too concerned with loss to take worthwhile risks.**

3. *Anchoring Bias*: the tendency to rely too heavily on the first piece of information received when making decisions, when all information should be considered. **Indicative of someone giving disproportionate weight to an initial piece of information.**

4. *Overconfidence Bias*: the tendency to underestimate risks and overestimate abilities, resulting in excessive risk-taking or overconfidence in financial decisions. **Indicative of someone equating investing success with success in other parts of life.**

5. *Framing Bias*: the tendency to be influenced by how information is presented or framed. *For example, an investor is presented with the following investment options regarding a 10-year U.S. Treasury bond: a) The bond offers a 10% fixed return yearly. b) The investor's money will double in 10 years.*

The first option is phrased positively for those seeking a secure, steady income stream. In contrast, the second option may have negative connotations if investors are reluctant to lock up their money for 10 years.

Understanding these biases and how they influence our income beliefs is paramount, since they can affect how we approach and arrive at solutions, whether buying a home, paying for a college education, or deciding how to source income in retirement. Although awareness alone does not guarantee success, it reduces the chances we'll make erroneous planning decisions since we know our tendencies and how they affect our decisions.

Armed with this insight, we'll be in a much better position to sidestep errors and mistakes that can plague retirement, such as choosing the wrong strategy, ignoring risks, overpaying taxes, or introducing inefficiencies.

Despite our best efforts, biases influence our income beliefs, which inform our decisions and influence our retirement planning outcomes.

A confirmation bias could lead someone to conclude that spending from invested assets is the only way to fund retirement when better alternatives exist.

Due to a loss aversion bias, someone might invest too conservatively, prioritizing capital preservation over growth. This could result in their portfolios not keeping up with inflation over time, thus eroding their purchasing power.

You can fall victim to overconfidence bias by incorrectly believing you can fund retirement using an income-focused investment strategy when a total-return strategy is more practical.

A person with framing bias might discount creating time-segmented buckets of retirement income as an acceptable funding strategy because they perceive it as too conservative and a loss of control.

An anchoring bias may lead people to cling to losing solutions that performed well in the past or prematurely abandon winning strategies that haven't delivered results yet.

Income beliefs have a strong influence on financial decision-making, which in turn affects income preferences.

As we work through retirement income planning, we must consider how these income beliefs impact income preferences.

What are Income Preferences?

They describe how someone feels about using their financial resources to generate a steady cash flow during retirement. They can be shaped by various factors, including biases, beliefs, cultural and societal norms, personal experiences, and financial education. Their impact on retirement is undeniable. Importantly, they can assist us in finding the most appropriate income-generation method, indicate how much and for how long we can spend, and predict whether our efforts will be successful.

Whether consciously or unconsciously, they play a key role in retirement income. Their impact can be felt in how someone prioritizes sources of income, invests and manages their savings, addresses the most important risks, and which solutions are used to transform wealth into income to meet retirement spending goals. We should take them into consideration when deciding how to allocate and use our financial resources in the way that is most comfortable for us.

This chart shows typical income preferences as a range from one end of the spectrum to the other for each line.

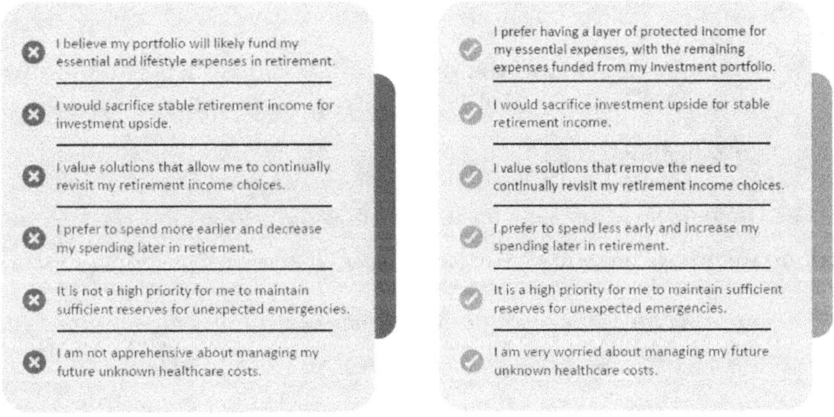

Income strategies based on considering preferences, beliefs, and biases heavily influence favorable retirement spending outcomes. Besides determining how much to save for retirement, deciding how to turn what you have saved into income will likely be the most crucial retirement planning decision you will ever have to make.

Income preferences reflect your concerns, goals, and priorities for creating retirement income.

We will have a whole subchapter dedicated to helping you identify your income beliefs and preferences. First, we will explore the relationship between income preferences, styles, and strategies and their impact on retirement spending.

Preferences, Styles, and Strategies Matter

A person's income preferences, associated style, and preferred strategy in retirement are interconnected and a vital component of ensuring financial stability and achieving retirement goals. These are closely linked when it comes to retirement.

- ➢ **Income Preferences** refer to the views someone holds on how they desire to use their financial resources to generate a steady cash flow in retirement.

- ➢ **Income Style** defines a particular philosophy for sourcing retirement income in accordance with a person's income preferences.

- ➢ **Income Strategy** refers to a specific solution to balance goals and protect against risks associated with an income style.

Income preferences reflect the concerns, goals, and priorities for creating income during retirement. A particular income style can be determined based on these preferences, and the income strategy that best aligns with that style is chosen. Two broad factors, *Probability-Based vs. Safety-First* and *Optionality vs. Commitment,* are influenced by income preferences and have the greatest predictive power on income style. By examining these two factors we can largely surmise how someone feels about using their financial resources to generate steady cash flow during retirement.

The Probability-Based factor assumes positive market returns from invested assets will subsidize future expenses. It focuses on leveraging the long-term growth potential of a diversified investment portfolio or assets with the expectation of growth to fund retirement.

This will appeal to those who believe in the long-term growth potential of the financial markets to provide a continuous and sustainable retirement income stream.

Key characteristics of the Probability-Based factor include:

> ***Withdrawal Strategy***: Taking systematic payouts from the investment portfolio to meet income needs.

> ***Risks***: Exposure to market fluctuations results in spending volatility.

> ***Flexibility and Growth***: Solutions that provide flexibility and growth potential are preferred over those that do not.

> ***Net Worth vs. Stable Income***: A willingness to forego stable income for investment upside.

In contrast, the Safety-First factor emphasizes funding essential retirement expenses to the greatest extent possible from guaranteed income sources. It stems from a belief that contractual-based income sources help protect income needs regardless of the economic outlook throughout retirement. These income sources are characterized by less flexibility and limited growth but greater downside spending protections. Compared with non-guaranteed income sources characteristic of the Probability-Based factor, these relatively secure sources are less sensitive to market swings, resulting in more predictable spending. These include defined benefit pensions, annuities with lifetime income protections, government bonds held to maturity, and Social Security.

Key characteristics of the Safety-First factor include:

> ***Withdrawal Strategy***: Seek reliable and predictable income from sources contractually obligated to provide a fixed stream of payments throughout retirement.

> ➢ *Income Floor*: Aim to establish a secure floor of income to cover essential expenses to maintain a desired lifestyle even in challenging economic times.

> ➢ *Risks*: Level lifetime income payments reduce the risk of outliving assets but increase the risk of inflation since payments may not keep pace with rising living costs.

> ➢ *Net Worth vs. Stable Income*: Willingness to forego investment upside for stable income.

Because many retirees have accumulated assets for retirement in defined contribution retirement savings accounts, such as 401(k)s or IRAs, a Probability-Based factor is generally preferred over a Safety-First factor. Still, it's important to remember that they aren't mutually exclusive and can be combined to maximize the benefits of each. The choice often depends on personal factors such as income, expected expenses, health status, family situation, risk preference, etc. The first projects income, the second guarantees it.

Next, we must consider the second factor of Optionality versus Commitment. This reflects someone's desire to keep options open and maintain flexibility to adapt to changing external conditions and personal circumstances versus a preference for locking in a long-term solution that eliminates the need to revisit the strategy.

A key characteristic of Optionality is embracing strategies that maintain flexibility to make new choices in the face of evolving economic or personal circumstances.

A hallmark of Commitment is determining strategies upfront that solve a lifetime income need and removing the burden of having to do so in the future.

The following attributes characterize the Optionality versus Commitment factors.

Commitment

> *Inflexible Withdrawal Strategies*: Locks in income less flexible to adjust to changing income needs.

> *Fixed Income Investment Focus*: Requires investing in fixed-income securities, such as annuities, bonds, or certificates of deposit, that provide stable payments.

> *Higher Inflation Exposure*: Level income payments may not keep up with rising prices of goods and services.

Optionality

> *Flexible Withdrawal Strategies*: Increased flexibility to adjust withdrawals to adapt to changing income needs.

> *Diversified Investment Portfolio Focus*: Places emphasis on maintaining a diversified portfolio to maximize investment growth.

> *Higher Market Exposure*: A focus on growth potential and flexibility with an increased vulnerability to market volatility.

> *Lower Inflation Exposure*: Increasing prices of goods and services may be kept in check by flexible income payments.

In contrast to Probability-Based & Safety-First factors, which are not mutually exclusive and can be combined as needed, Optionality and Commitment are mutually exclusive, reflecting distinct income factors that do not overlap.

The two choices often depend on risk tolerance, desire for payment guarantees, and flexibility requirements.

Income styles are formed by the intersection of Probability-Based vs. Safety-First (PS) and Optionality vs. Commitment (OC) factors.

Other factors cannot be ignored, but these two are most predictive of someone's income style and subsequent income strategy. These other factors will be discussed later.

Using these two factor groupings, we can distinguish four income styles (or personalities) applicable to retirement income as indicated in Exhibit 1.0

1. **Probability-Based & Optionality (PO)** are characterized by solutions that source income from market-based assets focusing on total returns to maximize upside growth and investing flexibility.

2. **Probability-Based & Commitment (PC)** solutions combine contractually guaranteed income sources to build a floor of income to cover essential expenses while relying on non-guaranteed income sources to cover discretionary expenses.

3. **Safety-First & Optionality (SO)** solutions are characterized by establishing time-segmented layers of retirement income to last for a certain number of years, using fewer volatile assets with limited flexibility and low growth prospects for short-term spending needs, and assets with greater volatility, high flexibility, and increased growth potential for long-term spending needs.

4. **Safety-First & Commitment (SC)** solutions emphasize guaranteed income sources that provide downside spending protections for essentials with limited flexibility while deploying investable assets for discretionary expenses with greater flexibility.

Exhibit 1.0 Retirement Income Style Awareness Matrix

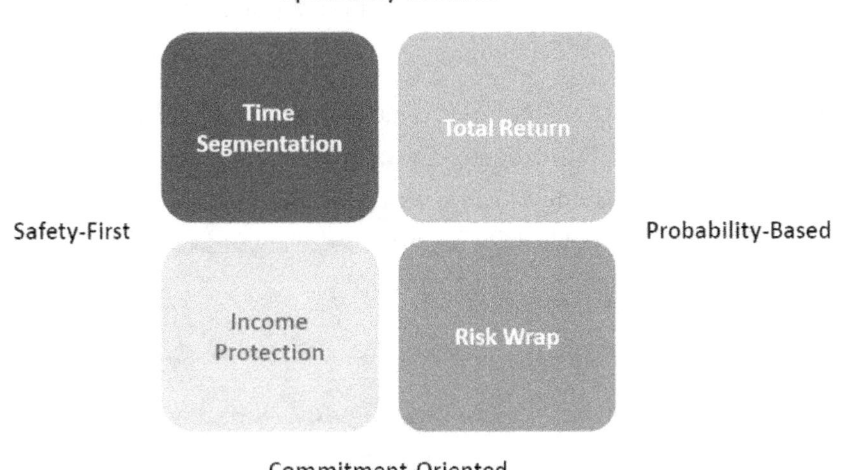

Source: RISA, LLC

In simple terms, Probability-Based vs. Safety-First (PS) describes the origin of retirement income, while Optionality vs. Commitment (OC) indicates the degree of flexibility desired.

My experience working with a couple, Justin and Renee, in their first year of retirement, exemplifies the importance of understanding where income comes from. They needed to be more aware of how fast their retirement savings were being spent as they were spending too much to maintain their lifestyle through retirement with their existing income stream. It became obvious that retirement would be anything but enjoyable without a substantial cash infusion or reductions in spending. Hearing their concerns, understanding their spending goals, and reviewing their assets made it apparent that their Total Return income strategy, indicative of the Probability-Based & Optionality income style that relies on reasonably good market returns to support spending, did not reflect their beliefs and preferences about income.

Through the assessment of their income preferences and identification of their income style, we were able to select and implement an income strategy aligned with their income preferences that would create income they couldn't outlive while maintaining a comfortable standard of living.

Four Secondary factors of Time-Based vs. Perpetuity (TP), Accumulation vs. Distribution (AD), Front-Loading vs. Back-Loading Income (FB) , and True vs. Technical Liquidity (TT) provide further refinement of income styles. While important, they have been shown to have less impact than the two primary income factors.

Time-Based vs. Perpetuity (TP)

Time-Based mindset focuses on funding fixed windows of time in retirement, while perpetuity-based mindset focuses on building income for life.

Accumulation vs. Distribution (AD)

Accumulation mindset emphasizes growing retirement assets, whereas distribution mindset implies maximizing portfolio distributions and income at the expense of maximizing returns.

Front-Loading vs. Back-Loading Income (FB)

A Front-Loading Income mindset would embrace structuring distributions to allow higher spending early in retirement, as opposed to a Back-Loading Income mindset that would prefer spending less in early retirement to avoid having to make spending cuts later.

True vs. Technical Liquidity (TT)

Those who prefer True Liquidity would like to have assets earmarked as reserves for future unexpected spending while those who prefer Technical Liquidity would rather raise cash for unexpected expenses from assets that are earmarked for other goals, as necessary—with an understanding that cuts may then need to be made elsewhere.

Exhibit 1.1 represents the mapping between retirement income beliefs & preferences and income styles & income strategies in light of the factors we discussed earlier.

Notice the beliefs and preferences on the left-hand side each impact your personal income style to result in an income strategy. These strategies are explained below the chart. Even though an income style helps you identify how you want to generate income in retirement, it won't tell you how to achieve it.

You'll need to match your income style with the appropriate income strategy. Doing so increases the likelihood that you will adhere to the strategy when you are tempted to abandon it, because you'll understand why you chose it in the first place.

Exhibit 1.1

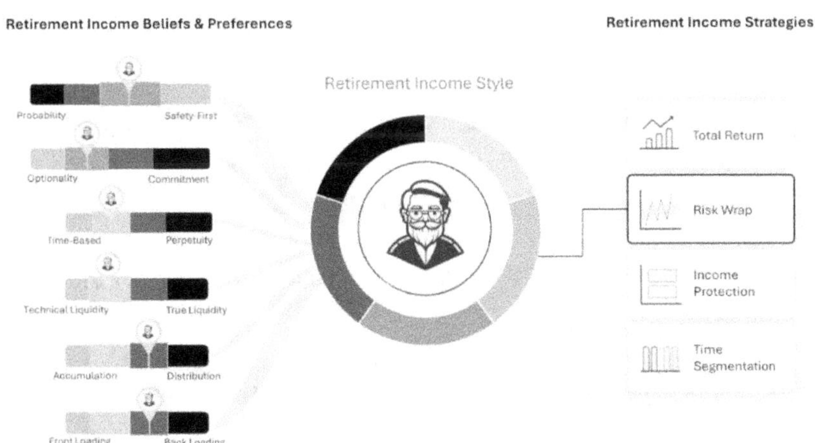

Source: RISA, LLC

INCOME STRATEGIES

- ➤ **Total-Return**: This strategy relies on systematic withdrawals from a diversified investment portfolio to meet essential and discretionary spending.

- ➤ **Risk-Wrap**: This strategy seeks to build a secure floor of income through income sources, offering guaranteed lifetime withdrawal benefits for essential spending needs combined with a diversified investment portfolio to meet discretionary spending needs.

- ➤ **Income Protection**: This strategy uses guaranteed income sources like Social Security, pension benefits, and annuities that provide a lifetime stream of income to cover essential spending needs, combined with a diversified investment portfolio to meet discretionary spending needs.

- ➤ **Time Segmentation**: This strategy divides financial assets into segments to provide income during predetermined time periods. Short-term segments hold the most secure income sources to meet immediate spending needs, intermediate segments hold moderately secure income sources for near-term spending needs, and a diversified investment portfolio is held in the long-term segment for distant spending needs.

Overall, income preference, style, and strategy are important when planning retirement income.

Understanding these concepts and how they relate can help individuals make more informed decisions regarding how to generate income from their financial resources.

A diagram of the relationship between income strategy and style is shown in Exhibit 1.2

Exhibit 1.2

Source: RISA, LLC

What Income Preferences Mean for Spending

Several plausible approaches exist to solve the retirement income puzzle. Still, one that aligns with retirement income preferences and style is the best place to start. The significance of retirement income preferences on retirement spending can be seen in several ways:

1. *Income availability*: Retirement income preferences can impact the availability of income. For example, someone more reliant on fixed levels of income from guaranteed sources such as annuities, pensions, or Social Security benefits may have less income to spend than someone reliant on investments that offer higher growth and spending potential.

2. *Income predictability*: Retirement income preferences can also impact income predictability during retirement. For instance, someone with guaranteed sources has a predictable income stream throughout retirement. In contrast, someone who relies on invested assets may experience more volatility in their income, resulting in less predictable income.

3. *Income flexibility*: Retirement income preferences can also impact income flexibility. Guaranteed income sources like annuities and pensions may provide a guaranteed income but limit flexibility to adjust the amount. Market-based invested assets offer greater flexibility to adjust spending as needs change due to their growth potential.

4. *Income sustainability*: Retirement income preferences can also impact the reliability of income. Someone who receives protected income sources that provide lifetime benefits is less concerned with running out of money, while someone drawing income from volatile invested assets is frequently concerned about running out of money.

5. ***Retirement costs:*** Retirement income preferences can also impact the overall cost of retirement. For example, someone with an annuity to hedge the risk of outliving their ability to pay for retirement may do so at a much lower overall cost than someone trying to insure against this risk alone.

6. ***Income strategy:*** Retirement income preferences can determine the most appropriate solution to generate income from assets.

It's important to note that retirement income preferences can change over time due to personal factors such as income, expected expenses, health status, family situation, and risk preference, and individuals may need to adjust their retirement income strategy and plan accordingly.

Assess Your Income Beliefs to Determine Your Preferences

Turning your financial resources into income is straightforward but not easy. But if you intend to fulfill your retirement objectives in a way most aligned with how you feel, you must engage in the right approach.

Without question, the primary goal in retirement is to have enough money for as long as retirement lasts. This differs greatly from the goal before retirement, where accumulating enough wealth to maintain spending during retirement took precedence. As important as that goal was then, the focus now shifts to preserving and using that wealth to create predictable and reliable income in retirement.

Your best chance of creating lasting income in a manner you are most comfortable with is to understand your income preferences. I might sound like a broken record here, but it's vital to overcome our biases, be open to new ideas, and be willing to adopt new techniques.

How you decide to pay yourself in retirement is made all the more difficult because traditional tools, like risk tolerance questionnaires (RTQ) used to quantify investment risk, often overlook the things that matter in retirement, such as having to spend down assets over an unknown period of time, which can have a greater impact on income than investment risk alone.

These tools, by design, hyperfocus on a single aspect of retirement – market volatility – at the expense of other factors such as spending longevity, inflation, healthcare, and spending shocks (greater than anticipated spending needs).

Investment risk is important, especially for investment-based retirement spending strategies, but it shouldn't be the driving factor when planning retirement income. Given their flexibility, time horizon, and outlook on market volatility, RTQs are intended primarily to determine how to position investments to reach a specific spending goal. They generally do this well. Their main shortcoming as a tool for retirement spending is the assumption that you will use distributions from a diversified portfolio of investments to fund spending goals and that market volatility is the *only* risk of consequence to spending while ignoring other risks, such as living longer, unexpected expenses, and rising living costs.

We need a fresh approach to assess our retirement income mindset and attendant behaviors for our retirement income plans to be effective. With the current tools available, this is not an easy proposition.

We financial planners and our clients have seen how the traditional RTQ is ineffective for identifying the full breadth of income mindsets and financial behaviors in retirement, by its singular focus on investment risk.

To be effective, any method must succeed in profiling income *preferences*.

In the past, we have used a set of questions to generate a collection of answers, which we then map to an income personality and translate to an income strategy. The process is tedious, error-prone, and time-consuming.

Our search for a better income preference profile tool led us to the Retirement Income Style Awareness (RISA) profile tool that helps retirees translate their income preferences into actionable solutions to source income comfortably, courtesy of Retirement Researcher. It allows us to reach a higher level of accuracy in a fraction of the time it would normally take to do it manually. It has worked well for us, and clients who have taken it have given positive reviews.

It appeals because it puts the clients front and center, rather than the financial planner. It's also a brief, 20-minute online assessment that can be completed at your convenience, and that's a win for everyone.

Disclaimer: Retirement Researcher and I have no relationship beyond vendor and customer. I am not compensated in any way for using their profile tool. My practice uses many vendors, including them. My experience using the product has led me to conclude that it provides the most accurate opportunity for measuring how a person feels about generating income in retirement from their financial resources.

This income preference profiling tool is best viewed as a counseling session between you and your retirement income plan. It leverages scientific, agnostic, and iterative processes, eliminating doubts about the right retirement style for your unique situation. The outcome is less prescriptive and more of a solution to solve a particular need for how you are most comfortable paying for retirement costs.

Moreover, it's unique in its ability to capture the multidimensional aspects of a retirement income plan that's shown to be reliable and valid by identifying the following:

> ➢ Retirement Concerns
>
> ➢ Retirement Income Styles
>
> ➢ Preferred and Appropriate Retirement Income Sources

With that background, let's examine how it works. The RISA is a brief questionnaire where individuals are asked questions to identify income preferences to determine how they want to fund retirement. This results in a snapshot of the retirement income style and strategy most comfortable for the individual.

The concept is vital for all retirees. Aligning yourself with a plan that matches your style is crucial to success. It increases your chances of sticking to your plan and enhances your retirement prospects.

Knowing how you want to spend in retirement rests on your ability to profile your income beliefs and identify your retirement income preferences.

To learn more about your income preferences, I am offering the questionnaire and free RISA profile to you. Please visit: **https://account.myrisaprofile.com/invitation-link/VV6C7RYOHV** to obtain your RISA Profile report without cost.

Next, we'll shift from the theoretical underpinnings to the practical application of using this profiling tool to help the Banners, our fictitious married couple, assess their income beliefs and preferences to identify a retirement income strategy that reflects their beliefs and preferences.

Case Study: How the Banners Identify Their Income Preferences, Style, and Strategy

Let's discuss a few details about the RISA before we move on to the case study. Generally, it is most useful for those 5-7 years on either side of retirement. It can be taken individually or jointly. For couples who prefer to complete it separately, they can analyze the results collectively to find a solution that works for both spouses.

Let's say the spouses have divergent opinions about how to fund retirement: one believes in the potential of market returns to provide enough income, while the other believes that market returns are unpredictable and would prefer more reliable funding sources. A compromise in this situation would be to shift savings from bonds to protected income sources unaffected by market ups and downs to meet core spending needs, while maintaining allocations to assets with greater growth expectations to meet secondary spending needs.

Now, on to the case study. In this scenario, we were approached by the Banners, a married couple in their late fifties looking for ways to use their financial resources to generate steady cash flow in retirement. David, an account executive at a large pharmaceutical firm, and Dawn, a lifelong primary school teacher, have saved well and accrued pensions and Social Security to prepare for retirement. They own their own home, have no debt, and expect to be healthy moving forward. Their children have established careers and families of their own. They aim to retire within five years and expect retirement to last for many decades.

After hearing about the 4% rule, which identifies the maximum withdrawal amount from savings as a percentage of retirement date assets over a thirty-year retirement, they questioned whether they could rely on it because some research suggested it was too high or, in some cases, too low. [1]

It was important to them to get a second opinion and to evaluate their planning efforts to determine if they were on the right track to retire and reach their spending goals.

Their online search for spending in retirement led them to our firm, where they learned about our focus on helping people approaching retirement determine how to generate steady income from their financial resources to support themselves when they are no longer receiving a paycheck. After speaking with them and discussing their concerns about retirement spending and the 4% rule specifically, we shared how we work with people like them to determine an appropriate and preferred method of sourcing retirement income.

During our discussion, we explained how we don't believe an advisor or anyone else should dictate how someone sources retirement income, no matter how knowledgeable or well-intentioned. A person's choice of using their assets to fund their retirement is best left to them alone.

This idea intrigued them, and they wanted to learn more. After explaining to them how my firm was equipped to help people make informed decisions about how to source income in retirement, they agreed to become clients and begin planning their retirement income.

While the RISA can be taken together, in our experience, each spouse is better served to take it separately. Spouses are free to think through and express their true desires without outside interference. We assured David

---

1 Rodeck, David, "The 4% Rule Gets a Closer Look," Kiplinger, October 2022, The 4% Rule Gets a Closer Look.

and Dawn that we routinely help couples combine different retirement income plans into a unified solution. Upon hearing this, they agreed it would be best if they each took it separately.

Although the results were revealing to the Banners, our familiarity with the tool allowed us to help them deepen their understanding during a meeting.

At this meeting, two things happened. First, they recognized the significance of how assessing their income biases and beliefs, not those of others, better informed what kind of income strategy they'd prefer. Secondly, the fact that perceived income preferences often differ from real income preferences was a huge surprise.

Before working with us, they thought they would land somewhere in the Probability-Based & Optionality income style (think: 4% spending strategy) since they had accumulated savings in a diversified investment portfolio. They assumed they would spend it in retirement.

The results, however, revealed something altogether different. Their responses indicated a preference for securing a base of income to fund core spending needs consistent with the Safety-First factor. It was equally telling that they were more inclined to lock in a strategy to solve for lifetime income upfront than to keep their options open to adapt to changing economic conditions and circumstances consistent with the Optionality factor. Lastly, while they preferred protected income sources like Social Security, pension benefits, or an annuity for funding core spending, they were open to less secure sources for funding non-essential spending.

By profiling their retirement income preferences, the Banners discovered that they prefer to receive income from guaranteed income sources to meet basic spending while using non-guaranteed income sources for discretionary spending. They prefer retirement income sources that offer contractual payment obligations in advance rather than opting for less secure sources with no payment commitments to cover essential expenses, and they remain open to using less secure income sources for non-essential expenses. This is closely associated with the **Safety-First & Commitment** income style representative of the Income Protection income strategy, which stands in stark contrast to the 4% spending strategy reflective of the Probability-Based & Optionality income style they initially thought to be best for retirement.

It's like saying green is your favorite color but only wearing blue.

In further discussions with the Banners, they expressed concern over stories about retirees who were unfortunate enough to enter retirement during the 2008 financial crisis and how they had to scale back retirement expectations and, in some cases, delay retirement altogether due to a reduction in their portfolio. This was a fate they wanted to avoid. They were relieved to learn there were alternative retirement funding strategies that instead relied more on secure, stable, and sustainable income sources instead of a riskier investment-based funding strategy dependent on market dynamics.

Once there was consensus on their income style, we posed one final question: How would they have known that drawing income from their portfolio wasn't their only option or their preferred retirement funding option? They shrugged their shoulders in unison.

MARK'S KEY TAKEAWAYS

- ➢ Retirement income should be sourced according to your own preferences, not those of other people or outdated methods.

- ➢ There are many ways to fund retirement, but it is vital to have the appropriate tool to determine how to do so.

- ➢ The income strategy you perceive may differ from the one you prefer.

CHAPTER 2

Income Strategy is Key

Learning Objectives

➢ Income Strategy is the Key to Effectively Turn Assets into Income

➢ Four Strategies to Turn Assets into Income

➢ Fitting Style and Strategy is Important

➢ Case Study: How the Banners Ensured the Right Strategy to Style Fit

People who have saved and accumulated for retirement will be faced with the challenge of determining how to generate income during retirement. The threat to Social Security's solvency and the absence of pension plans have placed additional pressure on retirees to turn their savings into sustainable income for an ever-lengthening retirement period.

Assets can be used to generate income in retirement in a variety of ways. A critical part of determining how to do this is to assess income beliefs and preferences. As we climb the retirement ladder, the first rung represents saving before retirement, and the second, third, and fourth rungs represent income beliefs, preferences, and style. We now take a small step towards retirement income security and a giant leap toward a successful retirement by examining the fifth rung, where income strategies reside. Establishing an appropriate solution to generate income in advance of retirement will be essential to retirement success.

We'll review the income strategy landscape to understand the various options better, how they align with income preferences and styles, and the importance of aligning income styles and strategies. We'll wrap things up by revisiting the Banner case study to review their income strategy and how they ensured it aligned with their income style.

Income Strategy is the Key to Effectively Turn Assets into Income

Putting assets to work to generate income is easier said than done. It does not matter whether you follow a formal or a less formal strategy to accomplish this. Whatever approach you choose, you must determine how to combine, coordinate, and utilize your assets to meet spending goals while minimizing risks to them. It will be much easier to achieve if one of the four common income strategies is employed. We will focus on these strategies because the retirement income planning profession considers them viable solutions for creating income from assets. The means employed are less important than the outcome in retirement since income outweighs all other factors.

Let's examine their objectives in more detail to understand why income strategies can be so useful for retirement income. Seeing them from this perspective builds appreciation and encourages their use.

Starting with the first objective, we must determine how to utilize our assets to generate income to meet spending goals. Recall the four spending goals in retirement are *longevity* to cover day-to-day essential living expenses, *liquidity* to deal with unexpected expenses, *lifestyle* to pay for the things that make retirement enjoyable, and *legacy* to ensure that future generations have what they need. A failure to achieve any of these goals, particularly longevity, would be devastating.

Choosing how to use your financial resources is your most important decision in retirement.

Retirement financial security depends on ensuring the chosen income strategy meets this goal.

A well-crafted asset-to-spending goal pairing will be a cornerstone to any income strategy. The goal is to pair low-payment flexible spending goals with high-payment reliable assets and high-payment flexible spending goals with low-payment reliable assets.

For example, a spending goal to fund day-to-day living expenses that must be paid is paired with high-payment reliable assets (annuities, bond ladders, pensions, and Social Security). These offer payment guarantees in the form of stable and in some cases lifetime income. A liquidity spending goal with increased payment flexibility could be coupled with assets with reasonable payment reliability, such as CDs, simple income annuities, savings, life insurance cash value, etc.

Conversely, lifestyle and legacy spending goals with some payment flexibility can be sourced from low-payment reliable assets, like invested assets or other assets such as business interests, collectibles, commodities, cryptocurrencies, real estate, etc., that are expected to grow in value but not guarantee payments.

A second objective is to consider how the income strategy manages the risks that could undermine the ability to meet spending goals. An income strategy that generates income at the appropriate levels when needed without accounting for what can undermine its ability to do so over the long run may not be ideal. Retirement comes with plenty of risks that can hinder meeting spending goals. Whether it's an extended life expectancy, higher inflation, unexpected spending shocks (more than planned expenditures), or losing a spouse that has not been accounted for, it can result in assets earmarked for a particular spending goal being diverted away to meet expenditures, undermining financial security and quality of life.

You will need to assess your particular risks and put in place a plan to mitigate their impact on spending goals.

For instance, those who worry about outliving their assets may want to fortify their income strategy with assets that deliver lifetime benefits. When inflation is a concern, ensuring assets keep pace with rising costs of goods and services is paramount.

When dealing with the potential loss of a spouse, it is important to maximize survivor benefits on assets that are likely to pay lifetime income to meet the surviving spouse's income needs.

Retirement income strategies are an ongoing process to balance goals and protect against risks.

Having a risk plan ensures your spending goals won't be compromised to a level that would reduce your standard of living, no matter what life throws at you.

The importance of understanding your income beliefs and preferences becomes apparent here. We gain insight through them into which risks are of greatest concern and how we prefer to manage them. The methods we choose inform an appropriate income strategy.

After ensuring the income strategy addresses these two primary objectives, you can consider secondary objectives such as maximizing efficiencies and managing taxes.

It is important to consider taxes at all stages of life. It is imperative to reduce tax liabilities if one wishes to sustain assets and maintain spending potential, since less tax paid results in more available to spend. Integrating tax strategies that generate income in an efficient manner will be crucial.

As you strive to do more with your resources, it is imperative to explore and employ those strategies that maximize their use to make your strategy as efficient as possible. Planning for retirement income requires finding ways to do more with less because resources are finite.

Our discussion of risks and these secondary objectives will be expanded upon in Chapter 4. Our focus now is examining the various income strategies we can use to create income.

Four Strategies to Turn Assets into Income

Various approaches are available for converting assets into income. Our focus will be on four widely recognized strategies. Regardless of the method used to convert assets to income, all aim to create income to live off during retirement. While no one strategy will work for everyone, the best strategy for your retirement rests solely on how you prefer to receive income in retirement.

We will examine each income strategy on the two broad factors of *Probability-Based* vs. *Safety-First* and *Optionality* vs. *Commitment* discussed in a previous chapter. The RISA lets you identify what income preferences align with which income styles and strategies based on your beliefs about retirement income.

Remember, income styles can be categorized as follows:

- ★ Probability-Based & Optionality
- ★ Safety-First & Optionality
- ★ Probability-Based & Commitment
- ★ Safety-First & Commitment

The most widely accepted approach to funding retirement is to save and build assets in a diversified investment portfolio characteristic of the Probability-Based & Optionality income style. This may be a good approach for some, but it may not be for all. Although it is a popular strategy, only 33% of retirees plan to use it, according to a study by Retirement Researcher.[2] This means the majority expect to fund their retirement in other ways and acknowledges that retirement often extends beyond an investment challenge. We'll begin our review of income strategies with this one as it's arguably the most well-known.

There will be many who will need to consider how to create income beyond their investments.

This is where the nest egg concept came about, where you save and invest wisely to fund your retirement. It's characteristic of the Probability-Based & Optionality income style representative of a **Total Return** income strategy that reflects a preference for sourcing income from assets with growth potential, while at the same time retaining flexibility to adapt to

---

2 Murguia, Pfau, "How Retirement Income Preferences Inform Retirement Income Styles," Retirement Income Institute, November 2022, How Retirement Income Preferences Inform Retirement Income Styles.

changing personal circumstances. This strategy is based on the belief that market returns can subsidize future spending.

This income strategy is predicated on using market returns to source income and has broad appeal to those comfortable funding retirement using withdrawals from assets with the expectation of growth. Those who tolerate fluctuations in spending due to market volatility and aim to retain the flexibility to adapt to changes in their circumstances will value this strategy. It is the most flexible of the four strategies, with the greatest spending potential but also the greatest risk, owing to the unpredictability of market returns.

An example of this strategy would be someone who believes in the growth potential of the financial markets and who would invest their savings in a diversified portfolio to grow them to pay for future expenses with no constraints to alter things according to economic or personal circumstances.

In Exhibit 2.0, we can see how income styles are plotted on the income style continuum, moving from the left, indicative of least income certainty and most flexibility, to the right, indicative of most income certainty and least flexibility.

Exhibit 2.0

At the other end of the income style continuum is Safety-First & Commitment. It differs considerably from the Probability-Based & Optionality income style, reflecting a strong preference for protected income sources that offer more income certainty and less flexibility to accommodate change. This income style aligns with the **Protected Income** strategy, which utilizes the most reliable sources of income to fund essential income needs while committing to less flexible solutions that remove the need for continuous revision. It relies not on market returns to fund spending but on relatively secure income sources like annuities, pensions, and Social Security. Building a secure income floor for essential spending using secure lifetime income provides greater downside spending protection. Among the income strategies, it provides the greatest spending certainty and offers the least flexibility. This strategy advocates relying on contractually guaranteed income sources to fund essential expenses and using market-based income sources to fund non-essential expenses.

Someone using this strategy would accumulate retirement savings in income sources like annuities, defined-benefit pensions, and Social Security that come with guaranteed lifetime payouts irrespective of market fluctuations.

Located immediately to the right of the Probability-Based & Optionality is the Probability-Based & Commitment income style geared towards individuals who prefer some market exposure with a willingness to commit to solutions that maintain a floor of income to meet essential expenditures. This is indicative of the **Risk Wrap** strategy, which combines investment growth potential through investment upside with lifetime income benefits from contractually guaranteed income sources. Those seeking upfront spending protection for essential expenses while maintaining flexibility to invest assets to fund non-essential expenses with constraints that limit market exposure will favor this income strategy. An individual following this strategy does not want to rely completely on the market to fund their retirement.

This strategy enables someone to invest a portion of savings in a diversified investment portfolio to capture market returns to meet discretionary spending while also designating savings to lifetime income to meet essential spending.

Landing to the left of the Safety-First & Commitment income style is the Safety-First & Optionality income style, which reflects a desire to ensure secure funding of essential expenditures and flexibility in adjusting solutions to changing economic or personal circumstances. It's characteristic of the **Time Segmentation** (i.e., bucketing) strategy that segments assets according to the time horizon of spending goals. Utilizing assets for their intended purpose is the goal. Assets and liabilities are paired so that low-growth and risk-free assets are allocated to short-term spending needs, low-risk assets with moderate-growth to near-term spending needs, and higher-growth and riskier assets to long-term spending needs. To mitigate the impact of poor market returns during the Fragile Decade (the 5 years leading up to and following retirement) this strategy emphasizes securing the most reliable funding for immediate expenditures while retaining less reliable funding for non-immediate expenditures.

This strategy's Safety-First and Optionality aspects are expressed in deploying more secure income sources like Social Security or bonds or annuities to cover short- and near-term income needs while simultaneously maintaining the flexibility to allocate long-term spending to assets with higher growth potential. Funds spent down from shorter-term buckets may be gradually replenished by longer-term buckets.

In practice, a person using this strategy would segment their savings across various assets where the timing of their spending goal and the asset's payout coincide.

Many strategies are available to turn your assets into income. It's important to carefully evaluate each strategy based on your income beliefs and preferences to determine the appropriate income strategy that will benefit your retirement most.

Fitting Style and Strategy is Important

Aligning your retirement income style with your retirement income strategy is paramount to ensure a successful and fulfilling retirement. Your retirement income style reflects your preferences and beliefs toward generating income during retirement. In contrast, income strategy encompasses the specific plan and actions you take to generate income and manage risks throughout your retirement years.

Matching your retirement income style with your retirement income strategy is essential for several reasons. First, it helps ensure the chosen strategy aligns with your income preferences and goals. This alignment enhances peace of mind and confidence in your retirement income plan and increases the likelihood you will stick with the plan.

It is more likely that you will stick to your strategy and benefit from it if your income style and strategy are well aligned.

Moreover, aligning your retirement income style with an appropriate income strategy ensures you generate an income stream that makes sense for you in retirement. Understanding your income preferences and style makes it crystal clear why you have the income strategy you have. Just knowing that removes all doubt and second-guessing. You no longer need to rely on someone else's opinion about the best income strategy for you.

Lastly, aligning your retirement income style with your retirement income strategy results in a personalized approach to your retirement income planning. A tailored strategy can be developed by considering your unique preferences, needs, wants, and goals. Personalizing retirement income planning represents a paradigm shift in retirement planning that only benefits your retirement.

Case Study: How the Banners Ensured the Right Strategy to Style Fit

We emphasized to the Banners the importance of aligning income strategies with income styles. A mismatch between style and strategy can lead to costly mistakes, constant revisions, diminished confidence, and missed opportunities, often resulting in an undesirable retirement outcome.

But this is easier said than done, especially when you rely on traditional tools that focus on quantifying your feelings on investment risk and ignore other risks like spending flexibility and durability that matter much more than how your investments perform. Trusting outside advice, often tainted by bias, can be equally detrimental.

By leveraging a profiling tool, such as the RISA, the Banners only had to rely on themselves to decide on the best approach.

Let's review the various components of the Banners' RISA profile report to understand what it revealed about their income preferences and style based on their income beliefs. Their results clearly show how they feel about sourcing income during retirement.

Exhibit 2.1 shows a strong affinity for the Safety-First & Commitment income style based on the primary RISA factors.

Exhibit 2.1

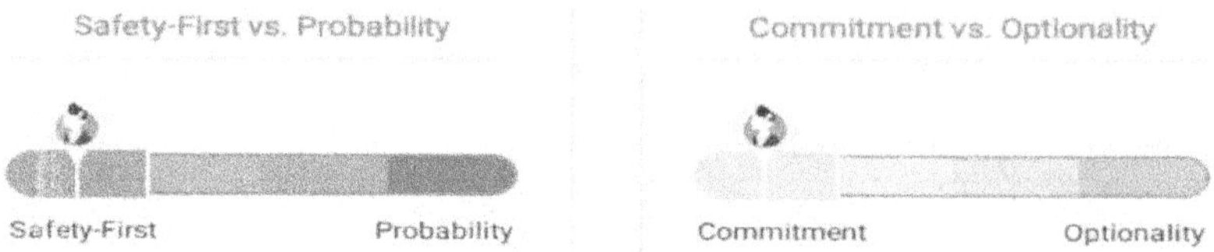

Source: RISA, LLC

Reviewing the answers to key questions in Exhibit 2.2, we can better understand their assessed income style. This demonstrates the power of asking the right questions correctly to determine income beliefs.

Exhibit 2.2

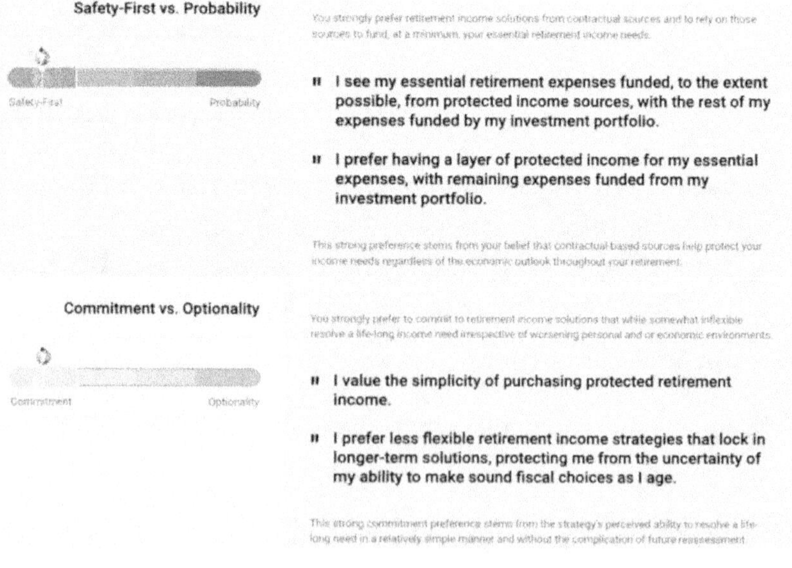

Source: RISA, LLC

According to Exhibit 2.3, their responses place them in the Safety-First & Commitment quadrant of the RISA Matrix.

Exhibit 2.3 - RISA Matrix

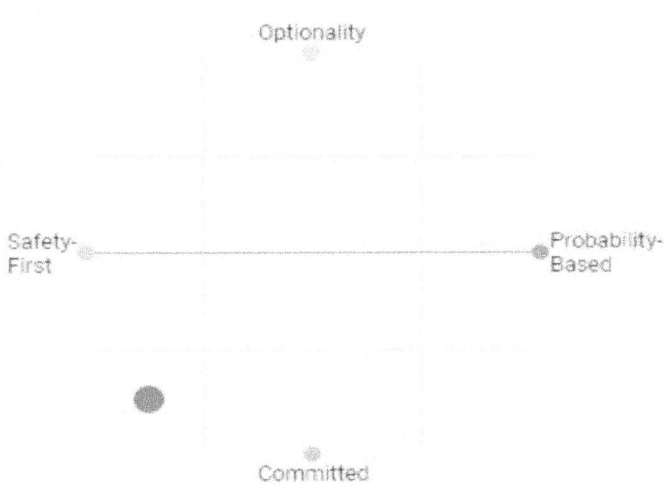

Source: RISA, LLC

Exhibits 2.4 & 2.5 illustrate their responses to secondary RISA factors influential to income style.

Exhibit 2.4

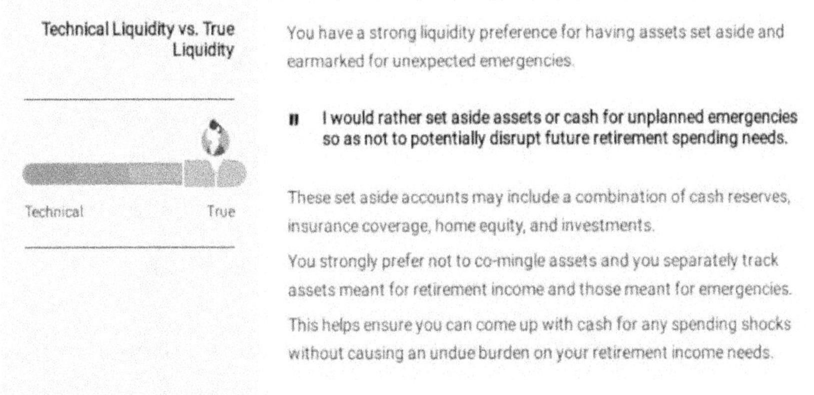

You have a strong liquidity preference for having assets set aside and earmarked for unexpected emergencies.

■ I would rather set aside assets or cash for unplanned emergencies so as not to potentially disrupt future retirement spending needs.

These set aside accounts may include a combination of cash reserves, insurance coverage, home equity, and investments.

You strongly prefer not to co-mingle assets and you separately track assets meant for retirement income and those meant for emergencies.

This helps ensure you can come up with cash for any spending shocks without causing an undue burden on your retirement income needs.

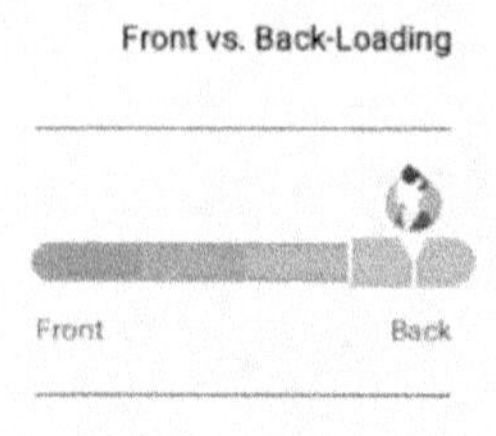

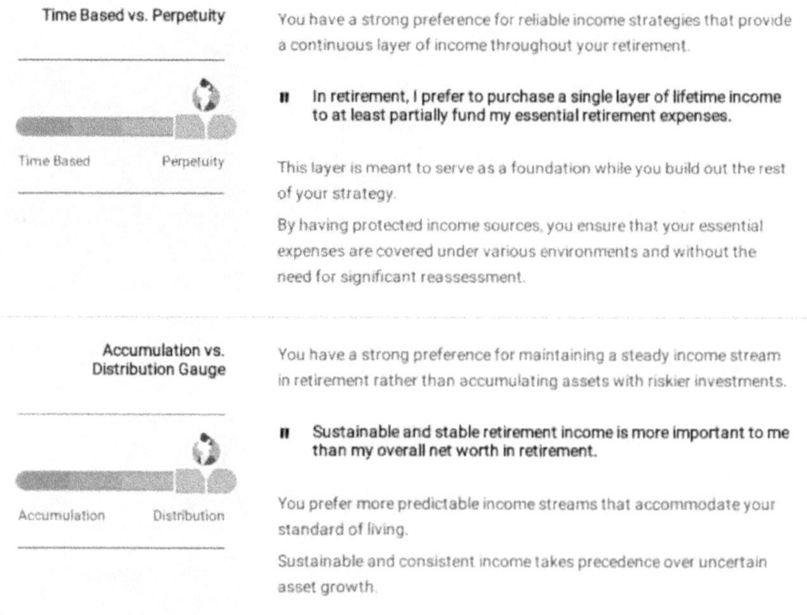

You have a strong preference for spending less early in retirement to avoid significant spending cuts as you age.

■ I prefer to spend more during my later retirement years rather than having to make future spending reductions because I've overspent early in my retirement.

A more conservative lifestyle early in retirement leads to greater satisfaction because you can protect yourself from potential spending reductions later.

You prefer maintaining a lower standard of living early in retirement and are willing to increase it as you age if your assets increase.

You also don't want to be a potential burden to anyone because you overspent early in retirement.

Source: RISA, LLC

Exhibit 2.5

You have a strong preference for reliable income strategies that provide a continuous layer of income throughout your retirement.

■ In retirement, I prefer to purchase a single layer of lifetime income to at least partially fund my essential retirement expenses.

This layer is meant to serve as a foundation while you build out the rest of your strategy.

By having protected income sources, you ensure that your essential expenses are covered under various environments and without the need for significant reassessment.

You have a strong preference for maintaining a steady income stream in retirement rather than accumulating assets with riskier investments.

■ Sustainable and stable retirement income is more important to me than my overall net worth in retirement.

You prefer more predictable income streams that accommodate your standard of living.

Sustainable and consistent income takes precedence over uncertain asset growth.

Source: RISA, LLC

Using the RISA Matrix, Exhibit 2.6 illustrates how the Banners' Safety-First & Commitment income style correlates with the Protected Income strategy.

Exhibit 2.6

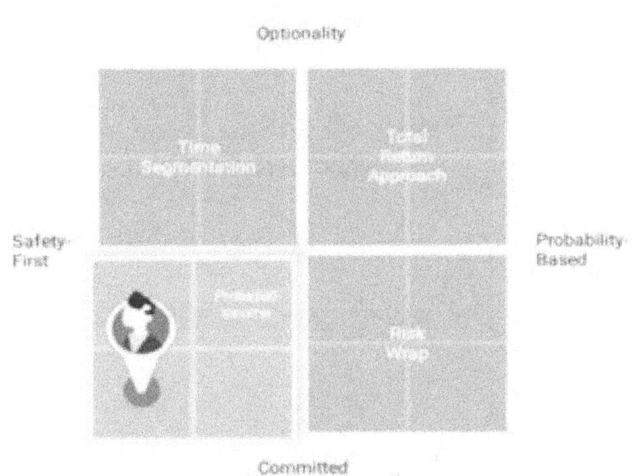

Source: RISA, LLC

Exhibits 2.7 and 2.8 illustrate how the RISA helped the Banners to understand their income preferences, styles, and strategies in relation to their concerns around the four primary spending goals.

Exhibit 2.7

Retirement Concerns

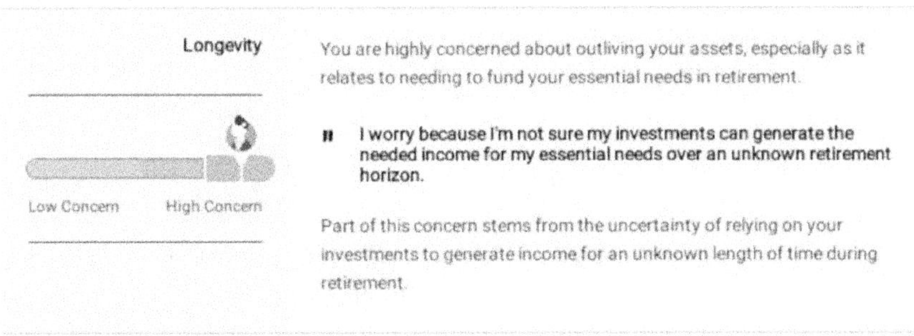

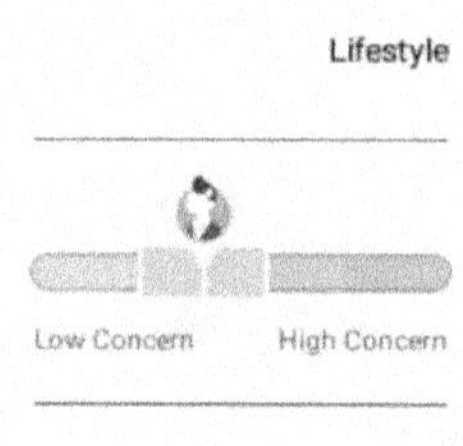

Source: RISA, LLC

Exhibit 2.8

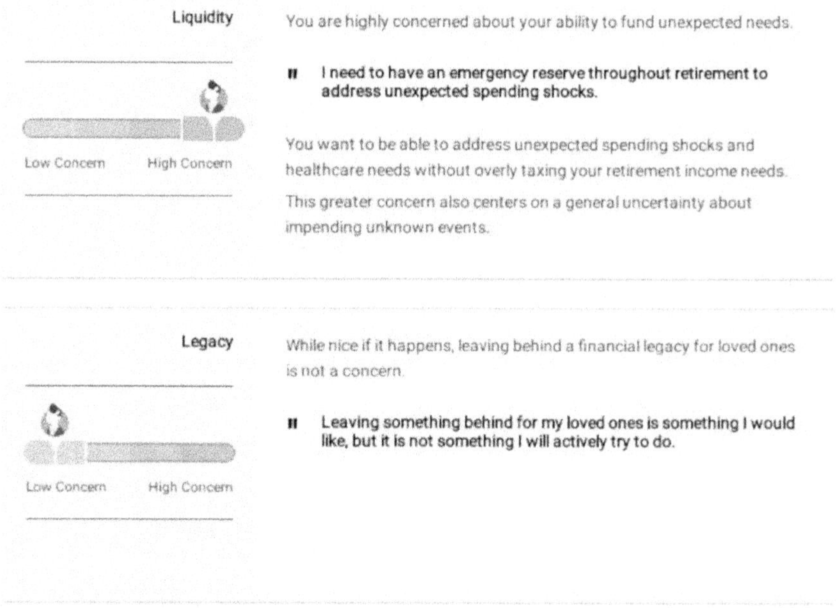

Source: RISA, LLC

It would be an understatement to say David and Dawn were stunned by these results. But the results speak for themselves. While discovering their *actual* income style and strategy, they realized it was quite different from what they had *anticipated*.

After giving it more thought, they realized that the Total Return income strategy did not align with their Safety-First and Commitment income style. A better fit for them was the Protected Income strategy that stresses using more secure income sources to pay for retirement. Looking back, it was their best retirement decision.

Rather than facing retirement with uncertainty about how they can reliably use their financial resources to meet spending needs over a potentially long retirement period amid changing economic and personal circumstances, they have the assurance that their income strategy, a key piece of the overall retirement income plan, is aligned with the way they feel most comfortable funding retirement spending. Confidence and contentment rush in to replace uncertainty and uneasiness. Upon determining that their income strategy fits their style, the planning process for incorporating it into a broader retirement income plan can begin.

While a great deal of planning remains, from developing a Social Security claim strategy, making decisions related to Medicare and other health insurance, addressing risks, structuring income to maximize tax efficiency, and optimizing efficiencies to increase spending potential, the foundational retirement income planning decision of turning assets into income has been resolved.

By profiling their income beliefs, the Banners learned several important lessons:

> It helped initiate further discussion and exploration of their true preferences around retirement income.

> It helped identify the right income strategy based on how they truly felt about what they thought or heard was best.

> It helped them recognize that no income strategy is right for everyone, regardless of what someone says.

> ➤ It helped them realize the right strategy may be entirely different from what they think is right.

> ➤ It helped them understand that planning retirement income should be guided by their income preferences.

> ➤ They realized the importance of having the right tool for the job.

In Chapter 5, we'll investigate how the Banners implemented their chosen strategy to fit the broader picture of retirement income planning.

MARK'S KEY TAKEAWAYS

> ➤ Don't underestimate the power of the right tool.

> ➤ Consider your income beliefs and preferences to determine the income strategy that best suits your style.

> ➤ Choosing how to fund your retirement is your most important retirement decision.

CHAPTER 3

Quantify and Match Assets With Liabilities

"There's only one corner of the universe you can be certain of improving, and that's your own self."

— ALDOUS HUXLEY

Learning Objectives

- ➤ Retirement Income Security
- ➤ Assumptions are Key
- ➤ A Systematic Approach to Identifying and Quantifying Assets and Liabilities
- ➤ How Asset-Liability Matching Can Benefit Retirement
- ➤ How to Calculate Your Retirement Financial Position
- ➤ Case Study: How the Banners Quantified and Matched Assets and Liabilities and Determined Their Retirement Readiness

You have to do a lot right before retirement to be ready. You must build a base of assets to spend from when you are no longer working. Once you have done this, you must determine how to use those assets to generate income for retirement.

Next, you must determine how much retirement will cost and how you plan to pay for it. By evaluating your needs, wants, and means, you can determine whether retirement is realistic for you. Simply put, you must settle the asset and liability sides of your retirement balance sheet to know whether your retirement is financially feasible. Setting realistic retirement spending goals (liabilities) and then assessing available means (assets) to pay for them is an essential step in the planning process for reaching retirement goals.

Having enough income to cover retirement costs when needed is a top retirement goal and risk.

Many people do the previous steps well, but I have found that too many miss the vital step of matching assets to liabilities. Asset-liability matching is not just about generating retirement income to pay for the costs of retirement, it is about ensuring assets and liabilities are appropriately matched to maintain income stability. This means ensuring liabilities with limited payment flexibility are matched with high-payment reliable assets. Reliable assets are those that have a high reliability of meeting payment expectations.

Effective retirement income planning requires managing cash flow to ensure a steady income stream throughout retirement. You will gain a higher level of comfort when you know what assets will be used to pay for each liability in retirement. This starts with identifying each liability's funding need, priority, and timing and then determining which assets meet each liability's need, priority, and timing so that they can be structured accordingly.

Matching assets and liabilities offer many benefits, from knowing upfront whether liabilities are realistic and how they will be paid to identifying funding deficiencies and surpluses to ensuring reliable funding is in place to meet essential expenditures. Asset-liability matching will tell the story of how you will most effectively fund your retirement using your financial resources.

Retirement Income Security

The most important goal and risk in retirement is having enough income to cover retirement costs. Understanding and planning for the 5 key components of retirement income planning (Exhibit 3.0) are key to ensuring retirement income security.

Each of these components is fundamental to retirement income security. We'll focus on the assets (income sources and assets to generate income) and liabilities (spending goals) in this chapter, and we'll cover risks and strategies to increase retirement income in the following chapter.

Exhibit 3.0

Assumptions are Key

Planning assumptions impact retirement costs and outcomes. A shorter planning horizon, a lower spending rate, favorable investment returns, and lower inflation will reduce costs and generally result in better outcomes. However, while overly optimistic assumptions will lower costs, they may produce unfavorable outcomes should any or all of them not come to pass. Making realistic assumptions about your life expectancy, spending rate, market performance, and inflation is essential to planning a successful retirement.

Realistic assumptions about expected spending and inflation rates, as well as life expectancy, could yield better outcomes in our efforts to achieve objectives when planning for retirement.

Retirement is an expensive proposition. It is generally the largest purchase someone will ever make. With rising medical and long-term care expenses, longer life expectancies, rising inflation, a comfortable retirement can seem out of reach for anyone but the wealthy. It's not all doom and gloom, though. Researchers have found that using realistic assumptions such as income replacement rate, inflation, and life expectancy for key costs in retirement can reduce cost estimates by 20 to 25 percent.[3]

It's a common practice to assume an income replacement rate of 80 percent, average consumer price inflation rates, and a 30-year life expectancy once retired. While these are common, they may not be accurate. When planning a retirement, it's crucial to use realistic assumptions that reflect experience.

---

3 Retirement Researcher, "Ten Reasons Why the 4% Rule is Too Simplistic for Retirement Planning", Vienna, VA: Retirement Researcher, 2018, Ten Reasons Why the 4% Rule is Too Simplistic for Retirement Planning

These can include:

> ➤ ***Replacement Ratio***: 80 percent is a good starting point, but the rate needed to maintain a post-retirement lifestyle comparable to a pre-retirement lifestyle can range from 54 percent to 87 percent of final income.

> ➤ ***Inflation Rate***: Spending rates through retirement generally do not keep up with inflation. Real spending tends to decrease over retirement, but some increase later due to rising medical costs. Assuming uniform inflation-adjusted spending each year overstates retirement costs.

> ➤ ***Life Expectancy in Retirement***: Actual life expectancies can vary widely for retirees—consider personal health and family health history, as well as life expectancy at retirement age, not at birth. You should also consider income, wealth, and education, which correlate with longer life expectancies. It's important to consider the possibility that you will outlive your wealth.

No one ever gets everything they want in life, so they must choose carefully. Reasonable assumptions will help quantify retirement expenses to know whether retirement as envisioned is attainable. Realistic assumptions are crucial to achieving favorable retirement outcomes.

A Systematic Approach to Identifying and Quantifying Assets and Liabilities

One of the most powerful things you can do if you're not already retired is to make a retirement plan. Many simply throw money at their portfolio, hoping everything will work out. You cannot develop a plan unless you know what you are trying to accomplish. You will need to know how much you want to spend and what you can afford to begin building a roadmap to navigate your retirement successfully.

Determine the assets available for retirement

Taking into account your assets will assist you in determining how much you can spend on retirement. This involves quantifying financial resources that can be used to pay for your liabilities.

This process can be approached in various ways. Use whichever method suits you best, but here are the steps I take with my clients.

Our goal is to get a better understanding of the assets that are available for spending.

To get started, you should gather the following information.

> ➤ *Compile a List of Accounts*: Make a comprehensive list of all your retirement accounts, including employer-sponsored plans (401(k)s or 403(b)s), individual retirement accounts (IRAs) , pension plans, annuities, and any other investment or savings intended for retirement.

> ➤ *Determine Current Balances*: Gather the most recent statements for each retirement account to determine current balances. This information will provide a snapshot of the value of your assets at the present time.

> ➤ *Consider Other Financial Assets*: Identify other financial assets that can contribute to your retirement income. These may include taxable investment accounts, savings accounts, certificates of deposit (CDs), real estate properties, or business interests. Determine their approximate values based on current market conditions or professional appraisals.

> ➤ *Include Social Security Benefits*: Social Security benefits are important to many individuals' retirement income. Estimate the value of your Social Security benefits by creating an account on the Social Security Administration website (ssa.gov) or using

online calculators that consider factors such as work history and projected retirement age.

➤ ***Assess Other Retirement Income Sources***: Consider any additional sources of retirement income, such as inheritances, rental income, cash-value life insurance, or income from part-time work during retirement. Determine the expected values of these income streams based on relevant documents, projections, or professional advice.

➤ ***Account for Non-Financial Assets***: While not directly financial, non-financial assets can also contribute to retirement. These may include property you plan to downsize or sell, possessions with significant resale value, or other valuable assets. Estimate their potential values or consult with professionals to get accurate appraisals.

The next step is to arrange the information to understand each asset and how it fits into your funding strategy.

Clients and I find it helpful and valuable to create a balance sheet (spreadsheet) to catalog assets according to Income Sources Currently Available for Retirement Income Needs (assets expected to produce a future income stream) and Assets Used to Generate Retirement Income (assets that can be converted into future income streams).

The Income Sources Currently Available to Meet Retirement Income Needs balance sheet tabulates the available income sources for retirement income needs.

Listing each asset's source, amount, duration, reliability, and payout option is helpful.

Exhibit 3.1 illustrates what this might look like.

Exhibit 3.1

Income Sources Currently Available to Meet Retirement Income Needs					
Source	Amount	Duration	Reliability	COLA	Payout
Social Security	Benefit Statement	Payable for life	Secure	Yes	Life Annuity
Qualified Defined Benefit Pension	Benefit Statement	Payable for life	Secure private backing by PBGC up to $5,420 per month	No	Lump-sum, Single Life, Joint and Survivor, Guaranteed Payment Annuity
Annuity	Benefit Statement	Payable for life	Provider claims paying ability	Yes	Lump-sum, Single Life, Joint and Survivor, Guaranteed Payment Annuity
Non-Qualified Employer Plan	Benefit Statement	Salary Continuation for stated number of years or payable for life	Not as secure with qualified plans	No	Lump Sum, Salary Continuation
Part-time Work	Varies	Ability to work and availability of work	Varies because a lot can go wrong	Yes - pay increases	Monthly
Business Interest	Varies	Buyer's ability to pay installments	Based on financial viability of buyers	No	Lump Sum or Installment Payments
Rental Income Rentals Vacation homes	Varies	Based on ownership	Based on tenant's ability to pay	Yes	Monthly payment, potential capital gains at sale

From your initial asset-gathering effort, you'll need to create another balance sheet limited to those assets that can be converted into income. The Assets Used to Generate Retirement Income balance sheet lists the asset's value, timing (availability), reliability, and payout method. Exhibit 3.2 shows an example of this.

Exhibit 3.2

Assets Used to Generate Retirement Income				
Asset	Value	Timing	Reliability	Payout
Employer retirement plans (401k, profit sharing)	Account balance, Future contributions, Investment returns	As early as 59 ½ or retirement, whichever is earliest	Secure	Some plans offer lump sum or annuity
Self Employed (SEP, SIMPLE, Solo 401k)	Account balance, Future contributions, Investment returns	As early as 59 ½ or retirement, whichever is earliest	Secure	Lump sum
IRA / Roth IRA	Account balance, Future contributions, Investment returns	As early as 59 ½ or retirement, whichever is earliest	Secure	Lump sum
Deferred Annuities	Account balance; investment returns	As early as 59 ½ or retirement, whichever is earliest	Secure	Lump sum or annuity
Brokerage accounts Mutual Funds, Stocks, Bonds	Account balance; investment returns	Anytime	Less secure	Lump sum
Real estate holdings Vacation homes / business interests	Market valuation	Buyer availability	Less secure	Lump sum or installment
Cash value life insurance	Policy cash value	Assuming cash value anytime	Secure	Lump sum loan
Home Equity, Downsize, Reverse Mortgage	Market value - loan balance	As early as age 62	Secure	Lump sum Annuity
Unused emergency fund provide funds for unexpected risks and expenditures	Account balance	Anytime	Secure	Lump sum
HSA, Pay for medical Expenses	Account balance	Anytime	Secure	Lump sum
Collectible	Market Value	Buyer availability	Secure	Lump sum

Remember that quantifying your retirement assets is an ongoing process. Regularly review and update the values of your assets as circumstances change, such as market fluctuations or major life events.

Calculate the cost of retirement

Identifying how you'll pay for retirement will only get you halfway there. You need to know if you can afford this next phase of your life. That starts with a thorough expense analysis to estimate expected retirement liabilities.

The task of quantifying retirement costs is much more challenging than quantifying assets. That's because longevity is the most significant factor affecting retirement costs. When you don't know how long retirement will last, it's difficult to predict how much it will cost and how much money you will need.

Medical advances and better lifestyle choices are enabling retirees to extend life. In addition, many people are retiring at a younger age, increasing their costs even more.

While living a long life is wonderful, it does come with a price. The length of retirement is hard to predict, but reasonable expectations need to be set if retirement planning is to be effective. Precision isn't necessary. Establishing a number you are comfortable with and fine-tuning it as necessary is important. Consider your health, family history, and lifestyle factors when projecting your retirement duration. The goal is to get in the ballpark of a reasonable number you can live with, recognizing that the outcome is a coin flip. A failure to accurately estimate the length of retirement can have grave consequences. When you assume a shorter retirement, you run the risk of depleting assets if you live longer than you expected. Meanwhile, assuming longer retirements entails living on less money than possible, which can harm quality of life.

Various tools can provide more accurate longevity estimates depending on personal circumstances. It can be done in minutes and at no cost with one of my favorite tools made freely available by the American Academy of Actuaries and the Society of Actuaries Longevity Illustrator (see Chapter 3 resources). These tools help retirees develop personalized estimates for their longevity based on a few questions about age, gender, habits, and overall health. It's a simple way to refine longevity estimates. Use it as a starting point and adjust based on your circumstances.

If you're reading this book, you're likely not like the average American. You're probably educated, make good health and lifestyle choices, and are wealthier than most. Those factors indicate that you should plan for at least a 30-year retirement and consider being prepared for more. Having identified longevity as the main driver of retirement costs, we next focus on other factors.

How much you can spend in retirement is an age-old question that doesn't have a clear answer. However, one clear thing is that spending without a plan can be risky. A spending plan, or budget, can help you determine if you're ready for retirement, set expectations around spending, and regulate spending to maintain a standard of living without running out of money. It is an essential component of a comprehensive retirement income plan. That said, there isn't a universal way to build a budget or spending plan that works for everyone because no two people will spend alike. Let's start with some general guidelines to get in the ballpark of a realistic budget and adjust it as needed to arrive at a reasonable baseline amount.

Creating a budget is a complex process. It's time-consuming and tedious, but the rewards can be substantial. To simplify this process, three common methods can be employed to help determine income needs to support a target retirement lifestyle and ensure financial security. Let's review them.

Income Replacement Method

This is a simple method that avoids making a budget by following a replacement rule for retirement spending. Estimate income based on a percentage of the pre-retirement income you will likely need to maintain a similar standard of living in retirement. The ratio most commonly cited is 70 to 85 percent of pre-retirement income to account for retirement savings, taxes, and work-related expenses. Remember that this rate can range from 54 percent to 87 percent of final income.

The Paystub Rule

The next method bases retirement income needs on your paycheck. It starts with current after-tax income and refines the amount needed to determine an income need.

Here's an eight-step process to get you started.

- Start with a paystub.
- Identify take-home pay after deductions.
- Calculate monthly take-home pay (bimonthly).
- Identify whether take-home pay satisfies income needs.
- Reduce income needs when mortgage and other debts are paid off.
- Decide if you want to maintain the same level of spending and standard of living in retirement.
- Add an inflation factor to account for rising costs (2-3%).

Detailed Income Method

This may be the most accurate of the three, but it requires a thorough analysis of the expenses and goals to include and exclude. Start with an estimate of the income you think you'll need, focusing on essential, discretionary, one-time expenses and taxes. Then, consider expenses that will drop off or change in retirement and factor in significant lifestyle changes.

It's tempting to throw down a big round number and call it a day, but you'd be short-changing yourself. Your retirement is best served by a detailed accounting of expenses that approximates future expenses based on current spending after accounting for the inclusion and exclusion of future expenses.

I have developed a system that simplifies the retirement costs calculation to help clients who choose the Detailed Income Method to assess and organize their retirement liabilities. For those familiar with Maslow's Hierarchy of Needs pyramid, a theory in psychology proposed by Abraham Maslow in 1943 suggests human needs can be organized into a hierarchy, with certain fundamental needs taking precedence over others. The hierarchy is typically depicted as a pyramid in Exhibit 3.3 with five levels.

Exhibit 3.3

Maslow's Hierarchy of Needs Pyramid

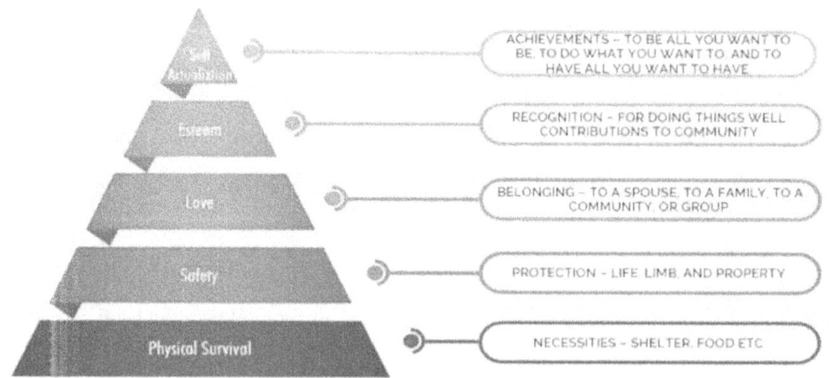

Using retirement income as a reference point, I have created the Retirement Hierarchy of Needs Pyramid based on Maslow's Pyramid, as depicted in Exhibit 3.4

Exhibit 3.4

Retirement Income Hierarchy of Needs Pyramid

We will now examine what each of these levels means in the context of retirement.

Survival Money

What is the monthly cost of survival?

Survival money is the income you have to have to make ends meet. How much do you need simply to survive each month: is it $3,000?

Or $15,000? This would be your survival cost if you stripped away the frills and thrills and just paid the survival bills. These include daily living expenses such as food, mortgage/rent, utilities, health, clothing, personal care, transportation, and taxes.

Taxes play a big role in retirement. How the money was saved makes a huge difference. Imagine if you spent your whole life diligently saving everything in your 401(k). When you spend that in retirement, a portion of the income will be taxed at ordinary income rates. On the other hand, if you'd been saving everything in a Roth IRA, your retirement income would be untouched by taxes.

Taxes matter, and if you don't include them in your analysis, you are missing out on a pretty massive piece of the picture.

Safety Money

Things don't always go as planned in life. Unexpected events happen. To meet life's unexpected turns, you need safety money. We are surrounded by circumstantial, familial, physical, and relational risks. These are all of the things that can go wrong. Leading retirement risks are running out of money, paying for healthcare, rising prices, volatile markets, losing a spouse, and financial needs within the family.

To estimate your safety income, you must understand the risks specific to your situation. It's a worthwhile exercise to identify where the vulnerabilities exist. Are there cracks in your financial foundation? Take the time to calculate the monthly cost of building a fence of emotional safety around your survival. The money needed to guard against these risks is your safety income. We'll talk more about specific risks unique to retirement a bit later.

Freedom Money

This is the money to do everything that brings you enjoyment and fulfillment. What are the activities and places that bring joy to your life?

Travel, adventure, and personal growth/education are considerations when calculating the income needed to fund your freedom. This is your fun bill – the reward you look to after all the years of working.

Gift Money

After meeting those needs, income can be used for the people and causes that you care deeply about. This includes giving to loved ones and the next generation. You may also wish to support causes and charities that connect with your heart and purpose.

Dream Money

Dream money is the income to pay for the things you've always dreamed of being, doing, and having. Some would call it their bucket list. What do you want to be? What do you want to do? What do you want to have?

Ultimately, estimating retirement costs involves assessing your expected expenses in retirement. While everyone's situation is unique, here are some key considerations to remember as you climb the pyramid to estimate costs:

> ***Evaluate Your Current Expenses***: Start by examining your current monthly expenses. Review your bank statements, credit card bills, and other financial records to know how much you spend on entertainment, food, healthcare, housing, transportation, utilities, and other essential and discretionary expenses. This will serve as a baseline for estimating future retirement expenses.

> ***Consider Inflation***: Remember that the cost of living typically increases over time due to inflation. When estimating retirement costs, factor in a reasonable inflation rate to account for the rising prices of goods and services. Historical average inflation rates can provide a starting point for your calculations.

> ***Identify Changes in Expenses***: Certain expenses may change during retirement. For example, you might have paid off your mortgage by then, lowering housing costs. On the other hand, healthcare expenses may increase as you age. Consider how your expenses might change and adjust estimates accordingly.

> ***Account for Health Care Costs***: Healthcare expenses can be significant during retirement. Consider the cost of health insurance premiums, deductibles, co-pays, and any anticipated out-of-pocket costs for medications, equipment and doctor visits. Research average healthcare costs for retirees and consider any specific medical conditions or needs you may have.

> ***Plan for Taxes***: Understand how taxes will impact your retirement income. Some sources of retirement income, such as Social Security, pensions, and withdrawals from traditional retirement accounts may be subject to taxes.

> *Anticipate Long-Term Care Expenses*: Long-term care can be a significant expense during retirement. While not everyone will require long-term care, it's important to consider the potential costs and incorporate them into your estimates.

A useful way to think about retirement liabilities is to consider them in terms of spending goals, of which there are four. Meeting the four retirement income goals, as illustrated in Exhibit 3.5, and managing the four risk categories is essential for securing retirement income. The quality of retirement and satisfaction with it will be greatly influenced by how well this process is navigated.

Exhibit 3.5

These retirement spending goals roughly correspond to the Retirement Income Hierarchy of Needs pyramid. In tandem with the other considerations, these can be transformational, as they can help uncover answers to the following questions:

> How much will future expenses likely be?

> What current expenses are likely to disappear?

> What is truly essential?

> How much is discretionary versus aspirational?

- ➢ What could I live without?
- ➢ What risks could I face in retirement?

There are many ways to cut up your liabilities, but it boils down to figuring out how much you want to spend in retirement and smoothing out one big wrinkle: taxes. We'll cover taxes in a later chapter. You'll want to account for all the expenses in retirement to develop realistic spending expectations. Ultimately, the goal is to have enough to cover everything comfortably when needed. If by some chance you come up short, separating essential and discretionary expenses could be immensely helpful.

We indicated at the outset that quantifying your liabilities wouldn't be easy. But if you want a secure and fulfilling retirement, you'll need to know how much it will cost.

When looking far into the future, forecasting living costs is significantly more challenging due to inflation, taxes, and unexpected expenses. For this reason, we are providing our Calculate Income for Life workbook to help organize your retirement finances in a way that puts first things first, clarifies what you can and can't pay for at this time, and offers peace of mind for the needs you can meet. This workbook will walk you through each level of the Retirement Hierarchy of Needs (see Chapter 3 resources) and record and tally the retirement costs. Refer to Exhibit 3.6 for the sample workbook output. A number of clients have also expressed satisfaction with the Alliance Lifetime Income Retirement Income Security Evaluation (RISE) Score® (see Chapter 3 resources) for determining whether they're on track with their retirement income and how well it will cover their basic needs. This is your retirement income credit score.

You must carefully estimate the retirement costs in terms of monthly and lump sum amounts across the retirement needs hierarchy. This workbook will help you calculate the monthly and lump sum amounts required to fund retirement. Remember, expense planning is an ongoing process.

Review and adjust your estimates periodically as you approach retirement and as circumstances change throughout retirement.

With these two key data points in hand, we are now able to assess our financial readiness for retirement based on what it will cost and what is available to cover those costs. Only through this level of detail can we determine if retirement is feasible as we envision it. Your retirement costs and what you have available to cover them will take on greater significance when we look at how the Funded Ratio (courtesy of Retirement Researcher) is used to assess your readiness for retirement as you envision.

Exhibit 3.6

Retirement Income Hierarchy of Needs Pyramid

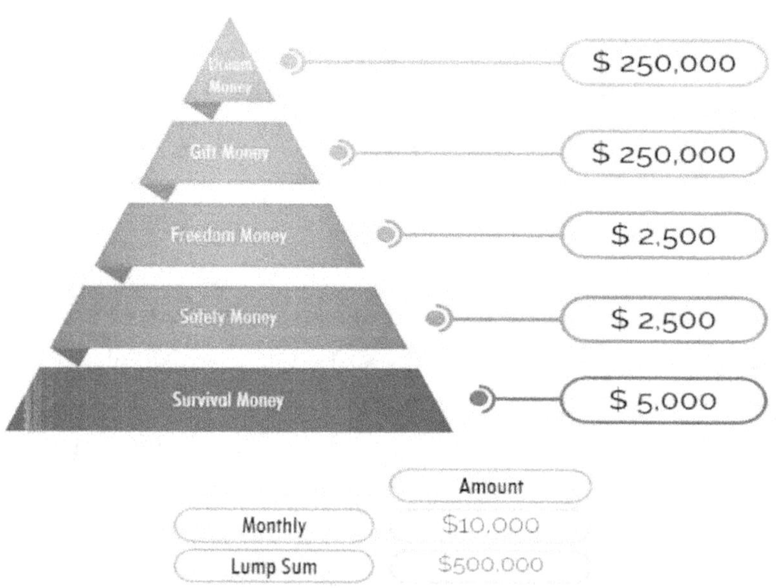

Having quantified the retirement cost (liabilities) and the available assets to fund those liabilities, we now focus on asset-liability matching to ensure the right assets and liabilities are matched and learn why it's a crucial step in the retirement income planning process.

How Asset-Liability Matching Can Benefit Retirement

An essential ingredient to achieving a desired lifestyle during retirement is having income to spend when needed. This depends on how well you pair your assets with your liabilities. The asset-liability matching process ensures that assets are optimized from a usability perspective to effectively manage liabilities. In simple terms, asset-liability matching involves strategically aligning your assets with the liabilities or financial obligations you expect to have in retirement.

Often overlooked, this step is crucial to retirement income planning. It is common for many people to assume that retirement is a given if they have sufficient assets to cover their liabilities. This does not guarantee retirement security any more than owning a sizable nest egg guarantees never running out of money. The mistake many make is to view their financial resources as one big bucket. Taking this stance prevents you from discerning the strengths and weaknesses of each asset and deciding how to utilize them effectively. Rather, carefully evaluating each asset will reveal its characteristics to guide how to deploy it to effectively meet liabilities.

It will be crucial to have a clear understanding of your assets and liabilities to create a viable asset-liability model. As we saw earlier with assets, liabilities also have a profile that reveals characteristics such as amount, duration, flexibility, risk, and timing that inform which assets are appropriate funding vehicles. Knowing each liability's profile will help you make informed decisions about which assets might be suitable for funding it.

The process of matching assets and liabilities can be summarized as follows:

Determine Each Asset's Characteristics

For each asset on the balance sheet compiled earlier, determine its value, availability, duration, reliability, and payout. By doing so, you can better understand how to use each asset to its fullest potential. The valuation of assets will be determined by two separate methods based on the two categories. How these values are calculated will be discussed shortly.

Determine Each Liability's Characteristics

For each liability computed on the Retirement Income Hierarchy of Needs Pyramid, you'll need to determine its amount, duration, payment flexibility, and timing. Just as you calculated a lifetime projected value for your assets, you must also calculate a lifetime amount for your liabilities. We'll discuss how to accomplish this in the following section.

Align Funding Needs to Funding Sources

This is the most important step. Retirement income planning requires asset-liability matching to ensure that assets are sufficient to cover liabilities in a timely manner.

In retirement, your assets (such as savings, investments, pensions, real estate, and Social Security) are the financial resources you have available to generate cash flow to support your lifestyle.

On the other hand, your liabilities consist of your financial obligations such as daily living expenses, healthcare expenses, housing costs, and any outstanding debts.

While it's important to know how much retirement will cost and if there's enough to pay for it, you'll want to go further and determine the best way to structure your assets and liabilities in the most effective manner possible.

First, classify assets by their reliability of payment. This represents how reliable they are as an income source. We use a low, medium, and high taxonomy. In the next step, you want to determine how flexible each liability is regarding payment. For each liability, this represents the timeliness of payment. Using the same taxonomy, we classify payment flexibility into low, medium, and high categories.

From here, you'll want to pair assets and liabilities accordingly:

➤ **High-payment** reliable assets with low-payment flexible liabilities

➤ **Medium-payment** reliable assets with medium-payment flexible liabilities

➤ **Low-payment** reliable assets with high-payment flexible liabilities

By understanding and managing the relationship between your assets and liabilities, you can effectively make informed decisions to align your income and expenses in the best manner possible.

Overall, asset-liability matching in retirement provides a structured approach to align financial resources with obligations in the most effective way possible to ensure that individuals can meet their financial needs and goals throughout their retirement years.

 It allows for proactive planning, risk mitigation, and the optimization of resources, providing individuals with a greater sense of financial security and peace of mind.

How to Calculate Your Retirement Financial Position

As you look towards retirement, the first thing you should ask yourself is how you stand financially. This is important because you need to know if you are on a trajectory to achieve retirement goals. In the event that your efforts up to this point haven't put you on track for retirement, you will need to make the necessary adjustments to get things back on track.

It matters less how it's done and more that it's properly done. Getting to the same conclusion can be done in many ways. The Funded Ratio and Monte Carlo Analysis are two approaches that are commonly used. Despite their differences, both aim to determine whether available assets are sufficient to finance anticipated liabilities during retirement.

The Monte Carlo simulation assesses the probability that a financial plan will succeed under various scenarios related to investment returns, lifespan, and potential expenses. It helps in understanding the risks and potential outcomes associated with retirement decisions. One of the primary virtues of using Monte Carlo analysis for evaluating a retirement plan is that it frames the conversation in terms of the probability of success and failure rather than simply looking at how much wealth is left at the end of the plan. As a result, the focus of planning shifts from maximizing wealth to maximizing the likelihood of success and minimizing the risk of failure.

The Funded Ratio is a more straightforward and easier-to-understand measure of a retirement plan's ability to fund known spending liabilities. It describes the total value of the assets, which includes both current balances and the present value of future expected income, divided by the liability, or all current and present value of future expected spending. A funded ratio of 1.0 implies that an individual has just enough assets to fully fund retirement. A funded ratio greater than 1.0 suggests they have a surplus, while one below 1.0 implies a shortfall. In other words, if we assume the assets will grow at a conservative interest rate, your funded ratio is your income and assets to your future liabilities.

For purposes of this discussion, present value is a financial concept used to determine the current worth of a future sum of money or a series of cash flows, discounted (the opportunity cost of the money, the rate of return you could earn on alternative investments with similar risk) at a specific rate of interest. The idea is based on the time value of money, which suggests that a sum of money today is worth more than the same sum in the future due to its potential earning capacity or investment opportunity.

For instance, if you received $1,000 of income today, you could use that sum to pay for more than $1,000 of expenses 20 years from now because you could invest the money between now and then and hopefully increase its value.

The Funded Ratio measures the ability of a retirement plan to meet its future obligations. The purpose of this analysis is to determine if there is sufficient capital available *today* (assuming conservative future growth estimates) to cover *future* (assuming average inflation growth estimates) retirement liabilities in line with their current values or if there is a shortfall.

For this discussion, we will focus our attention on the Funded Ratio. A wealth of literature is available online to those who want to learn more about Monte Carlo Analysis and how it can be used to evaluate retirement readiness.

The Funded Ratio is typically expressed as a percentage and can be calculated using the following formula:

Funded Ratio = (Present Value of Retirement Plan Assets) / (Present Value of Retirement Plan Liabilities) * 100

The Present Value of Retirement Plan Assets includes the balances of investment accounts and the present value of all future income streams.

The Present Value of Retirement Plan Liabilities is the future value of all estimated retirement expenses. Because these costs will occur in the future, estimating them in today's dollars is necessary when comparing them with the Present Value of Retirement Plan Assets. Since the Funded Ratio captures the current state of retirement readiness, it is imperative to determine the current value of both assets and liabilities.

A Funded Ratio of 100% indicates the retirement plan is fully funded and has sufficient assets to cover its projected liabilities. A ratio above 100% suggests that the plan is overfunded, while one below 100% indicates an underfunded plan.

Monitoring the Funded Ratio is crucial in retirement income planning as it helps individuals assess their retirement preparation and, if needed, make necessary adjustments that may include delaying retirement, saving more, reducing expenses, taking more risks, and other measures as outlined in Exhibit 3.7. These can be a life raft for underfunded retirement plans.

Exhibit 3.7

INCOME SHORTFALL SOLUTIONS

If you have an income shortfall, there are 5 levers to pull to plug a funding shortfall

Determine Your Funded Ratio

Funded Ratio calculation is a relatively straightforward process. The devil is in the details of determining the Present Value of Retirement Plan Assets, such as the current value of IRAs and 401(k)s, as well as the present value of expected future income like pensions and Social Security, and the Present Value of Retirement Plan Liabilities. Once you have these values, it's a basic math calculation.

To begin, let's estimate the Present Value of Retirement Plan Assets, then move on to estimating the present value of retirement plan liabilities.

Calculating the Present Value Of Retirement Plan Assets will require adding up the current value of assets that don't produce a future income stream and calculating the present value of all assets that do.

The following formula reflects this:

Present Value of Retirement Plan Assets = Current Value of Assets + Present Value of Future Income Sources

---

For example, suppose a 65-year-old expects to receive a $2,500 monthly Social Security benefit.

According to the IRS Single Life Expectancy table in Exhibit 3.8, his life expectancy is 22.9 years. Divide that by 2 to arrive at his life expectancy factor or 11 years. If partnered, he would want to use a table representative of joint life expectancies.

Our calculation of Social Security's present value will be based on an ordinary annuity.

Social Security payments are typically made at the end of each period, monthly, making it consistent with an ordinary annuity.

Exhibit 3.8

IRS Single Life Expectancy Table

Age	Life expectancy factor	Age	Life expectancy factor	Age	Life expectancy factor
0	84.6	41	44.8	82	9.9
1	83.7	42	43.8	83	9.3
2	82.8	43	42.9	84	8.7
3	81.8	44	41.9	85	8.1
4	80.8	45	41.0	86	7.6
5	79.8	46	40.0	87	7.1
6	78.8	47	39.0	88	6.6
7	77.9	48	38.1	89	6.1
8	76.9	49	37.1	90	5.7
9	75.9	50	36.2	91	5.3
10	74.9	51	35.3	92	4.9
11	73.9	52	34.3	93	4.6
12	72.9	53	33.4	94	4.3
13	71.9	54	32.5	95	4.0
14	70.9	55	31.6	96	3.7
15	69.9	56	30.6	97	3.4
16	69.0	57	29.8	98	3.2
17	68.0	58	28.9	99	3.0
18	67.0	59	28.0	100	2.8
19	66.0	60	27.1	101	2.6
20	65.0	61	26.2	102	2.5
21	64.1	62	25.4	103	2.3
22	63.1	63	24.5	104	2.2
23	62.1	64	23.7	105	2.1
24	61.1	65	22.9	106	2.1
25	60.2	66	22.0	107	2.1
26	59.2	67	21.2	108	2.0
27	58.2	68	20.4	109	2.0
28	57.3	69	19.6	110	2.0
29	56.3	70	18.8	111	2.0
30	55.3	71	18.0	112	2.0
31	54.4	72	17.2	113	1.9
32	53.4	73	16.4	114	1.9
33	52.5	74	15.6	115	1.8
34	51.5	75	14.8	116	1.8
35	50.5	76	14.1	117	1.6
36	49.6	77	13.3	118	1.4
37	48.6	78	12.6	119	1.1
38	47.7	79	11.9	120+	1.0
39	46.7	80	11.2		
40	45.7	81	10.5		

Source: *IRS*

To represent the discount rate, we'll use a conservative treasury yield on a comparable debt of 2%. The setup in an Excel PV formula (rate, nper, pmt, end) where rate=2% (*discount rate per period*), nper=23 (*number of periods (in years)) expected to receive Social Security payments*), pmt=30,000 (12 x $2,500) (*amount of each Social Security payment to be received annually*), and end=1 (*payments received at the beginning of each period*) produces a $559,741 lifetime Social Security benefit representative of the current value of the future sum to be received.

You will have to repeat this for every income you will receive in the future and sum them along with your current savings to arrive at your Present Value of Retirement Plan Assets.

Because the funded ratio is a current snapshot of retirement readiness, both the Present Value of Retirement Plan Assets and the Present Value of Retirement Plan Liabilities must be represented in today's value or present value. Knowing the present value is not necessary for plan assets that have a current value and the cost of liabilities known upfront. In all other cases, it's required. Estimating the cost of retirement in today's dollars is necessary to determine whether current assets can cover future costs.

Next, let's shift our attention to assessing the costs of future retirement liabilities. We must employ the time value of money future value of an ordinary annuity calculation to estimate a future liability's value. The future value in the context of time value of money refers to the value of a sum of money at a specific future point in time. An inflation rate must be used instead of a discount rate for the future value of an ordinary annuity to reflect the growth in future expenses rather than a discount rate to reflect investment opportunity costs for the present value of ordinary annuity.

Assuming $10,000 of survival, safety, and freedom monthly living expenses from Exhibit 3.6, projected to rise at 2% annual inflation over a 35-year life expectancy factor, the setup in an Excel PV formula (rate, nper, pmt, end) where rate=2% (*inflation rate per period*), nper=35 (*payment duration in years*), pmt=120,000 (12 x $10,000) (*annual payment amount*) amounts to a $3,059,831 lifetime survival, safety, and freedom future expense total.

Pulling this all together, let's consider a simple example. For illustration purposes, let's assume there are $4,000,000 of Current Value of Assets from personal savings and $500,000 of Present Value of Future Income Sources from Social Security, totaling $4,500,000 of Present Value of Retirement Plan Assets.

Pulling data from Exhibit 3.6, the Present Value of Retirement Plan Liabilities amount to $3,559,831 comprising $3,059,831 of survival, safety, and freedom costs and $500,000 from dream and gift costs.

Plugging these values into the funded ratio formula yields the following ratio for this hypothetical retirement plan.

Funded Ratio = ($4,500,000) / ($3,559,831) * 100 = 126.41

This ratio affirms that this retiree's retirement is overly funded since assets exceed liabilities because the ratio exceeds 100. Said differently, more money is available than is required to fund retirement *as of today*. Importantly, asset growth assumptions are conservative.

Recall a funded ratio greater than 100 is overfunded by that amount and indicates the plan is flexible enough to increase spending in the event of a rise in expenses without compromising the quality of life. It's important to remember that due to the point-in-time nature of this calculation, it can only provide a picture of how the plan would work if retirement began today. No implication is made or suggested that this may remain accurate later in retirement.

There are a few caveats to remember when calculating your Funded Ratio.

> ➤ This is a point-in-time result demonstrating retirement based on assumptions about life expectancy, spending expectations, and assets for a hypothetical retirement if retiring *today* and does *not* say anything about the funded status of retirement in future years.

> ➤ It does not indicate whether retirement readiness will remain or change. Life is fluid. Changes in the Present Value of Retirement

Plan Liabilities or the Present Value of Retirement Plan Assets could alter the fund ratio.

> The funded ratio calculation should not be the only type of retirement-preparedness analysis you do. Additional tests with Monte Carlo simulations (or potentially historical simulations) can also be informative.

With a few pieces of information and some basic financial calculations, the Funded Ratio provides a quick and accurate measurement of retirement preparedness. Monte Carlo analysis is a more comprehensive and involved measure of retirement readiness, given that it accounts for other factors affecting retirements, such as inflation, investment growth, market volatility, and taxes.

Among the two methods, I prefer the Funded Ratio because it allows me to quickly gauge whether someone is on track to meet their spending expectations, given knowledge of their spending goals and assets they have on hand. Should a deeper investigation be warranted, a Monte Carlo simulation can be carried out for a more detailed assessment.

For those interested in calculating a funded ratio spanning multiple years in retirement, a free calculator is available through the Oblivious Investor (see Chapter 3 resources). When calculating your Funded Ratio this way, you should remember several things:

Discount rates matter. You can think of it as the return on your investment. By choosing a conservative rate, assets will grow slower, which may result in a lower, more realistic Funded Ratio. Assets will likely grow faster, and the Funded Ratio will likely improve if you pursue an aggressive rate of return, but it may not be realistic.

Should the return earned be less than the rate used in the calculation, an inaccurate and misleading result will be generated. In other words, we're assuming that the portfolio will earn this rate of return every year without fail. So, suppose you choose an aggressive discount rate (such as the return you'd expect from a portfolio with a considerable stock allocation). In that case, you're setting yourself up for failure if your portfolio happens to earn a lesser return.

Time horizons are important. The funded ratio depends on the discount rate and planning time horizon, so you should make reasonable assumptions about how long your savings must last. Planning for short time horizons can be quite beneficial, yet they can also set you up for failure if you live beyond them. In contrast, planning for a longer time horizon can reduce spending and quality of life, since more assets must be held aside to support spending for an uncertain period.

Case Study: How the Banners Quantified and Matched Assets and Liabilities and Determined Their Retirement Readiness

To have a comfortable and financially secure retirement, you must determine how you will receive income when you stop working. Knowing this will ensure that you can fund your retirement expenses in a manner that is most meaningful to you.

After devoting time to uncovering how you wish to pay yourself in retirement, the next crucial step on the retirement income planning journey is to crunch the numbers to determine if you're on track to retire in the way you envision.

To accomplish this, you must estimate your retirement expenses to determine how much they will cost and then determine whether you have the resources to cover them.

But before you take a victory lap, you should ensure your assets and liabilities are appropriately matched. By aligning your assets and liabilities on the key characteristics of duration, risk, and timing, you enhance the likelihood of achieving retirement goals and enjoying financial stability throughout retirement.

The Banners' Anticipated Retirement Liabilities

I haven't met many clients thrilled at the prospect of creating a budget during my years as a planner. Estimating expenses before or after retirement is about as enjoyable as giving a porcupine a backrub. It wasn't any different with the Banners. As a result of considering their options, David and Dawn chose to utilize the Calculate Income for Life online worksheets we use to help clients like them determine their retirement costs.

Exhibit 3.9

The Banners' Retirement Expense Pyramid

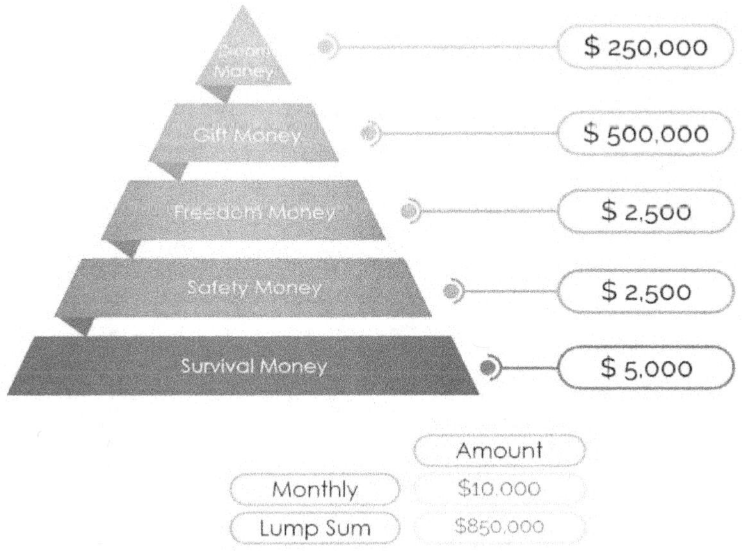

They both agreed that working through the workbook enabled them to consider costs they would not have considered otherwise. After a thorough examination of costs, they are now confident that they have accounted for the most consequential expenses. Exhibit 3.9 illustrates how their workbook output is mapped to their retirement expense pyramid.

A breakout of these retirement costs into the four retirement spending goals illustrated below would look like this:

➢ Longevity - $5,000/monthly for life

➢ Liquidity - $2,500/monthly for life + $50,000/one-time unforeseen expenses + $50,000/one-time expense of planned home repairs and upgrades

➢ Lifestyle - $2,500/monthly for life + $250,000/one-time expense

➢ Legacy - $500,000/one-time expense

Considering inflation is a constant threat to retirement security, we need to account for it when estimating the Banners' longevity and liquidity spending goals. Due to their recurring nature, these two spending goals are the most susceptible to cost increases.

We'll need to estimate the Banners' present value of all future retirement liabilities (longevity, liquidity, and lifestyle). Other income goals such as legacy and a portion of lifestyle spending goals are already based on today's cost and don't require a present-value calculation.

Key Assumptions:

➢ Retirement start date: age 65

➢ Retirement planning horizon: 35 years

➢ Inflation rate: 3% (long-term consumer price index cost of living increase)

DETAILED COST ESTIMATES FOR THE BANNERS' FOUR RETIREMENT SPENDING GOALS

Longevity:

This is a recurring spending goal estimated at $60,000 annual ($5,000 monthly) costs over 35 years, growing at 3% annual inflation.

Inputting these values into the HP 12C financial calculator Present Value where i=3%, n=35, pmt=60,000 yields the following income goal:

$1,289,233 lifetime funding need

Liquidity

This spending goal has recurring and episodic components. For the $2,500 monthly recurring expense, we will calculate the present value as we did for the longevity expense and add it to the $100,000 episodic expense component that already reflects a current value.

Recurring Expense: The $30,000 ($2,500 monthly) annual costs over 35 years grow at 3% annual inflation. Plugging these values into the HP 12C financial calculator Present Value where i=3%, n=35, pmt=30,000 yields a $644,616 income need for this component of the goal.

Episodic Expense: The $100,000 ($50,000 unplanned expenses and $50,000 planned home repairs and upgrades) lifetime income need.

Note: We elected to use the HP 12C financial calculator to calculate this component. Microsoft Excel, online calculators, and other financial calculators are all good options.

$744,616 lifetime funding need

Lifestyle:

This spending goal has recurring and episodic components as well, so we'll employ the same approach as we did with the Liquidity goal.

Recurring Expense: The $30,000 ($2,500 monthly) annual costs over 35 years, growing at 3% annual inflation. Plugging these values into HP 12C financial calculator Present Value calculation where i=3%, n=35, pmt=30,000 results in a $644,616 income need for this component of the goal.

Episodic Expense: The $250,000 lifetime income need.

$894,616 lifetime funding need

Legacy:

This spending goal is already stated in current value and no additional calculations are required.

$ 500,000 lifetime funding need

Exhibit 3.10 Present Value of Retirement Plan Liabilities summarizes the estimated lifetime cost of David and Dawn's retirement.

Exhibit 3.10

Present Value of Retirement Plan Liabilities

Liability	Costs
Longevity Income	$1,289,233
Liquidity Income	$744,616
Lifestyle Income	$894,616
Legacy Income	$500,000
Total Lifetime Cost	**$3,428,465**

The Banners' Anticipated Retirement Assets

Retirement costs are only one piece of the puzzle of retirement income. We will now turn our attention away from them to learn what's available to pay for them. As part of their planning process, David and Dawn will need to identify current sources of income and assets that can generate retirement income to meet their retirement spending goals.

CURRENT SOURCES OF INCOME

These are summarized in the Income Sources Currently Available to Meet Retirement Income Needs balance sheet in Exhibit 3.11.

Exhibit 3.11

Income Sources Currently Available to Meet Retirement Income Needs						
Source	Amount	Duration	Reliability	COLA	Timing	Payout
Dawn						
Social Security	$1,250/month	Payable for life	Secure	Yes	Age 67	Life Annuity
Pension	$1,500/month	Payable for life	Secure	No	Age 65	Joint and Survivor.
David						
Social Security	$2,000/month	Payable for life	Secure	Yes	Age 70	Life Annuity
Deferred Compensation	$1,750/month	payable for life	Less Secure	No	Age 65	Salary Continuation
Joint						
Rental Income	$1,000/month	20 years	Less Secure	Yes	Ongoing	Monthly payment + potential capital gains at sale

Because some of these income streams are expected to begin in the future for an indeterminate amount of time, we'll need to determine the present value of the expected future income stream before we can assess their retirement readiness. Here are the assumptions we will make:

Key Assumptions:

- ➢ Retirement start date: age 65
- ➢ Retirement Planning Horizon: 35 years
- ➢ Discount rate: 3% (conservative risk-free rate of return)
- ➢ Inflation rate: 3% (average long-term rate)
- ➢ Rental property ownership: 20 years
- ➢ Annual rent increase: 3%

DAWN'S ASSETS

Social Security

A $1,250 monthly benefit starting at age 70 produces a $322,308 estimated lifetime benefit using HP 12C financial calculator present value calculation where i=3% (discount rate per period), n=35 (number of periods (in years) expected to receive Social Security payments), pmt=15,000 (12 x $1,250) (amount of each Social Security payment to be received annually).

Pension

As a lifelong educator, she's entitled to a generous retirement pension that pays her $1,500 a month for life. During our consultation on her options, we advised her to choose the joint-life survivor option that pays out for whoever lives longer.

A $1,500 monthly benefit starting at age 65 produces a $386,769 estimated lifetime benefit using HP 12C financial calculator present value calculation where i=3% (discount rate per period), n=35 (number of periods (in years) expected to receive pension payments), pmt=18,000 (12 x $1,500) (amount of each pension payment to be received annually).

DAVID'S ASSETS

Social Security

A $2,000 monthly benefit starting at age 70 produces a $515,693 estimated lifetime benefit using HP 12C financial calculator present value calculation where i=3% (discount rate per period), n=35 (number of periods (in years) expected to receive Social Security payments), pmt=24,000 (12 x $2,000) (amount of each Social Security payment to be received annually).

Deferred Compensation

As a long-time senior-level executive at his company, he is eligible for a robust deferred compensation plan that will pay him $1,750 a month for the rest of his life beginning at retirement.

A \$1,750 monthly benefit starting at age 65 produces a \$451,231 estimated lifetime benefit using HP 12C financial calculator present value calculation where i=3% (discount rate per period), n=35 (number of periods (in years) expected to receive deferred compensation payments), pmt=21,000 (12 x \$1,750) (amount of each deferred compensation payment to be received annually).

CO-OWNED ASSETS

David and Dawn own a rental duplex in a nearby city that generates \$1,000 in net monthly rental income. It is expected that they will liquidate the property in 20 years.

Assuming a \$12,000 net annual rental income with a 3% annual rental increase over the next 20 years, this produces a \$178,529 estimated benefit using HP 12C financial calculator present value calculation where i=3% (annual rent increase), n=20 (number of periods (in years) expected to receive rental payments), pmt=12,000 (12 x \$1,000) (amount of rental payments to be received annually).

Exhibit 3.12 shows the Banners' present value of current income sources available to meet retirement income needs.

Exhibit 3.12

Present Value of Income Sources Currently Available to Meet Retirement Income Needs

Asset	Value
Dawn	
Social Security	\$ 322,308
Pension	\$ 386,769
David	
Social Security	\$ 515,693
Deferred Compensation	\$ 451,231
Joint	
Rental Income	\$ 178,529
Total Lifetime Value	\$ 1,854,530

ASSETS AVAILABLE TO TURN INTO INCOME

In Exhibit 3.13 we've compiled a list of the Banners' assets available to turn into income. Among these are retirement and personal savings accounts, real estate, cash-value life insurance, and cash.

It is not necessary to convert these accounts to their present value amounts since they are all valued in today's dollars. We simply have to total the account values to arrive at the grand total amount, which we determined to be approximately $2.45 million.

Exhibit 3.13

Assets Used to Generate Retirement Income				
Asset	Value	Timing	Reliability	Payout
Dawn				
403(b)	$500,000	As early as 59 ½ or retirement, whichever is the earliest	Market performance	lump sum or annuity
Roth IRA	$250,000	As early as 59 ½ or retirement, whichever is earliest	Market performance	Lump sum
David				
401(k)	$500,000	As early as 59 ½ or retirement, whichever is earliest	Market performance	Lump sum or annuity
Roth IRA	$250,000	As early as 59 ½ or retirement, whichever is earliest	Market performance	Lump sum
Joint				
Brokerage account	$250,000	Anytime	Market performance	Lump sum
Rental Equity	$100,000	Buyer availability	Secure	Lump sum
Cash value life insurance	$50,000	Assuming cash value anytime	Secure	Lump sum loan
Home Equity	$500,000	Buyer availability	Secure	Lump sum
Cash Savings	$50,000	Anytime	Secure	Lump sum

Totaling the Banners' $1,854,530 of Present Value of Income Sources Currently Available to Meet Retirement Income Needs and the $2,450,000 Current Value of Assets Available to Turn into Retirement Income amount to a little over $4,304,530 dollars available to fund their retirement.

By analyzing the Banners' spending goals and resources available to meet those goals, we have compiled key financial components of their Retirement in the Retirement Fact Pattern presented in Exhibit 3.14.

Exhibit 3.14 Banners' Retirement Fact Pattern

Income-producing Assets	Asset Value	Cost Basis
Taxable Account	$250,000	$100,000
403(b)/401(k)	$1,000,000	
Roth IRA	$500,000	
Cash-value Life Insurance	$50,000	$15,000
Cash Savings	$50,000	$50,000
Primary Home Equity	$500,000	
Rental Equity	$100,000	

Income Sources at present		
Pension (David)	$1,750/monthly	
Pension (Dawn)	$1,500/monthly	
Social Security (David)	$2,000/monthly	Primary Insurance Amount
Social Security (Dawn)	$1,250/monthly	Primary Insurance Amount
Rental Income	$1,000/monthly	

Spending Liabilities	Annual Expense	Age Range	Inflation-Adjusted?
Longevity Spending	$60,000	65-75	Yes
Longevity Spending	$50,000	76-95	Yes
Liquidity Spending	$2,500/monthly		Yes
	$100,000	one-time expense	
Lifestyle Spending	$2,500/monthly		Yes
	$250,000	one-time expense	
Legacy Spending	$500,000	one-time expense	

Taxes	22% Federal | 8% State		

Now that we know what retirement costs and what retirement funds are available to fund them, we are in a position to assess their progress toward retirement using the Funded Ratio.

The Banners' Fund Ratio

Recall the Funded Ratio measures the readiness of a retirement plan to meet its future obligations. This helps determine whether there are sufficient assets to pay for retirement liabilities or if there is a shortfall.

The Funded Ratio is calculated using the following formula:

Funded Ratio = (Present Value of Retirement Plan Assets) / (Present Value of Retirement Plan Liabilities) * 100

Inputting in the values from the previous steps for the Banners easily allows us to determine if their retirement plan can meet its future obligations at this point in time.

*125 = ($4,304,530) / ($3,428,465) * 100*

Recall a funded ratio greater than 100% indicates that the retirement plan is overly funded and has sufficient assets to cover its projected liabilities with a surplus.

The results show the Banners have accumulated sufficient assets to meet their anticipated liabilities. Their retirement is currently overly funded with a **$876,000** surplus resulting from the $4,304,530 value of retirement plan assets minus the $3,428,465 present value of retirement plan liabilities. A modest amount. Depending on the changes in their assets or liabilities, this figure may move up or down. Even though they have an overly funded retirement, they will need to monitor it periodically to determine where they stand financially in retirement at any given moment. But we can safely assume that based on their spending goals, available funding, and length of retirement, they are financially prepared to retire!

The advantage of having an overly funded retirement is that it opens up opportunities to leverage surplus amounts to obtain more secure funding for essential expenses that have little or no payment flexibility.

We'll explore this in greater detail in the next section on Asset-Liability Pairings, where we aim to optimize the alignment of assets with future liabilities to help David and Dawn ensure they have enough reliable income to cover their essential or non-discretionary expenses and achieve their desired lifestyle during retirement.

THE BANNERS' RECOMMENDED ASSET-LIABILITY PAIRINGS

In my experience, most people planning for retirement don't view prioritizing retirement spending goals as a crucial component of a successful retirement income plan. Due to the fungible nature of money, many assume it is less important that funds are set aside for specific spending purposes, and more important that they are available when needed. This line of thinking comes with huge risks, since the greatest risk in retirement is the ability to source income to cover liabilities when needed. The failure to consider the strengths and weaknesses of assets and liabilities can lead to funding mismatches that pose a threat to spending goals and financial security. To ensure cash flow is available for spending when needed, retirees should incorporate an asset-liability matching strategy into their planning to ensure alignment between an asset's payment reliability with a liability's payment flexibility.

Our ability to make wise asset-liability pairing decisions will be greatly enhanced if we understand not just an asset's payment reliability, but also a liability's payment flexibility. With this understanding, we can plan how to effectively align assets and liabilities.

An asset's ability to generate income is measured by its payment reliability, while a liability's payment flexibility refers to its payment requirements. The goal is to match the most secure assets with the most essential liabilities; in other words, pairing high-payment reliable assets with low-payment flexible liabilities. By doing so, we can prioritize funding to the most crucial spending goals with the most secure assets to maintain quality of life and financial stability.

Employing a taxonomy for classifying an asset's payment reliability and liabilities payment flexibility will be necessary for guiding the asset-liability process. We'll classify assets as low, medium, or high payment reliability, and liabilities as low, medium, and high payment flexibility. High payment-reliable assets with contractual obligations to guarantee payment include annuities, bonds, pensions, and Social Security. In contrast, assets that offer low or medium payment reliability, such as business interests, employment, investments, and real estate, depend on personal, financial, and economic factors and cannot offer payment guarantees.

Exhibit 3.15 shows a breakdown of the Banners' asset payment reliability ratios. Two important insights can be gleaned from this analysis about their income composition. Most assets, 45%, have high payment reliability (i.e., they can easily be converted into income), while 14% and 41%, have medium and low payment reliability, respectively.

Exhibit 3.15 Asset Payment Reliability

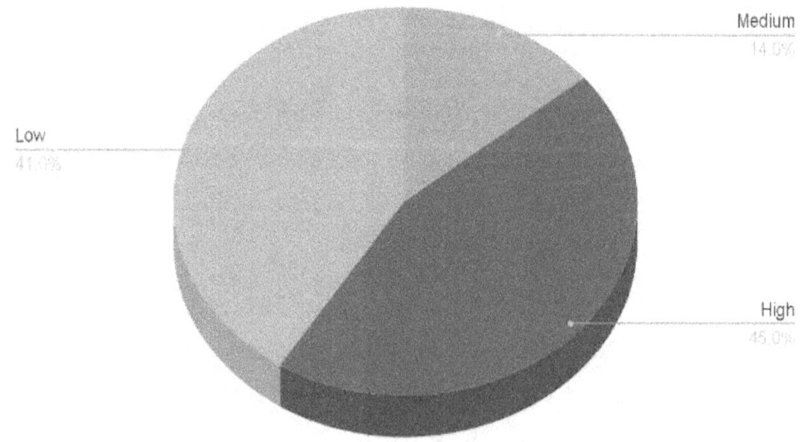

Banners' Asset Payment Reliability Composition

Asset	*Reliability*	*Amount*	*% of Total Assets*[1]
A	High	$1,954,000	45
B	Medium	$600,000	14
C	Low	$1,750,000	41

Percentage of $4,304,530 total assets[1]

A. Present Value of Income Sources Currently Available, cash-value life insurance, and cash savings

B. Primary home and rental investment property

C. Current Value of Income Sources that can generate income

To complete the asset-liability analysis, we will need to perform a similar evaluation on their liabilities to determine payment flexibility.

The Retirement Liability Balance sheet, as depicted in Exhibit 3.16, serves as the basis for our review of their liabilities. Using it, we can classify spending goals or liabilities according to payment flexibility, starting with longevity income, which includes essential expenses like food, housing, healthcare, and utilities, as "low-payment flexible" because those expenses must be paid.

Liquidity income is the money needed to cover unexpected expenses that may prevent other spending goals from being met. These are also classified as non-payment flexible liabilities that must be paid if and when they occur to maintain a desired standard of living. Lifestyle income reflects discretionary spending and is a medium- to high-payment flexible liability. Relative to all others, legacy income reflects the highest-payment flexible expense.

Exhibit 3.16

Retirement Liability Balance Sheet

Liability	*Costs*
Longevity Income	$1,289,233
Liquidity Income	$744,616
Lifestyle Income	$894,616
Legacy Income	$500,000
Total Lifetime Cost	**$3,428,465**

The chart in Exhibit 3.17 is a visual representation of the Banners' Retirement Liability Balance Sheet.

Exhibit 3.17 Liability Payment Flexibility

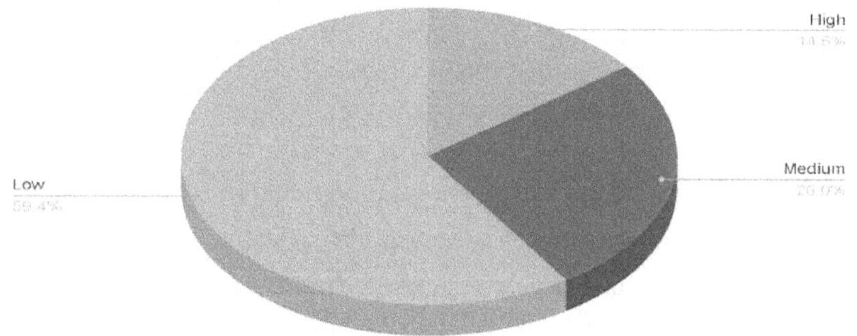

Banners' Liability Payment Flexibility Composition

Liability	*Flexibility*	*Amount*	*% of Total Liabilities*
Longevity	Low	$1,289,233	37.6
Liquidity	Low	$744,616	21.7
Lifestyle	Medium	$894,616	26
Legacy	High	$500,000	14.6

Percentage of $3,428,465 total spending liabilities

Based on this analysis, the following conclusions can be drawn:

> 59.3% of the liabilities are essential/non-discretionary and have limited payment flexibility while 45% of the assets have high payment reliability.

> Liabilities with low payment flexibility amount to $2,033,000 ($3,428,465 times 59.3%), while assets with high payment reliability amount to $1,937,00 ($4,304,530 times 45%).

> The amount of low-payment-flexible liabilities exceeds the amount of high-payment-reliable assets by $95,961 ($2,033,000 - $1,937,00), creating a secure income funding gap in this amount we'll need to address.

With this deeper understanding of the Banners' asset and liability composition, we can begin to think more strategically about how to structure their assets and liabilities to reliably fund essential spending needs.

However, before continuing, we should pause briefly to discuss a framework commonly used to accomplish this.

By utilizing the Retirement Income Optimization Map (RIO), in Exhibit 3.18, courtesy of Retirement Researcher, it is possible to visualize the relationship between assets, liabilities, and spending goals in retirement to guide our decision-making on arranging assets and liabilities to increase income security.

The framework will serve as a decision-making aid to guide our asset-liability pairings and remind us why we made these decisions in the first place.

Exhibit 3.18

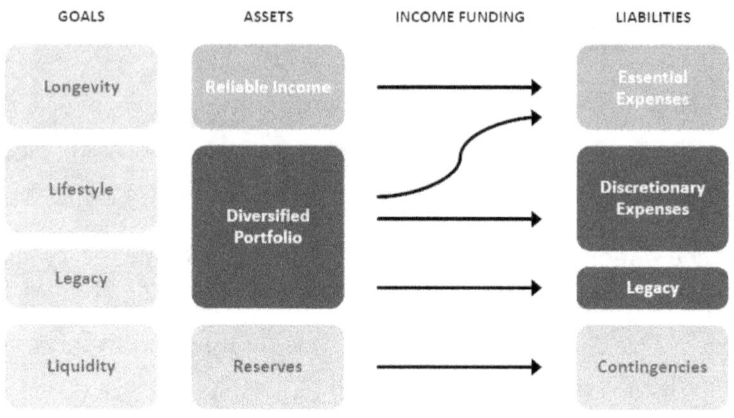

We can draw several conclusions from the RIO map:

> ➤ Longevity goals and liabilities associated with essential expenses are tightly coupled and should be funded with high-payment reliable assets.

> ➤ Liquidity goals and liabilities associated with contingencies are tightly coupled and should be funded with high-payment reliable assets.

> ➤ Lifestyle and legacy goals can be funded with lower-payment reliability assets.

With the Retirement Income Optimization Map to guide us and an understanding of the Banners' asset and liability composition, we are now in a position to determine the optimal asset-liability matching pairings.

They have an overly funded retirement of $876,025 (total assets $4,304,530 minus total liabilities $3,428,465). A primary concern is the approximate $96,000 secure income shortfall resulting from the

$2,033,000 ($3,428,465 times 59.3%) of low-payment-flexible liabilities minus the $1,937,000 ($4,304,530 times 45%) high-payment-reliable assets to fund them. Exhibit 3.19 illustrates how this shortfall results in a $96,000 (4.7%) funding deficit that poses a risk to reliable funding of essential expenses, considering that the Banners indicated their preference for funding essential expenses with secure income.

Exhibit 3.19

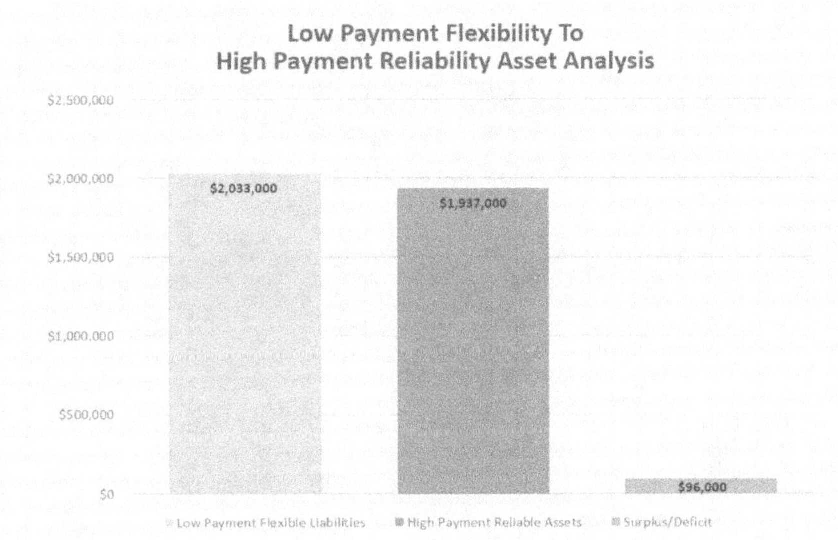

It's a straightforward solution. It will be necessary for them to redirect a portion of the surplus funds and any other funds in the underfunded amount from low-payment-reliant assets to higher-payment-reliant assets. By doing so, the imbalance will be corrected, and funding will be secured for essential expenses.

We proposed that the Banners acquire additional sources of secure income equal to the essential expense underfunded amount, with payments beginning at the start of retirement. Our discussion in the next chapter will elaborate on how we went about solving this need.

Based on an understanding of their asset and liability composition, the following asset-liability matching strategy in Table 3.20 would best serve the Banner household. In essence, the most secure assets go toward paying the most essential (longevity and liquidity) liabilities, while the least secure assets go toward paying discretionary (lifestyle and legacy) liabilities.

Table 3.20

Goal	*Asset*	*Liability*
Longevity	annuity, pension, social security, cash-value life insurance	essential
Liquidity	cash, CDs, short-term debt, line of credit, cash-value life insurance	contingencies
Lifestyle	diversified portfolio	discretionary
Legacy	diversified portfolio	discretionary

The Banner case study demonstrates the value of quantifying and matching assets and liabilities. Understanding the retirement costs and funding sources allows us to evaluate their retirement effort to date and gauge their readiness for retirement.

Moreover, while they are fully funded for retirement when considering their assets and liabilities broadly, they are underfunded with respect to funding essential expenses with reliable assets. It was only after a careful analysis of their asset and liability composition that this became apparent.

This underscores how important it is to understand your income preferences, so your assets and liabilities align appropriately. It is significant because David and Dawn's income profile results indicate a strong income preference to fund essential expenses with secure income.

An effective asset-liability matching strategy aims to uphold income preferences while keeping assets in a position to be utilized at optimal times to pay liabilities steadily and reliably to benefit the retirement household.

MARK'S KEY TAKEAWAYS

➢ Assess retirement readiness by quantifying assets and liabilities.

➢ Ensure proper asset-liability alignment.

➢ Address any asset-liability alignment funding gaps.

CHAPTER 4

Maximize Efficiencies, Mitigate Risks, and Manage Taxes

"The income tax created more criminals than any other single act of government."

— BARRY GOLDWATER

Learning Objectives

- ➢ Mitigating Risks to Preserve Assets and Protect Spending Goals

- ➢ Achieving Maximum Efficiencies to Lower Retirement Costs

- ➢ Managing Taxes for Greater Wealth and Increased Spending

- ➢ Case Study: How the Banners Mitigate Risks, Maximize Efficiencies, and Manage Taxes

Even the most well-crafted retirement strategies will encounter a range of potential risks. These can include extended life expectancy, market volatility, and spending shocks. Those risks mattered less before retirement because you were still working, weren't facing them, or had other means to deal with them unavailable in retirement. A key component of safeguarding spending in retirement is having a plan to mitigate the impact of risks.

Efficiency probably wasn't on the radar before retirement. Back then, the goal was to build as much wealth as possible and hope it would be enough to live on in retirement. Now, efficiency moves to the forefront because you are no longer working and building wealth, and it is important to make the most of what you have. Efficiency, when applied in the retirement income planning context, means using assets to maximize after-tax spending and legacy value.

Achieving greater spending potential requires mitigating risks, maximizing efficiencies, and minimizing taxes.

A change in the nature of income (for example, going from a paycheck to accessing retirement savings for income) alters the importance and impact of taxes.

Taxes are now levied on once tax-free income. Income sources that aren't perceived as taxable, like annuities, pensions, and Social Security, are potentially subject to taxation. Income that comes with mandatory withdrawal requirements complicates managing tax liabilities. It was never necessary for you to withdraw savings before retirement, but that changes during retirement. Taxes can constrain consumption and undermine preservation more than anything else in retirement. Many retirees are shocked by the toll taxes can take on their savings in retirement. For retirees concerned about potential tax exposure, planning from a tax-centric perspective may reduce tax liabilities, preserve assets, and increase after-tax spending.

In this chapter, we will review these three key elements of retirement income planning to better understand and appreciate the best strategies and techniques for ensuring a steady and reliable income throughout retirement.

Mitigating Risks to Preserve Assets and Protect Spending Goals

Life involves balancing caution and daring. Cautious enough to avoid costly mistakes, avoid burnout, and maintain a margin of safety, yet daring enough to bet on yourself to do the things you would regret not doing, and willing to face discomfort in the short term to learn and grow in the long term. Similarly, retirement will require you to balance (maintain a margin of safety) the risks (the caution) you face with the goals (the daring) that make it all worthwhile (grow in the long term).

You must use the same care, dedication, and effort to protect your assets as you did to grow them. Even if you have saved well for retirement, if you haven't identified and prepared for the risks you might encounter, the costs to cover the risks could eventually exceed the funds you have left to spend.

Some of these risks include extended life expectancy, rising inflation rates, falling markets, and soaring healthcare costs. One or more of these risks or several others could seriously compromise retirement income security. There will always be risks in life, and we cannot avoid them, but we can plan to minimize their impact when they show up, as they will. We must assess the relevant threats to determine if our financial foundation has any cracks, so we can make the necessary preparations to ensure income security in retirement.

Your ability to manage the four key retirement risks will determine whether you will have the income you need when you need it. These categories encompass all risks. Exhibit 4.0 highlights each of the risks, which includes longevity (living longer than expected), market volatility, inflation (increases in the price of goods and services), and spending shocks (events that result in higher-than-expected spending).

Exhibit 4.0

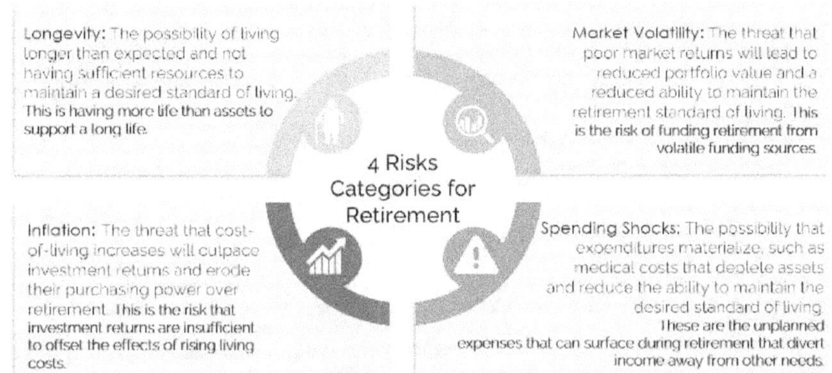

Any of these risks can negatively impact spending capacity, whether taken together or separately. Considering the uncertainties surrounding their occurrence, their impact on the household, and the means required, dealing with them can be challenging. But we should not let that deter us from finding ways to mitigate them.

Longevity

Longevity swings the biggest hammer of all retirement risks because it amplifies all other risks. A longer life expectancy increases vulnerability to market volatility because assets are at increased risk to market behavior since they have to be invested over a longer period to cover a greater life span. While aging is wonderful, it will add to your healthcare costs as the body and the mind deteriorate over time. The longer one lives; the more time inflation has to eat away at savings. Spending shocks are more likely to occur with a longer lifespan.

Having no idea how long retirement will last makes it tricky to calculate how much income is needed to live comfortably. Let's say you plan to live to 85. Your life span ends up being longer than expected, and you live to 95 or longer. Will you be able to extend your money's life by 10 or more years? Considering the unpredictability of life spans, it is not a question that anyone can answer definitively.

Among all the risks you will face in retirement, an unknown life expectancy is the greatest because it magnifies all other risks.

We can never pin down an exact number. To plan effectively for retirement, it will be necessary to come up with a reasonable estimate of how long life will last to know how much to save and to spend. We must consider the historical experiences of life expectancy, family and personal health history, and other lifestyle factors.

A good starting point is to understand the numbers that surround life expectancy. At 65, the average life expectancy for a man is 84.3 years, while for a woman, it is 86.6 years. Although these are useful references, they should be viewed cautiously, since half of the population lives shorter lives than the average, and the other half lives longer lives. A person's life expectancy is highly nuanced, so it is difficult to boil it down to averages.

The numbers look different when viewed from this perspective. Statistically, one in four people will live past 90, but only one in ten will live past 95. For example, a male born in 1961 has an average life expectancy at age 62 of 84. And for those still alive at ages 66 and 70, life expectancy extends to 85.3 and 86.2, respectively. In other words, longevity decreases with age while life expectancy increases. The probability of planning to live well into the 90s may be reasonable for individuals in good health who come from long-lived families and maintain healthy lifestyles.

There are no hard and fast rules for estimating life expectancy. It will always be an imprecise exercise to some extent. Below are a few common guidelines to consider when estimating how long you may live.

Longevity decreases with age while life expectancy increases.

PLAN FOR LONGEVITY

While the uncertainty of longevity cannot be eliminated, one can address this concern by setting realistic life span expectations. This begins by looking at life expectancy tables and considering personal and family health history and other factors. Here, it may be helpful to consult online calculators that are designed to consider personal factors, like the Living to 100 and the Social Security Life Expectancy calculators (see Chapter 4 resources).

The Social Security Life Expectancy calculator asks only gender and birthdate to generate average life expectancy estimates at various ages. This is only an average and should only be used as a starting point. Exhibit 4.1 illustrates what the output from the calculator would look like for a male born on January 1, 1961.

Long life expectancy comes at a high price. Unless you transfer the risk of a long life to an insurance company that can pool the risk of a long life among many individuals more efficiently than you can, the longer your planning horizon, the more resources you need to set aside, and the more conservative you need to be in your spending.

Exhibit 4.1

At Age	Additional Life Expectancy (in years)	Estimated Total Years
62 and 6 months[a]	21.1	83.6
67[b]	17.9	84.9
70	15.9	85.9

[a] Your current age.
[b] Your normal (or full) retirement age.

Note: The estimates of additional life expectancy:

- do not take into account a wide number of factors such as current health, lifestyle, and family history that could increase or decrease life expectancy.

- are based on
    - the sex and date of birth you entered (your cohort) and
    - information from our cohort life expectancy tables.
      (Some of the information can be found in the 2023 Trustees Report.)

Source: *Livingto100, LLC*

STRATEGIES FOR COUNTERING LONGEVITY

Lifetime Income

An effective strategy to reduce the risk of living too long is to secure income sources that will last a lifetime. Social Security payments can be deferred as a first step to increasing lifelong income. A second option is to choose life annuity payments from an employer-sponsored retirement plan rather than rolling them over to the self-managed investment account.

Many employees are unfamiliar with the life annuity option to create lifetime income and instead opt for the lump-sum option. An annuity, which transfers longevity risk to an insurance company that can manage it more effectively than a retiree, is another option to create a lifetime income stream. The cost of an annuity to insure against a long life is less than self-funding.

Investing in annuities is a way to buy future income using current income.

Here's an example to illustrate this. A 60-year-old couple with a need for a $30,000 annual income expects to live into their nineties and begins receiving payouts at age 65. Using an annuity to insure against this risk would cost them $372,367. If self-funding this spending goal for 30 years, this couple would need to set aside $900,000 ($30,000 annual payment times 30) to fund spending up to 30 years. In the event that they lived longer, their funds would be exhausted. Over half a million dollars at a minimum could be saved by using an annuity rather than self-funding to protect against a long life.

Income for an Indefinite Period

Besides annuities and Social Security, other reliable sources of income provide some protection from longevity risks that are not for life but can be for an indefinite period. For homeowners, reverse mortgages can provide monthly payments if the owner remains in the home. Additional possibilities for income sources that do not have a specified end date include rental income, dividend-paying stock, or active business interests capable of producing ongoing income.

Withdrawal Strategies

One of the most important questions facing retirees planning to use their investments to fund retirement is how to withdraw them sustainably without running out of money in retirement. There has been extensive research into Safe Withdrawal Rates (SWRs) that retirees can take, with perhaps the most famous study being Bill Bengen's paper suggesting that a person who withdrew 4% of their portfolio's value during their first year of retirement, then withdrew the same dollar amount adjusted for inflation in each subsequent year, would never run out of money by the end of a 30-year time horizon – even in the worst-case sequence of returns ever experienced in historical US data.[4]

Choosing an appropriate withdrawal rate can extend the life of assets. Still, it cannot completely protect a household from the perils of a longer life expectancy because no one knows how long that could be. It would also be incredibly inefficient to keep a large reserve of assets or restrict spending early in retirement. Doing so could lead to higher costs than needed and sacrifice the present for the future. It's a gamble that may not pay off if you live a shorter or longer life than expected. The key is to select a withdrawal rate that can be sustained over time without compromising quality of life. Funding retirement with an investment-based withdrawal strategy involves risks, and it's not without challenges. Sustainable withdrawal rates, according to research, are limited to a finite number of years, usually 30, and must be decreased over time.[4] For longer retirements, choosing a modest withdrawal rate, increasing the percentage of equities in the portfolio, and reducing the withdrawal rate when the market is down can improve sustainability.

Inflation

I call inflation and longevity "the power couple of retirement risk," because rising costs over an extended lifespan pose a formidable threat to retirement. Figuring out how to deal with inflation—and specifically how to generate inflation-adjusted income for as long as needed—is one of the greatest challenges retirees will face when deciding how to fund retirement.

---

4 Kitces, Michael, "What Returns Are Safe Withdrawal Rates REALLY Based Upon?," Nerds Eye View, August 2012, What Returns Are Safe Withdrawal Rates REALLY Based Upon?.

Though market volatility is much more impactful to an investment-based retirement funding strategy that depends on market returns to fund spending, inflation is likely to impact all retirement funding strategies. Inflation is particularly acute for an income strategy like Protected Income that relies on income sources that may not increase payment amounts with inflation. Inflation-resilient income strategies, such as Total Return, Risk Wrap or Time Segmentation income strategy, that rely on market returns that generally track better with inflation are less impacted.

The corrosive effect of inflation: $100,000 today will buy the same amount that $57,000 would buy in 2011. This means that due to inflation, the value of money has decreased, and it would take $100,000 in 2023 to buy what $57,000 could buy in 2011.

Inflation is a general increase in the cost of goods and services over time that reduces the purchasing power of money. Whether that money comes from annuities, investments, or real estate, inflation will negatively impact it unless adjusted to account for price increases.

As prices rise, the value of a dollar decreases, eroding the purchasing power of retirement income and causing an ever-increasing amount of additional assets to be consumed to keep pace, which, over time, decreases the base of assets available to fund retirement.

Inflation affects spending whether you are retired or not. Over the past half-century, inflation has averaged about 3.7%, but as Exhibit 4.2 illustrates, there have been times when it reached double digits. Although the Federal Reserve aims to keep long-term inflation at 2 to 3 percent, that's not always feasible.

Look at post-Covid events for a sense of how that could play out. Think about the challenges of trying to fund retirement on a fixed income with inflation nearly double what it is today.

Exhibit 4.2

Source: https://fred.stlouisfed.org/graph/?g=JlWz#0

WHY INFLATION MATTERS TO THOSE IN OR NEARING RETIREMENT

It is not retirement that is the goal line but transitioning and living at a desirable level in retirement. Increasing life expectancies may result in greater savings than originally anticipated. Furthermore, Social Security's annual cost of living adjustment (COLA) is generally determined by changes in the Consumer Price Index that fail to consider higher increases in other expenditures, like healthcare, that are often more impactful to retiree spending than other expenses. Long-term financial planning goals can be significantly affected by minor changes in inflation in the near term, placing increased emphasis on ensuring savings can keep pace with future inflation.

HOW INFLATION AFFECTS RETIREMENT INCOME PLANNING

Inflation erodes the value of money over time and reduces purchasing power. The same amount of money will buy fewer goods and services in the future than today. If your retirement income remains fixed, its purchasing power will decrease as prices rise, requiring an ever-increasing consumption of savings and accelerating asset depletion.

As we've seen earlier, a longer retirement period exacerbates the effects of inflation. That's because inflation compounds over time, meaning its impact on retirement income becomes more significant as the years go by. Planning for a longer retirement period requires accounting for the potential effects of inflation on income needs.

Inflation can also impact investment returns. If the returns on your investments do not outpace inflation, the real return (adjusted for inflation) may be lower than expected. This can affect the growth of retirement savings, potentially limiting the income generated from those investments and impacting spending.

Healthcare costs tend to rise faster than the overall inflation rate. Retirees often face higher healthcare expenses as they age, which can strain retirement income. It is essential to consider potential healthcare costs and factor them into retirement income planning.

Social Security inflation increases may not keep pace with all cost-of-living increases. Benefits are adjusted annually for inflation based on the Consumer Price Index for Urban Wage Earners and Clerical Workers (CPI-W). However, the adjustment may not fully keep up with the actual increase in living costs, especially healthcare, which has a higher inflation rate than the CPI-W, leading to a gradual reduction in the purchasing power of Social Security income over time.

If you rely on fixed-income investments like bonds, CDs, fixed annuities, or pensions for retirement income, inflation can erode the real value of the interest or income generated by these investments. Their fixed-amount payments may not keep pace with rising prices unless they have provisions for the cost-of-living increases to offset rises in living costs. This could reduce their value and, over time, result in a decline in your standard of living.

PLAN FOR INFLATION BY INTEGRATING THESE IDEAS

Model Inflation Rates to Understand Their Effects

A higher inflation rate won't benefit your retirement plan, but inflation will affect each plan differently. Understanding how inflation affects your plan will help determine your exposure.

Factor in inflation when estimating expenses. When calculating your retirement income needs, consider the potential impact of inflation on various expenses, such as housing, healthcare, and daily living costs. Plan for increasing costs over time to ensure your income is sufficient to meet future needs.

Retirement is not the same for everyone, nor will the impact of inflation be the same for everyone. Inflation affects goods and services differently. Rates can differ, so it's unreasonable to assume a universal rate.

Furthermore, not every person consumes the same goods and services or even the same amounts, so if you don't use or use less of them, any inflation increases may not be as significant. This emphasizes the significance of looking beyond headlines to determine which expenses personally will impact spending and calculating your inflation to know its true impact. To do this, you must determine which expenses are relevant and how susceptible they are to inflation.

A helpful tool for modeling this information is Michael Kitces's inflation calculator (see Chapter 4 resources).

Use Strategies That Either Hedge or Outpace Inflation.

With its cost-of-living adjustments, Social Security is an effective hedge against inflation; therefore, maximizing its benefits is the first step. Another effective hedging strategy is using inflation-protected securities like Treasury Inflation-Protected (TIPS) bonds, bills, and notes that earn higher coupon and principal payments as inflation rises.

An alternative to hedging is to employ strategies that outpace or outrun inflation. The stock market does not necessarily move with inflation like Social Security or TIPS, but it produces long-term returns that can outpace inflation over time. Research suggests a steady or increasing stock allocation in retirement in the vicinity of 50% to 75% is superior to a declining or static stock allocation strategy.[5]

Inflation is a critical factor to consider when planning for retirement. By accounting for it and taking appropriate steps to protect against its effects, you can help ensure your retirement income retains its purchasing power and supports your financial needs throughout your retirement years.

Market Volatility

Financing retirement with a probability-based income strategy will always be a gamble. As the name suggests, it will *probably* work, but it may not. Nevertheless, for those pursuing this income strategy, it is important to understand investing comes with many risks. Several of them are particularly relevant to retirement income planning. Among them are market risk (losses due to market fluctuations), interest rate risk (bond prices will vary due to fluctuating interest rates), and liquidity risk (not having assets available to cover unanticipated cash flow requirements). Of these, market and interest-rate risk represent the greatest threat to retirement income, as a growing number of retirees will depend on their investments to fund retirement since company pensions have all but disappeared and the solvency of Social Security is under threat.

Understanding the impact of market and interest-rate risk on retirement income planning is important before creating a mitigation strategy.

> ➤ *Market Fluctuations:* Market volatility can cause the value of investment portfolios to fluctuate. Suppose you rely on

---

5 Kitces, Michael, "Should Equity Exposure Decrease In Retirement, Or Is A Rising Equity Glidepath Actually Better?," Nerds Eye View, September 2013, Should Equity Exposure Decrease In Retirement, Or Is A Rising Equity Glidepath Actually Better.

investments for retirement income. In that case, a significant decline in the value of your portfolio during market turmoil may require you to sell more assets to achieve the same income that you would have achieved without the market decline. This causes assets to be consumed at an unsustainable rate, threatening long-term spending stability.

➢ ***Timing of Returns:*** Market returns are always important, but their order of arrival has an equally significant impact on long-term spending. The combination of income withdrawals and poor market returns, especially at the beginning of retirement, can drive the portfolio value so low there is no chance for recovery, no matter how well the markets subsequently perform. The confluence of poor market returns and withdrawals at inopportune times creates a rate of withdrawal the portfolio cannot sustain. Better known as sequence of returns risk, this is where the returns experienced early in retirement have a disproportionate impact on a portfolio's sustainability. Research suggests portfolio returns right before retirement have an outsized influence on retirement income sustainability.[6] A bear market or recession near retirement increases the risk of outliving assets far more than these events at any other time.

➢ ***Withdrawal Rate Risk:*** Funding retirement using an investment portfolio is complex and risky. Knowing how much can be sustainably taken each year to meet income needs over an unknown period is not easy. Taking out too much leads to running out of money. Taking out too little leads to spending cuts and reduced quality of life. It's a balancing act anyone wishing to fund a retirement budget through a portfolio must master. It is important

---

6 Katz, Michael, "Little-Known Risk Threatens Baby Boomers Golden Years," Plan Adviser, March 2022, Little-Known Risk Threatens Baby Boomers Golden Years.

to consider withdrawal rate risk the percentage of your portfolio you withdraw each year for retirement income without depleting your assets. If market volatility reduces the value of your investments, the same withdrawal rate may have a greater impact on the remaining portfolio balance. This can deplete your savings faster and increase the risk of running out of money during retirement.

➢ ***Diversification and Risk Management***: Market volatility underscores the importance of diversification and risk management in retirement income planning. A well-diversified portfolio across different asset classes can help mitigate the impact of market volatility by spreading the risks across a larger swath of investments, thus lessening the impact of any one investment.

➢ ***Required Minimum Distributions (RMDs)***: For individuals with traditional IRAs or employer-sponsored retirement plans, market volatility can affect the value of the assets subject to Required Minimum Distributions (RMDs) . If the value of the assets declines due to market volatility, it can affect the amount of the RMD and potentially impact retirement income.

➢ ***Psychological Impact***: Market volatility can create stress and anxiety for those who rely on their investments for income. Fear and emotional reactions to market fluctuations can lead to poor investment decisions, such as selling investments during market downturns, which can negatively impact long-term retirement income.

➢ ***Adjusting Retirement Plans***: Market volatility may require adjustments to retirement plans. If market conditions negatively impact your retirement income, you may need to reassess your spending, make spending cuts, or explore other options to generate additional income to maintain financial stability during turbulent times.

Those wishing to participate in the market to fund their retirement cannot avoid market or interest-rate risk (unless they purchase and hold individual bonds to maturity).

However, there are viable mitigation strategies to reduce its impact.

➤ Regularly review and rebalance your portfolio to align with your investment objectives and risk tolerance. Rebalancing ensures that your portfolio remains within your desired asset allocation, avoids overexposure to certain volatile sectors, and helps avoid knee-jerk reactions to short-term market fluctuations.

➤ Maintain a well-diversified portfolio that balances risk and return based on risk tolerance and retirement goals. Adjust the asset allocation as you approach retirement to reduce exposure to more volatile assets.

➤ Periodically review and adjust your withdrawal strategy to align with market conditions and portfolio performance.

➤ Consider flexible withdrawal approaches, such as dynamic spending rules that adapt to market volatility.

➤ Remember that retirement is a long-term journey, and market volatility is a normal part of investing. Stay focused on your long-term goals and avoid making impulsive decisions based on short-term market movements.

➤ It may also be beneficial to consider non-market-based income strategies (Protected Income) that rely more on income sources with lifetime income benefits and less on unpredictable market returns to fund spending.

➤ Explore guaranteed income options such as annuities or other guaranteed income streams to provide a steady and reliable income during retirement. These instruments can offer protection against market volatility by providing stable income regardless of market conditions.

> ➢ Spending from buffer assets (cash, home equity, and cash-value life insurance) uncorrelated to the financial markets can provide a cushion during market downturns and help avoid tapping into investments during periods of volatility.

While market volatility can pose challenges to retirement income planning, a well-diversified and well-managed portfolio, combined with a long-term perspective and a comprehensive retirement income strategy, can help mitigate the impact of market fluctuations and provide a more secure retirement income.

Spending conservatively and flexibly, managing a conservative portfolio, and accumulating buffer assets are proven methods to mitigate market volatility and sequence of returns risks.

Spending Shocks

If we could estimate the amount spent in each year of retirement, we would only need to account for a long-life expectancy, weak market performance, and rising inflation. Alas, retirement isn't so simple. For a full picture of retirement costs, we must also consider other factors hindering our spending ability. Factors affecting retirement spending plans are rising healthcare costs, long-term care, divorce, widowhood, change in public policy, cognitive decline, frailty, reduced earning power, early retirement, and changing housing requirements. Any of these can impact retirement spending just as much as an extended lifespan, poor market performance, or rising inflation.

Commonly referred to as spending shocks, these create higher than expected income needs. If not included in the budget, they can increase retirement spending, accelerate asset depletion, and threaten financial stability. Although life expectancy, market volatility, and inflation are universal concerns, spending shocks can vary based on the specific circumstances of each retirement. Consequently, each factor must be evaluated to determine its relevance, potential impact, and cost to make sure measures are in place if needed.

To that end, here are several common—yet unexpected—setbacks that can upend your retirement plan and some tips for better preparation.

HEALTHCARE EXPENSES

Healthcare expenses are often a significant factor in retirement income. According to a Fidelity Investment retiree health cost estimate, an average, healthy 65-year-old couple will need $315,000 (after taxes and excluding long-term care costs) to pay for medical expenses for the remainder of their lives. Based on a U.S. News & World Report, "Take Control of Your 6 Biggest Retirement Expenses," healthcare costs are the second largest expense in retirement. Many people are under the impression that Medicare will cover most of their healthcare costs during retirement. But the fact is, Medicare only covers about half.

As individuals age, healthcare needs often increase, and the costs associated with medical care, insurance, and long-term care can strain retirement budgets.

The fact that these expenses increase at a faster rate than general inflation makes them even more difficult to manage.

Drivers That Can Increase Healthcare Costs in Retirement

Healthcare costs tend to rise faster than general inflation rates, making it challenging to predict future expenses accurately. Prescription medications, medical procedures, and doctor visits can increase healthcare expenses during retirement.

Costs associated with medical care do not stop at the point of care. Health insurance premiums can take a significant portion of retirement income. While Medicare is available for individuals 65 and older, it doesn't cover all healthcare expenses. Retirees often need to pay premiums for Medicare Part B (medical insurance), Medicare Part C (medical insurance), and Part D (prescription drug coverage), as well as supplemental insurance (Medigap), to cover gaps in Medicare coverage.

Spending budgets can be blown out of the water by out-of-pocket expenses. Even with Medicare coverage, retirees often face out-of-pocket expenses, such as copayments, deductibles, and coinsurance.

Medicare typically covers only 80% of covered costs. A $10,000 covered procedure may leave you on the hook for $2,000 if supplemental coverage does not cover it. These expenses can accumulate over time, particularly for frequent healthcare visits or more extensive medical treatments.

Medical or unexpected health issues can create unforeseen medical emergencies, leading to substantial healthcare expenses not accounted for during retirement income planning.

These unforeseen circumstances can strain retirement budgets and require individuals to adjust their spending, tap into their savings, or divert income from other spending goals to cover the costs.

To manage the impact of healthcare expenses on retirement income, consider the following strategies:

> ➤ ***Estimate and Budget for Healthcare Costs:*** Research and estimate the potential costs of healthcare, including premiums, deductibles, and copayments. Incorporate these estimates into the retirement budget to ensure you set aside sufficient funds to cover healthcare needs.

➤ ***Optimize Medicare Coverage:*** Understand the different parts of Medicare (Part A, Part B, Part C, and Part D) and explore options to optimize coverage based on your healthcare needs. Consider Medigap or Medicare Advantage plans to fill gaps and potentially reduce out-of-pocket expenses.

➤ ***Research Health Insurance Options:*** Explore healthcare insurance options beyond Medicare, such as retiree health benefits or private health insurance plans. Compare premiums, coverage, and out-of-pocket costs to find the most cost-effective solution for your situation.

➤ ***Review Prescription Drug Coverage:*** Regularly review your prescription drug coverage to ensure it meets your needs and is cost-effective. Compare drug plans, consider generic alternatives, and discuss cost-saving options with your healthcare provider.

➤ ***Regularly Review and Adjust Retirement Plan:*** Periodically reassess your retirement income plan to account for changing healthcare needs, costs, and insurance coverage. Adjust your savings, budget, and investment strategies to accommodate healthcare expenses.

Long-term care services are typically not covered by Medicare, and individuals may need to rely on other sources of income. You must account for this potential health-related expense in the retirement budget, as a Morningstar report estimates that 70% of people turning age 65 will develop a severe long-term care need in their lifetime.[7] It is difficult to predict the income needed for long-term care, as it can be very costly if it does occur. It can be a substantial expense if you need assistance with daily living activities or care in a nursing home or assisted living facility in retirement.

---

7 Benz, Christine, "100 Must-Know Statistics About Long-Term Care: 2023 Edition,", September 2013, 100 Must-Know Statistics About Long-Term Care.

To manage the impact of long-term care expenses on retirement income, consider the following strategies:

- ➢ **Social Insurance:** Medicaid may become necessary if other savings and resources are exhausted. However, qualifying for Medicaid typically requires spending down assets to meet income and resource limits.

- ➢ **Long-Term Care Insurance:** Consider purchasing long-term care insurance to help cover the costs of future long-term care needs. Long-term care insurance can help protect retirement savings and provide a dedicated source of funds for long-term care services.

- ➢ **Hybrid Insurance Policies:** Explore hybrid insurance policies that combine long-term care coverage with life insurance or annuities. These policies provide benefits for long-term care services if needed but also offer a death benefit or annuity income if long-term care is not required.

- ➢ **Self-Funding:** Include potential long-term care costs in your retirement income planning and budgeting. Save and invest to set aside funds specifically for long-term care needs in case they arise.

- ➢ **Home equity:** For some, the home is their largest asset and a potential source of income. Reverse mortgages may provide an income stream that can be used to pay for long-term care.

- ➢ **Home Modifications:** Consider making home modifications that can enhance safety and accessibility, potentially reducing the need for long-term care services or delaying institutional care.

- ➢ **Utilize Community-Based Services:** Investigate community-based services and support programs that can assist with activities of daily living or home healthcare. These services may be more affordable than institutional care options.

Planning for long-term care expenses is a crucial aspect of retirement planning. By considering the potential impact of long-term care on retirement income and implementing appropriate strategies, individuals can better protect their financial well-being and ensure a more secure retirement.

DIVORCE AND DEATH OF A SPOUSE

The loss of a spouse or partner, whether by legal separation or death, is a major personal setback that, without planning, can also result in a decline in financial security.

When death comes before you realize your retirement plans, it can be devastating. A spouse's death has not only emotional consequences but also financial hardships. The death of a spouse usually results in a decrease in income, but that isn't usually the case for expenses. Social Security benefits could be reduced by up to a third or even half, depending on the situation. Pension benefits can be lost altogether if the single-life payout option is chosen. Also, a surviving spouse may be unable to manage finances independently, and they may be more likely to require expensive institutional care due to the loss of their caregiver.

> - It's particularly devastating for widows, since research suggests Boomer women may remain widowed for 15 to 20 years. Making matters worse, as widows age, their income declines, and their healthcare costs rise. This is especially troubling since it occurs when the widow's assets have been depleted from providing care during her spouse's last years. It's been shown that more than 40% of widows fall into poverty within five years of a spouse's death, while just 4% of non-widows experience unexpected poverty.[8]

> - Planning the right solution involves meeting the income needs of the surviving spouse. This can be done in various ways, but both

---

8 Littell, Hopkins, Pfau, "Retirement Income Process, Strategies, and Solutions" Bryn Mawr, PA: The American College Press, 2018.

spouses must participate in the retirement income planning process. To prepare the household for both the death of the first spouse and the life of the surviving spouse, a retirement income plan for married couples must consider many aspects.

While one spouse may take control of household finances in some married households, either because they desire to or are capable of doing so, or because their spouse lacks the capability or interest, it may not be beneficial, especially if they predecease the other spouse. A plan must also address this issue if one spouse is uncomfortable making financial decisions. Although delegation is important, since no spouse should bear all the responsibility independently, each spouse should become familiar enough with what the other spouse is doing to assist if needed.

Strategies to Protect a Surviving Spouse

For each spouse to be protected, it is crucial to ensure the proper estate planning documents like wills, trusts, and beneficiary designations have been completed properly to make sure the decedent's wishes are respected while safeguarding the surviving spouse.

Increasing income for a surviving spouse is essential to retirement income plans for married couples. Making smart claiming decisions to maximize Social Security survivor's benefits and choosing joint life options on annuity and pension benefits that pay out for the longer of a couple's joint life can increase retirement income to the surviving spouse.

Insurance planning takes on greater importance in a married household. Life insurance can provide income to a surviving spouse. A permanent life insurance policy bought on both lives can provide income to the survivor at the first spouse's death. If additional income is needed, the policy's cash value can be used to meet other income needs. Likewise, the surviving spouse has a greater need for long-term care planning since their spouse will no longer be there to care for them. In some long-term care policies, couples can pool benefits so the second spouse can access the remaining benefits when the first spouse dies.

When using retirement funding strategies like the Total Return, which rely on systematic withdrawals from a diversified investment portfolio, it is important to choose a withdrawal rate that is sustainable to support spending needs for the longest living spouse.

Work to meet income requirements for the longest expected life expectancy for both spouses.

And lastly, sufficient contingency funds should be set aside to meet the longevity uncertainty. A potential source of contingency funding would include using home equity through a reverse mortgage or simply selling the home to support alternative housing or care needs.

From triaging financial decisions and claiming life insurance death proceeds to applying for Social Security benefits and managing retirement savings, making the right financial moves early can set up a surviving spouse for greater financial stability later.

There is a growing trend of late-life divorces (known as gray divorces) which has crippling effects on both spouses. Retirees who separate at an advanced age often face rebuilding their lives with diminished resources, limited financial skills, and greater responsibilities.

There may be an impact on the division of retirement assets. During divorce proceedings, retirement assets such as pensions, 401(k) plans, individual retirement accounts (IRAs) , and other investments may be divided between spouses. This division can reduce retirement savings for both parties, potentially affecting their future income streams.

Moreover, increasing costs and risks due to the loss of spousal benefits, such as Social Security or a pension, must be considered. In divorce, these spousal benefits may be lost, leading to a decrease in overall retirement income. Some situations may result in one spouse's insurance coverage being nullified, increasing their risk and cost since the financial burden is no longer shared. Further complicating matters, a surviving spouse may lose death benefits if life insurance or annuity beneficiary designations are changed during a divorce.

A gray divorce can irrevocably change the composition of household expenses. After divorce, each spouse typically establishes a separate household, which can result in increased living expenses. Maintaining two households instead of one may require a higher income level to cover housing costs, utilities, insurance, and other expenses, potentially impacting retirement savings and income.

Social Security benefits may be affected by gray divorce. If the marriage lasted at least ten years, divorced individuals may be eligible to claim Social Security benefits based on their ex-spouse's earnings history. However, claiming these benefits can be complex, and specific criteria must be met.

Divorce at any time can trigger changes in retirement plans. Individuals may need to adjust their retirement plans, savings goals, and investment strategies. A divorce can lead to reassessing retirement timelines, goals, risk tolerance, and the need for additional savings or adjustments to investment portfolios.

To mitigate the impact of gray divorce on retirement income, it's advisable for individuals going through a divorce to seek the guidance of trusted advisers who can help navigate the complexities of dividing assets, analyze the long-term impact on retirement income, and develop a revised retirement income plan that aligns with the new financial situation.

PUBLIC POLICY

Policy decisions can have a significant impact on retirement income. Government regulations and programs can shape the retirement landscape by influencing retirement savings, Social Security benefits, healthcare costs, tax laws, and other factors that affect retirees' financial well-being.

> *Social Security Benefits*: Changes might include adjusting the retirement age, altering benefit calculations, or implementing changes to cost-of-living adjustments (COLAs) that may impact retiree income.

> *Health Care Policies*: Changes in the availability of affordable health insurance options, Medicaid eligibility rules, or prescription drug coverage, can also affect retirees.

> *Pensions*: Regulations on pension plans may dictate funding, benefit formulas, vesting rules, and other aspects that can influence the amount and security of retirement income.

> *Tax Laws and Rates*: Changes with these may affect the taxation of retirement account withdrawals, Social Security benefits, investment income, and other sources of retirement income.

> *Consumer Protections*: Regulations regarding financial products, investment advice, and fraud prevention can help safeguard retirees' savings and ensure they have access to suitable retirement income options.

It's important for individuals planning for retirement to stay informed about public policy developments and understand how they may affect retirement income sources and planning strategies.

COGNITIVE DECLINE AND FRAILTY

Rising life expectancy means many more Americans will reach old age. Living longer is undeniably positive, but it may force more people to face financial risks during their golden years that they might not be prepared for.

These late-life risks can include cognitive decline (a diminished mental capacity to carry out routine responsibilities of managing finances, maintaining a property, and running a household) and frailty (the inability to perform daily activities such as bathing, dressing, toileting, transferring, eating, and maintaining continence) (Exhibit 4.3).

Exhibit 4.3

Aging individuals risk high out-of-pocket healthcare expenses due to frailty and increased probability of financial mistakes, falling victim to fraud, and elder abuse due to cognitive impairment, especially when a financially savvy spouse dies early or becomes incapacitated.

Seniors are more likely than 40-somethings to fall victim to fraud. This may be because they overestimate their financial abilities but make common financial errors.

Personal finances are often not managed equally within the household. A surviving spouse can run into serious problems if no preparations have been made for the death of the spouse in charge of finances. It's easy for a surviving spouse to become vulnerable to financial predators and make mistakes regarding finances. It is common for survivors to become more vulnerable to fraud and theft as they age.

The afflicted may have difficulty making sound portfolio investments and withdrawal decisions as they age. While liquidity and flexibility are important, retirees should also prepare for the reality that cognitive decline will hamper the portfolio management skills of many as they age, increasing the desirability of advanced planning and automation for late-in-life financial goals.

The silver lining is these risks can all be addressed largely through appropriate risk management techniques. The first step in tackling these risks is developing a plan with appropriate strategies. We'll examine a few of them.

Cognitive Decline Can Be Managed in Several Different Ways

In times of need, making decisions with a trusted partner may involve bringing in a family member, hiring a money manager, or even hiring a corporate trustee. This is generally done by granting or appointing someone through a power of attorney to make financial or health decisions when you are no longer able to make decisions for yourself.

It is also possible to establish a trust to determine in advance how your personal affairs will be managed if you cannot decide for yourself. By following your wishes rather than relying on human judgment, the trust will handle your personal affairs according to your wishes.

Planning with the documents outlined here is crucial to avoiding a court incompetency hearing during which a guardian is appointed. It can also be helpful to simplify finances by using direct deposit for income payments and automatic payments for regular bills, and by choosing investment products that are easier to manage. Managing and withdrawing money from an investment portfolio to fund retirement may be difficult if cognitive ability declines. Income strategies that solve a long-term income need in advance and don't require overhead might be a better option.

Many Different Approaches Can Be Undertaken to Manage Frailty

The simplest solution is for families and friends to help out. As additional help is needed to handle chores no longer able to be done independently, outside help can be hired. Seniors hiring contractors and others for home maintenance need to be careful. This is an area of significant potential elder abuse, especially financially.

Retrofitting the home to make it more accessible for those with reduced physical abilities can allow them to age in place and reduce living costs.

It may be more appropriate for some to choose alternative housing. Townhouses and condominiums may offer maintenance services, senior housing may offer more comprehensive care, and continuing care retirement communities offer care to all ages and abilities. For some, house sharing can be an effective solution to share expenses and chores and reduce living costs.

The aging process may rob retirees of their ability to make their own decisions regarding their finances and health and expose them to abuse, so it is imperative to prepare a plan for delegating those responsibilities to trusted allies. The lack of a plan can add a more stressful personal impact to a difficult situation for retirees and loved ones. Taking no steps to plan for incapacity can lead to loss of dignity, unnecessary trauma for family members, and increased risk of elder abuse.

FORCED RETIREMENT, REDUCED EARNING POWER, AND LIMITED EMPLOYMENT

As soon as you leave your job, you are limited in earning an income, making the first day of retirement the riskiest. Many factors play a role in this. Some may be less prepared for retirement than expected and be forced to leave work because of declining health, a family member's health, or a company downsizing or insolvency. Others will have to rely on other sources of income that come with risk, since they are no longer receiving wages from an employer or income from a business. Finally, while many retirees hope to return to the workplace on a part-time basis at least, this may not be a reality because of factors beyond their control, including economic conditions, limited opportunities, and health, as well as a lack of interest in returning to the demands of the workplace.

Forced Retirement

The possibility always exists that work will end prematurely because of poor health, disability, job loss, or to care for a spouse or family member. This event can quickly derail a retirement plan. For example, Marge plans to work until age 65, but her long-time employer suddenly closes her office when she is 61. Very few employers need her skills, and she cannot find suitable employment. Not only are her plans to accumulate more funds for retirement or build Social Security benefits ambushed, but she may not receive or afford health care coverage until she is eligible for Medicare.

Research consistently finds that more than 40 percent of retirees retire sooner than expected. According to a Prudential study conducted in 2018, 51 percent of the oldest baby boomers had retired earlier than planned. Only in 23 percent of cases did the retiree want to retire. In the rest of the cases, health concerns were cited in 46 percent of cases, followed closely by job loss cited in 30 percent of cases.

Among the respondents to the EBRI Retirement Confidence Survey in 2018, 48 percent of retirees indicated they had retired earlier than planned, 41 percent retired due to health or disabilities, 26 percent due to downsizing or company closures, and 14 percent for caregiving responsibilities.

These numbers demonstrate the reality of forced retirement and its attendant risks to retirement security. For most, retiring at a later age won't be a reality. Even though this risk cannot be eliminated, there are methods to mitigate its impact.

An effective retirement income plan must account for the possibility of retiring earlier than intended. Modeling retirement at various ages can be an effective risk management tool to assess how different retirement start dates affect future outcomes. This could be accomplished by looking at multiple options such as these:

> ➢ A reduced, but adequate standard of living 10 years before the start of retirement

> ➢ A more comfortable standard of living 5 years before the start of retirement

> ➢ Desired standard of living at the planned retirement age

This planning has the benefit of promoting early savings and assessing what the final years of work can offer in terms of retirement.

Few would argue against the value of planning and preparing for a forced retirement. You can actively do something about it because planning is the one thing under your control. It will also be valuable to consider how to prevent or reduce the chance of this happening in the first place.

It is important to consider the following points to reduce the likelihood of being forced to retire:

> ➢ Learn about your employer's severance policy and consider negotiating for benefits to protect your income.

> ➢ Keep up with skills and learn new ones as you age to ensure that you remain valuable to your organization.

> ➢ Maintain professional networks into old age and keep a polished resume to be prepared for this contingency.

> ➢ Consider the impact of healthy lifestyle choices on your overall health: eating well, managing weight, getting ample sleep, and exercising regularly.

> ➢ Consider working less before fully retiring to extend the years you can work. You could take more time off, reduce your responsibilities, or cut back on your client load.

Reduced Earning Power

As soon as paid employment ends, earning power is reduced. When individuals transition from active employment to retirement, their income-earning capacity typically decreases. It is a natural consequence of leaving the workforce and relying on savings, pensions, and other sources of income instead of a regular paycheck. The value of fixed income sources such as annuities, pensions, and Social Security cannot be increased above their contractual rates, while assets with the expectation of growth, like stocks, bonds, and real estate, come with no guarantees of future earnings. While some retirees work part-time or in flexible arrangements to supplement their income, they typically earn less than when working full-time, resulting in diminished earnings potential.

Individuals need to plan for reduced earning power in retirement by saving and investing during their working years to build a sufficient base of assets to support spending needs. This can help provide a sustainable income stream to cover living expenses and maintain financial stability throughout retirement.

Reemployment Risk

Many retirees plan to work in retirement, but that may not be realistic for various reasons. Due to tight labor markets, poor health, and/or caregiving responsibilities, reemployment risk is the inability to supplement retirement income with employment.

This has been proven in research. A retirement confidence survey was conducted by EBRI that asked retirees how they feel about working after retirement. In every year's report, the total number of retirees who work in retirement is much lower than the pre-retirees who say they expect to work in retirement. For instance, in 2017, 79 percent of those still working expected to work after they retired, while only 29 percent of retirees worked.

Most survey respondents cited positive reasons for working. The majority (90 percent) said they wanted to remain active and involved at work, and 82 percent said they enjoyed working. Financial reasons also played a role in 67 percent of respondents' decision to work. 42 percent cited the need to earn a living as a reason for working, 23 percent wanted to make up for a decrease in savings or investments, and 13 percent planned to work to preserve health insurance.

Factors contributing to reemployment risk can include changes in career or industry where transitioning into a new field may result in lower earning potential or require acquiring new skills that can impact income levels and decrease earning capacity.

When individuals age, they may experience physical limitations or health conditions that affect their ability to work and earn income. Employment prospects among retirees vary depending on the demands for the retiree's skills, decreased marketability, or sparse opportunities. With advancing age, some retirees may face challenges in the job market, such as competing in a globalized economy and enduring age-related biases. These factors can limit employment opportunities and affect earning potential.

In light of the statistics, planning on earning significant employment income in retirement may not be realistic. It may be impossible to find work or to find employment at all. Rather than relying on the possibility of post-retirement employment to meet retirement goals, it may be better to postpone retirement from a career that pays better, offers health insurance, and provides other benefits.

Many retirees engage in an informal type of phased retirement by taking consulting positions, part-time jobs, or even turning their hobbies into profit-making activities, so exploring ways to grow alternate streams of income may be worthwhile.

SHIFTING HOUSING NEEDS

Deciding where you'll live is probably one of the most important retirement planning decisions. This shouldn't be surprising because where you live can impact overall living costs, healthcare quality, general livability, access to amenities, social connections, and happiness.

For several reasons, deciding where you plant roots during your twilight years is important to retirement income.

- ➤ ***Cost of living:*** The cost of living can vary significantly depending on the location. Choosing a place with a lower cost of living can stretch retirement income further, allowing someone to maintain a comfortable lifestyle and potentially save on expenses such as food, housing, taxes, healthcare, utilities, and daily essentials.

- ➤ ***Housing expenses:*** Housing is typically one of the most significant expenses in retirement. The choice of location can impact housing costs, including property prices, rent, property taxes, and homeowners' insurance. Selecting an area with affordable housing options or considering downsizing can help reduce housing expenses and generate more retirement income.

- ➤ ***Tax implications:*** Tax laws and rates differ across jurisdictions. Some states or countries have tax-friendly policies for retirees, such as exemptions on retirement income, lower property taxes, or favorable tax treatment on pension and Social Security benefits. Understanding the tax implications of different locations can help optimize retirement income and minimize tax burdens.

- ➤ ***Healthcare costs:*** Healthcare expenses increase in retirement, and access to quality healthcare services is crucial. Different areas may have varying healthcare systems, costs of medical care, and insurance options. Retirees should consider proximity to healthcare facilities, availability of specialists, and affordability when choosing a retirement location to help manage healthcare costs effectively.

- ➤ ***Social services and amenities:*** Retirement is a time to enjoy life, pursue hobbies, and engage in social activities not possible while working. Selecting a location with recreational facilities, cultural events, social clubs, and access to amenities like parks, shopping centers, entertainment, and restaurants can enhance retirees' quality of life. Engaging in low-cost or free activities can help retirees stretch their retirement income while maintaining an active and fulfilling lifestyle.

> ➤ ***Proximity to family and support networks:*** Being close to family members, friends, and support networks can provide emotional support and potentially reduce certain costs, such as caregiving expenses. In some cases, family or friends may be able to provide assistance or support, reducing the need for professional services.

Considering these factors when deciding where to live in retirement can help retirees make informed choices that align with their financial goals and lifestyle preferences. Thinking through the various financial impacts can provide valuable insights and guidance in assessing the financial implications of different locations and developing a retirement income strategy. There are many ways to decide where to live in retirement, some of which may be more valuable than others. That said, where you live in retirement doesn't boil down to a single financial decision. Costs and taxes are important, but so is being happy, healthy, and safe.

SPENDING PATTERNS

Retirement households are likely to experience both increases and decreases in spending levels, i.e., volatility or fluctuations, during retirement years. Therefore, it is important to consider these spending patterns to gain insight into how spending may change in retirement as well as inform mitigation strategies to cope with volatile spending. By planning for, and being ready to adjust to such fluctuations, retirees will be more likely to succeed in retirement.

Data shows that retirement spending generally decreases, but many retirement households will experience meaningful fluctuations rather than a continuous decline throughout their retirement. According to data from the Health and Retirement Study (HRS) and its supplement, the Consumption and Activities Mail Survey (CAMS), found that, on average, annual household spending declined by about 2% during retirement. But this decrease is not uniform for all retirement households.

As far as spending increases are concerned, 1 in 4 households experienced at least a 17% - 20% increase in annual spending over a two-year period and over 1 in 4 households experienced a spending increase between 25% and 50% from ages 65 to 90.[9]

Additionally, a number of households saw significant, long-standing increases in spending, with 15% still spending at the same level after four years. Although average spending increased as investable assets and household income increased, spending volatility did not fluctuate based on investable assets or income levels.

Interestingly, for households with annual incomes of less than $150,000, overall spending volatility was largely due to changes in nondiscretionary spending. For retirees with income levels above $150,000, the lion's share of volatility was due to changes in discretionary spending.[10]

Some level of spending variation is expected in retirement, but if it arises from spending shocks–unplanned increases in nondiscretionary or essential spending–that could become a true liquidity event and a cause of concern. Nondiscretionary spending— housing in particular— is the primary source of spending variability in retirement, but this varies with income.

Although health-related costs are typically the top concern when it comes to retirement expenses, data shows that housing is both the largest contributor to spending volatility and, by far, the largest spending category before and throughout retirement.

---

9 Banerjee, Sudipto, "Planning for Spending Volatility in Retirement,"
T. Rowe Price, September 2023, Planning for Spending Volatility in Retirement.
10 Littell, Hopkins, Pfau, "Retirement Income Process, Strategies, and Solutions" Bryn Mawr, PA: The American College Press, 2018.

In light of the variable nature of spending, many retirement households will experience "liquidity events," and need to have enough easily accessible liquid assets to meet these needs. To plan and prepare for these liquidity events, they will need to better understand their liquidity needs as they relate to the household to develop retirement income solutions that generate cash flows that address liquidity and growth to potentially enhance retirement outcomes. Increased spending on nondiscretionary expenses might require immediate cash. Retirees without adequate liquid assets might have to take untimely distributions from their longer-term investment portfolios that could lower the chance of enjoying a successful retirement.

Retirement spending can fluctuate greatly at any time, and increases may persist. Having adequate allocations of liquid assets can reduce financial stress during times of high spending. Strategies that incorporate different levels of assets or income requirements and personal risk factors could help address individualized needs. Considering the wide range of possible variations in spending increases, retirees will need to hold various amounts of liquid assets to cover potential shortfalls.

Findings show that a subset of retired households will experience variability in their spending, and many will adjust to these fluctuations. If retirees fulfill other retirement income goals with guaranteed income products, leveraging non-guaranteed retirement income products that can handle some volatility may be well-suited to address the liquidity and growth to counter spending variations that would otherwise compromise financial security and retirement satisfaction. It is crucial that income solutions take into account personal factors such as income, expected expenses, health status, family situation, and risk preferences before devising a solution.

Predicting every curveball life will throw at you is impossible, but even a small amount of forethought can make unexpected expenses more manageable. The potential dangers of any of them go beyond the household's fiscal health. The goal is that increased awareness of the gap between risk and protective measures will encourage retirees to take them more seriously and factor them into their retirement income planning. Increased awareness can lead to meaningful action to reduce the harmful effects of common retirement hazards.

Achieving Maximum Efficiencies to Lower Retirement Costs

Your greatest retirement risk is living longer than expected and running out of money, which means it's important to plan for a long retirement and utilize what you have to the fullest extent possible. Employing resources efficiently can lead to a higher lifetime spending level and a higher amount left to your heirs.

We know that meeting spending goals and managing risks largely depend on the sustainability of assets. Measures taken to increase portfolio longevity are paramount for retirements that depend on generating income through portfolio withdrawals. These measures include dynamic withdrawals, increased stock allocation, delayed Social Security claiming, variable spending levels, and integrating home equity. Together or separately, they work to extend the life of a portfolio.

Ignoring efficiency-enhancing actions can reduce portfolio sustainability and lead to a permanently reduced standard of living in retirement. This underscores the importance of finding ways to stretch resources to enhance retirement outcomes. As a force multiplier in retirement, efficiency creates opportunities to accomplish more with less to maximize the retirement experience than might otherwise be possible.

Making the most of what you have begins with an efficient retirement. That means obtaining the most after-tax spending and legacy values for a given base of assets. Efficiency is a hallmark of sound retirement income planning, where the goal is to maximize resources and income during retirement by leveraging various financial strategies effectively and optimally. Key components are carefully planning and managing retirement assets, income sources, expenses, investments, and tax strategies, ensuring that retirement income and resources are used wisely to meet financial goals and maintain a desired lifestyle.

Many efficiencies require a long-term focus to support a higher sustained living standard that often comes at the price of short-term sacrifices that can detract from their long-term benefits. By implementing efficient retirement planning strategies, individuals can strive to achieve financial security, protect their retirement savings from erosion, minimize unnecessary costs, lower the cost of retirement, and make informed decisions that align with their long-term goals and needs.

Common strategies include taking advantage of insurance-based income sources that mitigate longevity and market volatility risks while simultaneously reducing retirement costs and selecting Social Security benefit-claiming strategies that maximize inflation-adjusted spending and survivor benefits, as well as repurposing the home as something different from a legacy asset that passes from generation to generation to an asset-protection mechanism.

Exhibit 4.4 illustrates common strategies for promoting efficiencies that increase spending and accumulated legacy balances.

Exhibit 4.4

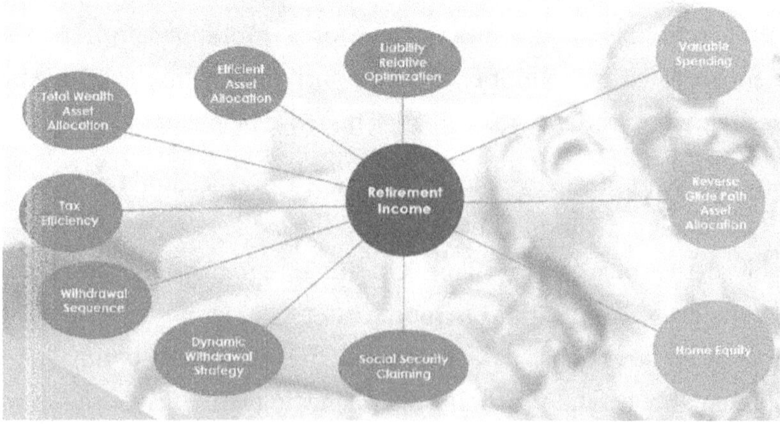

These are not pie-in-the-sky ideas. By effectively incorporating these strategies into a retirement income plan, they have the potential to boost spending, reduce risks, lower retirement costs, and enhance outcomes.

As Exhibit 4.5 illustrates, simply implementing 6 of these strategies alone can increase retirement income by 37 percent! The importance of this number cannot be overstated. Combining any of these strategies into a retirement income plan can significantly alter planning fortunes.

Exhibit 4.5

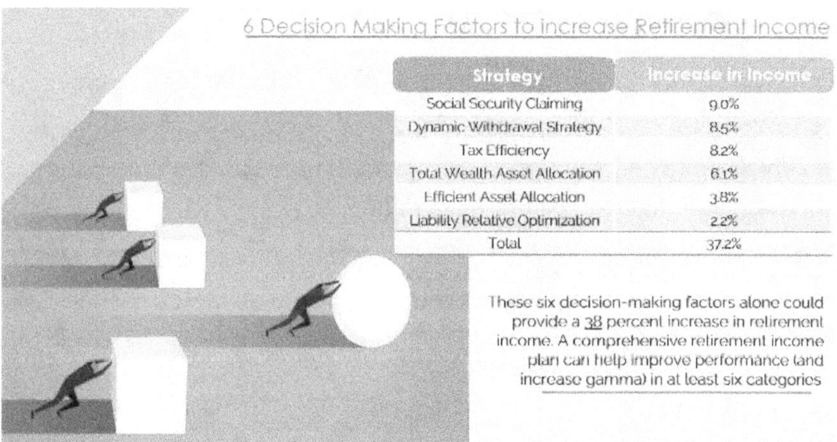

Strategy	Increase in Income
Social Security Claiming	9.0%
Dynamic Withdrawal Strategy	8.5%
Tax Efficiency	8.2%
Total Wealth Asset Allocation	6.1%
Efficient Asset Allocation	3.8%
Liability Relative Optimization	2.2%
Total	37.2%

It's important to note that the degree of retirement efficiency can vary depending on an individual's specific circumstances, goals, risk tolerance, and other factors. Some retirement strategies are more suited and appropriate to some retirements than others. The optimal retirement efficiency will depend on the needs and objectives of each individual.

A 37% increase in spending potential is achievable by incorporating a few key efficiencies.

When there are too many options, staying focused on the real goal can be difficult. This book doesn't have enough space to treat all ten efficiencies fairly. Thus, we will focus on the six decision-making factors that have a quantifiable impact on retirement income. That doesn't mean the remaining four cannot be as beneficial. Depending on your circumstances, they may be just as impactful. You can only determine which strategies are appropriate for your circumstances by carefully considering them, weighing their pros and cons, and measuring their effectiveness. Depending on your ability, skills, and time, the task may be easy or difficult.

SOCIAL SECURITY CLAIMING

Apart from choosing when to retire, another crucial decision people will face in retirement is when to claim Social Security. As pensions have virtually disappeared, markets continue to devalue investments, and home values rise and fall, the traditional funding mainstays people have relied upon are becoming less reliable. It will become increasingly important for retirees to make wise claiming decisions to maximize their benefits.

It will be extremely important to do this since approximately half of retirees rely entirely on Social Security, and up to a quarter depend on it for 90 percent of their income. It has been proven that delaying benefits can increase benefit amounts and lead to better retirement outcomes.

Some data suggests delaying benefits can result in an increase in benefits of about 7-8% for each year of deferral from age 62 to 70. Postponing claiming your Social Security benefits until age 70 can increase the monthly benefit amount by 76%, compared to claiming early at 62. In the process, you can increase inflation-protected income, lower portfolio withdrawals, and provide more opportunities to build tax diversification through strategic Roth conversions.

Among these benefits, lowering portfolio withdrawals is among the most important for portfolio longevity. On average, higher Social Security benefits require fewer withdrawals from portfolios since income needs can be easily met outside the portfolio. This also increases the amount of guaranteed income and the amount of inflation-adjusted income.

Guaranteed income offers stability not possible with market-dependent income. Many retirees today do not have other guaranteed lifetime income, and research has shown retirees with greater amounts of guaranteed income show more satisfaction, worry less, and show fewer signs of depression.[11]

As one of the few income sources that allows for inflation adjustments, delaying benefits also increases inflation-protected income. Unabated price increases can devastate a fixed-income retirement budget because incomes do not keep pace with increases in goods and services.

This leads to decreased purchasing power and increased spending requirements on other assets. A larger benefit that tracks inflation reduces the pressure placed on other sources of assets to fund retirement, thereby extending their life.

It's not just the individual who makes the claiming decisions that benefit. There are far-reaching consequences for their spouse as well. Because the amount, frequency, and duration of benefits are known upfront, the chance of mismanagement due to frailty, elder financial abuse, excess withdrawals, and market risk is reduced. Moreover, the surviving spouse will receive the higher of the two benefits following the death of the first spouse, making it crucial for the higher-earning or higher-benefit spouse to delay benefits to maximize survival benefits.

Here's an example:

A married couple each earns $60,000. When their total annual benefits are stated as a percentage of their $120,000 income, and each claim at age 62,

---

11 Littell, Hopkins, Pfau, "Retirement Income Process, Strategies, and Solutions" Bryn Mawr, PA: The American College Press, 2018.

Social Security replaces 23 percent of pre-retirement earnings. If they retire at age 66 and claim benefits, Social Security replaces 33 percent of pre-retirement earnings. If they retire at 70 and claim benefits, Social Security replaces 45 percent of pre-retirement earnings.

This couple only needs 80 percent of pre-retirement income ($96,000 annually) to meet their income needs. If they claim at age 70, Social Security meets 57 percent of their retirement need—and that is inflation-protected income!

It is important to remember that retirement efficiencies often involve short-term costs for long-term rewards. Delaying Social Security has long-term benefits for retirement, but in the short term, it increases dependence on other sources of income to cover spending. Preserving financial stability will require the construction of a "bridge" of income to offset the loss of Social Security benefits. The Social Security income bridge is the funding needed to replace the lost benefits in the retirement budget due to deferrals. Common ways to fund the bridge are continuing to work, using other assets, accessing home equity through a reverse mortgage with a line of credit distribution option, and taking withdrawals from the investment portfolio for a limited period. According to research, consuming other assets such as annuities and savings prior to drawing Social Security increases Social Security benefits and reduces withdrawals from other assets later in retirement, often resulting in increased growth potential for other assets, lower retirement funding costs, and enhanced planning outcomes.[12] Even though spending savings before Social Security seems counterintuitive, doing so could yield superior retirement planning outcomes.

For many, the Social Security claiming decision is one of the most important retirement income decisions because approximately two-thirds of retirees derive more than half of their income from Social Security.

---

12 Pfau, Wade, "Retirement Planning Guidebook" Vienna, VA: Retirement Researcher, 2021.

Unfortunately, many don't take the claiming decision seriously and take benefits as early as possible at age 62, leaving money on the table and forgoing a valuable risk management tool. The Social Security claiming decision must be part of a comprehensive retirement income plan.

DYNAMIC WITHDRAWALS

For retirement spending strategies relying on withdrawals from volatile investment portfolios, a flexible distribution strategy sensitive to market volatility is essential for preserving assets, maintaining spending power, and ensuring a comfortable lifestyle. Static withdrawal strategies that promote the consumption of assets irrespective of market performance can prematurely exhaust them and compromise financial security. This is particularly true around the retirement start date when poor market returns coupled with withdrawals can erode assets to such a low level, leaving fewer assets remaining to recover when markets improve. This is better known as sequence of returns risk, where market volatility at the start of retirement has a disproportionate impact on subsequent portfolio growth and sustainability than at any other time in retirement. The sequence of returns risk exacerbates market volatility, especially at the beginning of retirement, and must be considered for those who rely on market returns to finance retirement.

Market volatility will always be an existential threat to investment-based retirement funding strategies. It is impossible to eliminate this risk. Nevertheless, there are proven methods by which it can be mitigated. Common strategies include:

> ➤ Start with a lower allocation to equities around the retirement start date and gradually increase it over time to lessen the risk of withdrawing from a depressed portfolio during market downturns.

> ➤ When markets are down, adjust spending.

> ➤ Fund spending with income sources less dependent on the market, such as annuities, home equity, and life insurance cash value

➢ Supplement income with part-time employment.

➢ Consider income strategies less dependent on market returns and instead rely on protected sources of income that are immune to market fluctuations.

We invest for a purpose. And that purpose is to be able to fund our spending in retirement. But to do that effectively, we need to be able to spend from our investment accounts efficiently. One of the most effective approaches to spending efficiently (and hopefully ending up being able to spend more) is to use a dynamic spending strategy that reduces spending when the portfolio value drops and potentially increases spending when the portfolio value increases. This flexibility makes it possible to potentially spend more than a constant inflation-adjusted strategy that does not allow any flexibility, while still maintaining the same overall risk regarding running out of money.

Managing withdrawals over an unknown retirement period will also be a challenge for many. Unlike annuities, defined benefit pensions, and Social Security that provide recipients with steady benefits for as long as they live, employer-qualified retirement saving plans like 401(k)s and Individual Retirement Accounts (IRAs) provide little guidance on how to turn accumulated assets into income. As a result, retirees have to decide how much to withdraw each year and face the risk of either spending too quickly and outliving their resources or spending too conservatively and consuming too little. Research has found people who fear they will exhaust their savings and cannot cover health care expenses will cut back on spending, increase retirement costs and reduce the standard of living.[13] The use of assets in this way is inefficient. Embracing a dynamic withdrawal strategy will be important for those pursuing a Total Return income strategy.

---

13 Silvestrini, Elain, "The Annuity Puzzle," Annuity.org, Nov 2023, The Annuity Puzzle.

Here are some examples of dynamic withdrawal strategies.

> *Percentage of Portfolio Method*: In this approach, retirees withdraw a fixed percentage of their portfolio each year. For example, retirees might withdraw 4% of their initial portfolio value annually. The actual dollar amount will fluctuate based on the portfolio's performance, ensuring that larger withdrawals are taken in times of market growth and smaller ones during downturns.

> *Floor and Ceiling Strategy*: This strategy establishes a "floor" for the minimum annual withdrawal, ensuring retirees can cover essential expenses. A "ceiling" is also set for the maximum annual withdrawal to prevent overspending during periods of strong portfolio performance. Over time, the floor and ceiling amounts adjust based on changes in account value and inflation.

> *Dynamic Spending Rule*: This rule considers changes in the retiree's age, market conditions, and portfolio value to determine the annual withdrawal amount. It might involve a formula considering life expectancy, asset allocation, and economic indicators.

> *Guyton-Klinger Rule*: This rule utilizes a set of criteria to adjust annual withdrawals based on market performance and portfolio values. It includes specific guidelines for increasing or decreasing withdrawals over time, depending on various economic indicators and percentage changes in the portfolio.

> *Hybrid Strategies*: Many retirees use different withdrawal strategies to create a personalized approach that aligns with their financial goals and risk tolerance. Although not a dynamic spending strategy in a true sense, a dynamic spending level that varies spending levels based on behavior instead of market performance can benefit retirement.

According to a study done by Morningstar, assuming level spending over retirement overstates the costs of retirement and shortens portfolio longevity. Even without accounting for market behavior in retirement, behavioral-based withdrawals can reduce retirement costs and increase a portfolio's life.

Common examples include the Retirement Spending Smile, or the "Blanchett Spending Smile" created by David Blanchett, Managing Director and Head of Retirement Research for PGIM DC Solutions. His research has shown the benefits of spending in a "smile" pattern, where spending is highest during the first ten years, lowest over the following ten years, and up again in the latest years, instead of a steady rate of spending.

A second behavioral-based withdrawal method is Retirement Spending Stages, which create three stages of retirement spending, where expenses are reduced downward at each stage. The first stage begins at retirement, and the last stage ends at the end of the plan.

Retirees need to sequence withdrawals in a manner that suits their specific circumstances, risk tolerance, and financial objectives and adapts to changing economic conditions in retirement to preserve spending power and potential through various market environments for as long as retirement. Choosing dynamic withdrawals, whether market-sensitive or behavioral-based, should be unique to your needs.

TAX EFFICIENCY

Taxes may be one of the few aspects of retirement that retirees have some control over as markets fluctuate, inflation rises and falls, and longevity is uncertain. It will be important to look for ways to minimize taxes in retirement.

Various strategies can be used to extend retirement income through careful tax planning. When deployed effectively, these strategies can extend portfolio life and income sustainability, lower taxable income, and save on Medicare tax, Social Security tax, and possibly net investment income tax.

Tax efficiency often requires strategically paying more taxes today to enjoy substantial future tax reductions. A common practice is accelerating the payment of taxes when tax rates are low to avoid paying higher taxes later. Roth Conversions effectively maximizes tax rate arbitrage by shifting income from higher to lower tax rates.

Tax alpha, the additional return an investment strategy can generate by minimizing tax liabilities, is often overlooked when building portfolios. Bonds are tax-inefficient, as coupons are taxed yearly as ordinary income, meaning they are taxed at the individual's marginal tax rate. Stocks (including mutual funds and Exchange-Traded Funds (ETFs) that trade like stocks)) are more tax efficient because capital gains are only realized upon selling the stock, and if held for a year or more, gains are taxed at the lower long-term capital gains rate. Tax efficiency can be improved by the appropriate placement of assets based on the tax characteristics of the account. Many investors naively allocate the same proportion of asset allocation across accounts rather than allocating for tax efficiency.

These are just a few strategies and techniques to improve tax efficiency and retirement outcomes. The next section will cover this vital area of retirement in greater detail.

TOTAL WEALTH ASSET ALLOCATION

A holistic view of wealth is crucial for portfolio construction for those reliant on portfolio returns for income. Most individuals only examine financial assets like a 401(k) or IRA when making asset allocation decisions. Invested assets, however, are only part of retirees' wealth. Department of Labor data shows that the median wealth of married couples age 65 and older is $192,000 of home equity and $92,000 of non-equity wealth. According to a survey conducted by the U.S. Census Bureau, the present value of Social Security benefits is often a retiree's largest retirement asset. Exhibit 4.6 demonstrates the importance of Social Security and home equity as a retiree's most significant retirement assets.

Exhibit 4.6

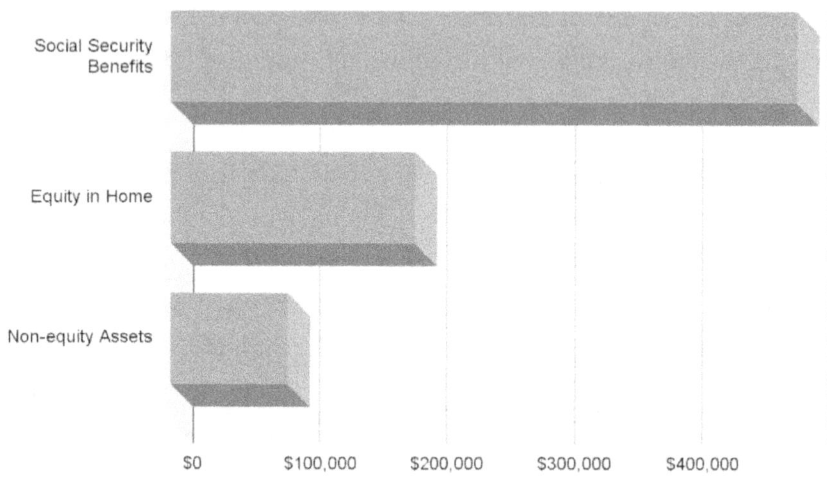

Source: Net Worth Data from the U.S. Census Bureau, Survey of Income and Program Participation, 2008 Panel, Wave 10; Present value of Social Security benefits based on a worker with $60,000 of wage, and a same aged nonworking spouse. The worker's PIA is estimated at $1,557. Benefits are claimed at 66 and the worker dies at 84 and the spouse at 89. Present value as based on a 0% real rate of return (a current approximation of the risk-free rate of return).

Since these assets comprise a large portion of household wealth and carry unique risks, they should affect all retirement income decisions, particularly for the portfolio.

For instance, a retiree receiving 80 percent of their retirement income from Social Security (with attributes similar to bonds) may have a more aggressive portfolio than one receiving only 20 percent. Likewise, those fortunate to have protected income sources like annuities and pensions can invest more aggressively than those with fewer guaranteed income sources who must invest more cautiously, as they stand to lose more and face higher spending cuts in a market downturn.

The key takeaway is that all assets on the household balance sheet should be considered when building a portfolio. Leveraging the strengths of one asset to either augment the strengths or counteract the weaknesses of another asset is an example of efficient asset use.

Embracing a holistic approach to asset allocation, where all assets play a role in decision-making, can improve efficiency and achieve more successful outcomes. The whole is greater than the sum of its parts.

EFFICIENT ASSET ALLOCATION

Efficiency is achieving an end goal with minimal effort or waste. An efficient retirement is a retirement approach that optimizes the use of resources to meet retirement goals with minimal risk and resources. An efficient retirement isn't just about having sufficient funds; it's also about using those funds wisely and maximizing their use to increase overall well-being during the retirement years. The idea is to take advantage of what is available to the fullest extent possible.

There is no one-size-fits-all solution for the efficient allocation of financial resources. The optimal use of resources will vary depending on the circumstances and goals of each individual. To begin the efficiency conversation, it will be helpful to review the areas often overlooked to evaluate how efficiency can be incorporated into a retirement income plan.

Asset allocation is an essential part of investment-based retirement income strategies for growing and conserving assets to sustain spending and manage risks. The right combination of stocks and bonds is commonly assumed to be key for this type of funding strategy. Though that is true, we have learned that deploying assets in ways not commonly used can yield similar or better results. Research demonstrates the most efficient way to fund retirement is through stocks and annuities, not stocks and bonds. Despite the fact that annuities can improve portfolio sustainability, reduce risks, and simplify asset management is not enough to encourage retirees to use them to create additional sources of secure income at a potentially lower cost. Choosing to skip annuities when evidence indicates their inclusion increases efficiency in terms of spending capability, and the ability to leave a legacy not possible with stocks and bonds alone leads to the annuity puzzle.[14] It is an inefficient use of assets to disregard annuities.

Annuities can play a key role in retirement income planning, as unlike other income sources they can provide regular payments over a specified period. These payments can be made for a specified period or for the rest of your life. The insurance company agrees to make payments for as long as needed after you pay them a lump sum of money.

It matters less how annuities are incorporated into a retirement income plan than that they are included at all. Unfortunately, many retirees opt to systematically draw down their savings or take lump sum distributions when annuitizing could be a better option. An annuity can be a form of longevity insurance and one of the few ways to protect against outliving your assets because payments are guaranteed for life. On top of that, purchasing an annuity transfers the overhead of creating income from assets to an insurance company that can do this more efficiently than one individual. Managing investments wisely can be challenging as cognitive abilities decline. Annuities solve this challenge and many more while improving overall efficiency. Retaining a portion of savings in an annuity can contribute to more efficient retirements and better retirement outcomes.

The home is the largest balance sheet asset for many retirees. It is unfortunate that many see it as a resource used only after all other assets

---

14 Silvestrini, Elain, "The Annuity Puzzle," Annuity.org, Nov 2023, The Annuity Puzzle.

are exhausted. This reasoning is flawed, as strategic use of home equity to create income should not be overlooked. It can help you delay Social Security and increase benefits, supplement retirement spending during market downturns, secure more reliable sources of income, or reduce withdrawals to increase portfolio sustainability. Incorporating home equity intelligently and efficiently into a retirement income plan can translate into more favorable outcomes with better allocation and use of an already available resource.[15]

The following sections provide practical guidance on improving efficiency with annuities and housing wealth.

Using Deferred Income Annuities (DIA) to Lower Retirement Costs

Using DIAs can effectively lower retirement costs and provide a steady income stream during retirement. DIAs are an annuity where the income payments start at a future date, typically many years after the annuity is purchased. Allocating a portion of savings to a DIA, particularly for those worried about investment risk in the near term or running out of money later in life, can reduce the expected costs of funding retirement income.

To justify the purchase of a DIA, there are several factors to consider.

> ➤ Purchasing a DIA secures a guaranteed income stream that starts at a predetermined date in the future, such as age 80 or 85. This future income can act as a safety net, ensuring you have a source of funds for as long as you live, regardless of market conditions.

> ➤ It is one of the most effective ways of reducing the risk of outliving your retirement savings. DIAs protect against this risk by offering income payments that continue for the rest of your life, no matter how long you live.

---

15 Pfau, Wade, "Improving Retirement Income Efficiency Using Reverse Mortgages," Forbes, Improving Retirement Income Efficiency Using Reverse Mortgages.

> Because the income payments from DIAs start later in life, they generally offer higher payout rates than immediate annuities (which start paying right away). The longer the deferral period, the higher the monthly income payments.

> Part of each income payment from a DIA is considered a return of principal, which means it's not subject to income tax. This can make the income more tax-efficient than other retirement income sources like withdrawals from traditional IRAs or 401(k)s.

> DIAs can complement other sources of retirement income, such as Social Security, pensions, and investment income. By providing a guaranteed income stream, they can help cover essential expenses, allowing you to be more flexible with other assets and investments.

> With a DIA, you know exactly how much income you'll receive in the future, providing peace of mind and making it easier to plan your budget in retirement.

> Knowing you have a DIA to rely on in the future can reduce the need to keep large cash reserves for unexpected expenses. This allows you to invest more assets for potential growth without worrying about immediate income needs.

> People who are risk-averse and prefer portfolios with low stock allocations are more likely to be attracted to DIAs. Shifting lower-risk assets like bonds to a DIA involves fewer tradeoffs, as DIAs provide bond-like returns with longevity protection.

Enhancing Retirement Outcomes with Investments and Income Annuities

Meeting retirement spending goals sustainably and preserving assets for contingencies and legacy are top goals. There are several different tools for meeting these objectives, ranging from investment portfolios to insurance products. Many people view these choices as either/or, but they are complementary as an integrated approach that draws from investments, and insurance can create more efficient retirement outcomes than either alone could. Certain approaches to building retirement income strategies offer increased efficiency—greater spending and a higher legacy.

A sequence of returns risk goes beyond investment risk to amplify the importance of portfolio returns in the short period around the retirement date. Poor market returns at the start of retirement can derail the plans for some retirements without necessarily implying an economic catastrophe for the general population. Pooling these risks across groups of individuals, as defined-benefit pensions and insurance companies do, helps manage this vulnerability better than a retiree can do alone.

Market volatility is not the only risk retirees have to deal with. They also have to deal with the risk of a long life. It is impossible to predict how long life will last. Still, risk pooling enables many people to share the burden of covering costs associated with risks to avoid a costly retirement resulting from living longer than expected. An income annuity allows those with shorter retirements to subsidize those with longer retirements. The subsidies (mortality credits) from the income annuity make a big difference for those who live long lives. There is an advantage to pooling your risk when uncertain about which group you will fall into. Compared to self-funding to manage longevity risks, using an annuity to pool or spread the risk among other individuals can reduce costs to manage a long life as the costs to insure against a long life for a single member are shared by all members in the pool.[16]

The composition of retirement assets can positively impact the bottom line. However, evidence suggests retirees with higher amounts of annuitized assets spend more than retirees whose wealth consists

---

16 Finke, Pfau, "Reduce Retirement Costs with Deferred Income Annuities Purchased before Retirement," Financial Planning Association, July 2015, Reduce Retirement Costs with Deferred Income Annuities Purchased before Retirement.

primarily of non-annuitized assets. Marginal estimates suggest that investment assets generate about half of the additional spending as an equal amount of wealth held in guaranteed income, suggesting that by shifting non-annuitized wealth into annuitized wealth, retirees could spend twice as much each year per dollar of savings.

The low spending rate among retirees who hold wealth in investments rather than guaranteed income suggests significant opportunities for retirees to increase annuitized wealth through delayed Social Security claiming or private income annuities.

The benefit of pooling longevity risks through an annuity can result in a 35% increase in retirement income over self-funding. However, due to their reluctance, retirees are not using income annuities as much as they optimally should. This is partly attributable to the annuity puzzle that poses this question: if the benefits of annuity ownership outweigh the benefits of not owning them, why do so few own them?[17]

The lack of liquidity and control could be one reason. Purchasing an annuity involves paying a lump sum to an insurance company in exchange for a promise of a monthly payment throughout life. Because this is a contract between you and the insurance company, no changes are possible. Another concern is that many believe they will not live long enough to recoup their investment. Life is unpredictable. We've all heard stories of people signing the contract one minute and being hit by a bus and losing everything the next moment. Another barrier to their adoption is the perceived financial risk of the company not being able to make good on their promise to make payments well into the future. There is a risk with doing anything in life, and annuities are not risk-free. However, unlike investments in financial markets, where you can lose everything, if an insurance company fails, the state protects policyholders. Every state, along with the District of Columbia and Puerto Rico, has a State Guaranty Association. This nationwide safety net

---

17 Silvestrini, Elain, "The Annuity Puzzle," Annuity.org, Nov 2023, The Annuity Puzzle.

ensures that your qualifying annuity policies will be protected if your insurance company becomes insolvent.

While these concerns are valid and cannot be eliminated, and appropriate measures exist to mitigate them, retirees should seriously consider allocating a portion of their retirement assets to some form of annuity to reduce market and longevity risks. Using sophisticated optimization techniques for retirement investment, one study found the best return/risk portfolios consisted of the following options:

> - Stocks (S&P 500)
> - Bonds (TIPS)
> - Fixed single premium immediate annuities
> - Variable annuities with guaranteed living benefit riders

Regardless of risk preferences, research shows that a 90% stock and 10% allocation to a fixed single premium immediate annuity (SPIA) even dominated a 100% equity portfolio in terms of return/risk tradeoffs. Fixed SPIAs dominated all other non-equity assets. The best asset combinations were always fixed SPIAs and equities, with no allocations to bonds, inflation adjusted SPIAs, or variable annuities.[18]

Using Reverse Mortgages to Increase Retirement Income

Home equity is an untapped source of retirement income that can benefit spending and legacy while improving the use of other assets for retirees. It can make the difference between running out of money in retirement or maintaining a desired spending level.

Conventional wisdom encouraged preserving housing wealth as a last resort option in retirement. If it was not needed, the home could be left as a legacy.

---

18 Pfau, Wade, "Retirement Planning Guidebook" Vienna, VA: Retirement Researcher, 2021.

Research suggests reverse mortgages provide an opportunity to strategically spend available equity in retirement to increase spending and enhance the sustainability of other assets. This viewpoint can result in more efficient use of available assets to support greater spending and higher legacy amounts.[19]

For a significant number of retirees' homes, equity represents two-thirds of retirement assets. Making smart decisions about home equity integration into a retirement income plan may be more important than deciding how to invest and distribute other assets. These considerations can include spending home equity to extend the life of a portfolio, supplementing retirement income, creating an income bridge to delay Social Security benefits, and reducing expenses.

Reverse mortgages may help retirees preserve their investment portfolio by allowing them to access equity in their homes. They may benefit from potential market growth and reduce sequence-of-returns risk by requiring less withdrawal from investment accounts in the early retirement years when markets decline.

Reverse mortgages can provide additional cash flow to retirees with limited savings or investment income to cover living expenses, healthcare costs, and other expenses.

Using funds from a reverse mortgage can increase retirement income and lower reliance on other assets.

A reverse mortgage can provide an income bridge during the early retirement years for those who wish to delay claiming Social Security benefits. Using reverse mortgage funds to cover living expenses allows retirees to maximize their Social Security benefits.

---

19 Garland, Susan, "Reverse Mortgages Are No Longer Just for Homeowners Short on Cash", New York, NY: New York Times, April 2022, Reverse Mortgages Are No Longer Just for Homeowners Short on Cash

Using home equity makes intuitive sense since many people consider it their biggest asset. There is, however, a lack of clarity regarding how and why it should be used in practice. Using an example, we can better understand how and why it might be useful.

An excellent way to determine whether home equity should be included in a spending strategy is to see how it impacts withdrawals from a portfolio. As a general rule, anything that reduces the amount taken from a portfolio should be beneficial. It will be especially beneficial for retirement spending that's dependent on investment income.

We can answer this question by looking at the sustainable withdrawal rate for investment portfolios combined with home equity across three different strategies for incorporating home equity into retirement income plans, to determine whether asset depletion occurs.

To understand how to apply these strategies, we'll look at a study by Sacks and Sacks published in 2012. The goal of this study was to examine three strategies for using home equity as a reverse mortgage credit line to increase the safe maximum initial rate of retirement income withdrawals from the portfolio. They analyze how home equity impacts the portfolio and spending.

The strategies are as follows:

1. The last resort strategy is to spend from a reverse mortgage after exhausting all other assets.

2. A coordinated strategy involving the establishment of a reverse mortgage at the start of retirement and the timing of reverse mortgage withdrawals to coincide with negative investment returns.

3. A spend-first strategy involves establishing a reverse mortgage at the start of retirement and spending it down before beginning withdrawals from the portfolio.

The results provided a great deal of insight.

➤ Monte Carlo simulations were conducted to quantify spending among the strategies, and strategies (2) and (3) were found to have a higher chance of success and last longer than strategy (1).

➤ Moreover, their study found that households following strategies (2) and (3) are twice as likely to have a higher net worth after retirement (the value of their remaining financial portfolios and any remaining home equity) than those following strategy (1) of saving the home equity as a last resort.

➤ When withdrawal rates are 4.5% to 7%, a coordinated strategy is 67% to 75% more likely to result in higher residual net worth after thirty years than reverse mortgages as a last resort. Home equity spending did not ruin the possibility of leaving an inheritance. As it turned out, it was the exact opposite.

This study's results are not surprising. Scenarios (2) and (3) protect a retirement plan from the debilitating sequence of returns risk, one of the most important factors to consider when making a sustainable retirement plan from an investment-based income strategy. In times of market declines, retirees who spend down home equity last are more likely to deplete other assets earlier and lock in market losses and failure.

When home equity is used first, option (3) leaves the financial portfolio alone, giving it a better chance of growing in the meantime. As a result, retirees can continue spending the same amount in retirement while utilizing a lower withdrawal rate from their larger portfolio when home equity has been exhausted. There are some costs associated with reverse mortgages, but the benefits to retirees and their beneficiaries outweigh these expenses.

In option (2), retirees use reverse mortgages only if their portfolios have declined.

It is clear from the Sacks and Sacks study that not all retirees should consider reverse mortgages, but those who intend to remain in their homes should consider them more than as a last resort.

LIABILITY RELATIVE OPTIMIZATION

In terms of efficiency, liability-relative optimization (LRO) is the least understood strategy for increasing efficiency. Quite rightly so. Despite understanding each word's meaning, it's unclear what they mean collectively. Ultimately, it matters less what they are than how they benefit retirement. Those adopting a Total Return income strategy will find it especially useful.

LRO involves optimizing an investment portfolio. It utilizes the underlying principles of Modern Portfolio Theory (MPT), a framework used for constructing and optimizing investment portfolios, but extends it in ways that benefit investing in retirement. MPT's main goal is to maximize a portfolio's expected return for a given level of risk or minimize the risk for a desired level of return.

In Chapter 2 we reviewed four common income strategies retirees can use to draw down their assets. Their primary task is to balance the income needs with the risks that would prevent the needs from being met. Implicit in these strategies is the need for some portion of retirement savings to be invested in equities—stocks, mutual funds, and Exchange-Traded Funds (ETFs).

It's commonly believed a retirement portfolio needs an equity element to keep pace with inflation, secure growth, and provide sufficient capital for an indefinite time period. With no equity allocation, you risk exhausting retirement funds more quickly than you anticipated. Even if you have covered a significant portion of your income needs with lifetime annuities, it is important to have a growth element in your portfolio. The equities address the risk of inflation, and the annuities hedge the risk of living too long.

The traditional framework for portfolio optimization depends only on three factors:

1. Expected returns

2. Standard deviation (risk)

3. Correlation: a measurement of the relationship between two or more assets and their dependency. Asset allocation aims to combine assets with low correlations so that the impact of the negative movement in one asset is offset by an opposing move in another asset, thereby reducing the overall impact on the portfolio.

The goal of retirement investing is to maintain assets in a manner that generates income to maintain desired spending. As such, LRO introduces a fourth factor, inflation, to account for the desire to spend at levels sensitive to rising prices. From an investment standpoint, it stresses using asset classes that account for and combat inflation. Someone unfamiliar with this concept would only focus on growing their assets rather than building them with the goal of long-term inflation-protected income in mind. Investing with inflation in mind is essential to maintain and grow the real value of investments over time to support spending during retirement.

If robust returns, appropriate levels of risk, and the right combination of investments were all that was needed to grow assets to support spending at desired levels, you could concentrate on them alone. However, because inflation gradually increases the price of goods and services, countermeasures are needed to maintain purchasing power and avoid excessive spending. We must be mindful of how inflation erodes the purchasing power of money over time and that the same amount of money today will buy fewer goods and services in the future.

To invest with inflation in mind, measures must be taken to counteract its effects. Generally, these measures are implemented using the following strategies:

> Diversifying the investment portfolio across different asset classes can help mitigate the impact of inflation. Asset classes such as equities (stocks) have historically shown the ability to outpace inflation over the long term.

> Fortifying the portfolio with inflation-protected securities like Treasury Inflation-Protected Securities (TIPS) or inflation-linked bonds that adjust principal and payments based on changes in inflation provides a hedge against rising prices.

> Dividend-paying stocks can be particularly attractive during periods of inflation. Companies that consistently pay dividends can provide a steady income stream that may keep pace with inflation.

> While cash provides liquidity and stability, holding excessive amounts of cash can erode purchasing power in an inflationary environment. Consider keeping an appropriate emergency fund but invest the rest in assets that have the potential to outpace inflation.

> Roth accounts allow tax-free withdrawals in retirement, which can be advantageous during inflationary periods when taxes may be higher.

> ➤ Holding a reduced amount of stock in retirement can shorten the life of a portfolio as it will not produce returns at the levels needed to keep pace with inflation. One way to protect against inflation is to hold 50% to 75% of the investment portfolio in stocks. This is superior to a declining or steady stock allocation strategy.

> ➤ Periodically rebalancing the portfolio to maintain the desired asset allocation ensures that investments align with risk tolerance and long-term goals while accounting for changes in market conditions and inflation expectations.

It's important to remember that all investments carry some level of risk, and there are no guarantees in the financial markets. It's crucial to align investment strategy with risk tolerance, time horizon, and financial goals.

Finally, you don't want the inflation tail to wag the overall financial well-being dog, so strive to develop a personalized investment plan that addresses inflation concerns and supports your overall financial well-being.

Efficiency in retirement involves careful planning, informed decision-making, strategic implementation of strategies, regular monitoring, and adjustments to ensure that your retirement income is effectively managed to support your desired lifestyle and financial security in the most efficient manner possible.

Managing Taxes for Greater Wealth and Increased Spending

The key to retirement income is to keep more of what you have. In the end, it doesn't matter how you do it. Whether it is creating efficiencies that reduce spending needs, mitigating the costs of risks, or managing taxes to decrease tax liabilities, the means are less important than the outcome. After covering risks and efficiencies, our focus now shifts to tax management.

When less income is paid into the IRS coffers, there is more income to support spending. The key to managing taxes is to plan ahead. It involves analyzing your retirement income plan and overall situation from a tax perspective and then employing tax management strategies to minimize unnecessary taxes.

Due to the nonlinearities that retirees face with their taxes, such as Social Security tax torpedoes, Medicare IRMAA surcharges, preferred income stacking, and the surprises associated with required minimum distributions, tax planning is essential.

A carefully crafted tax strategy can help your retirement income plan achieve the best tax outcomes based on your specific goals, current tax rules, and tax filing status. It can also help you with:

➤ Claiming all the tax credits and deductions you are eligible for.

➤ Maintain compliance and prevent costly filing errors.

➤ Make tax-smart decisions throughout the year.

Managing your tax burden, enhancing your total returns, and increasing spending and legacy values can be achieved by using tax planning strategies and techniques that include:

➤ Tax-Advantaged Accounts

➤ Portfolio Efficiency

➤ Prioritizing Tax-Exempt Income Sources

➤ RMD Management

➤ Tax Rate Arbitrage

➤ Estate & State Taxes

➤ Tax Law

TAX-ADVANTAGED ACCOUNTS

Understanding and utilizing retirement savings accounts appropriately can maximize your savings and minimize your tax burden, positively impacting spending and legacy. Since retirement accounts have differing tax treatments, it is important to know the tax implications of investing in or withdrawing from them to maximize income and minimize taxes.

How Tax Treatment Affects Where You Save

Your decision on where to save should be based on current and future tax rates. You should not assume that personal income tax rates or the rate your income is subject to tax will be lower during retirement.

The reason is that predicting tax rates is nearly impossible, and those who hold most of their savings in tax-deferred savings accounts may have a higher tax rate in retirement than they had while working. It's important to remember that tax-deferred accounts that include 401(k)s, IRAs, and the like, receive non-taxable contributions and are taxed accordingly at the time of withdrawal, often at higher rates than expected.

Tax implications of taxable accounts are also important to consider. Contributions are made after tax and are not subject to tax when withdrawn. Taxes will still apply to earnings, however. Unlike tax-deferred accounts that defer or postpone the taxes until withdrawal, taxable accounts have different tax treatments that imposes taxes before and during withdrawal. The tax is assessed on all account profits (dividends, interest, and capital gains), regardless of whether they have been distributed to the account owner.

Tax-exempt accounts, such as Roth IRAs and Roth 401(k)s, have their own rules. These accounts receive after-tax contributions that grow tax-deferred and allow tax-free distributions when certain conditions are met.

The Health Savings Account (HSA) offers a triple tax break in that it accepts pre-tax contributions, provides tax-deferred growth, and permits tax-free withdrawals under certain conditions.

GUIDELINES FOR REDUCING TAX LIABILITY THROUGH TAX ACCOUNT DIVERSIFICATION

> ➢ **Prioritize Tax-Deferred Accounts:** Do this when the tax rate at contribution is higher than the tax rate at withdrawal. It makes more sense to pay taxes in the future when they are lower than pay them today when they are higher.

> ➢ **Prioritize Tax-Exempt Accounts:** Do this when the tax rate at contribution is lower than at withdrawal. It's better to pay taxes now when they are lower rather than later when they may be higher.

> ➢ **Prioritize Taxable Accounts:** Do this only after exceeding the contribution limits to tax-deferred and tax-exempt accounts and extra funds are available. These are most suitable if future tax rates are expected to be higher than those currently in effect. Estate planning considerations may also support their use as assets passed on at the death of the account owner may be taxed more favorably.

The most appropriate accounts in which to invest and save will depend on the current and future tax rates. In the absence of a crystal ball, diversifying savings across several accounts to take advantage of their tax treatment can provide a hedge against tax risk inherent to all investments.

PORTFOLIO EFFICIENCY

Market fluctuations, inflation, and taxes are some of the biggest factors to consider for a successful retirement. But while the markets and inflation are generally out of your control, taxes can be managed with proper planning. Investing in various tax-advantaged accounts and following an appropriate withdrawal plan are examples of portfolio efficiencies that can lower tax liabilities and extend retirement savings. Key portfolio efficiency strategies are asset location and tax-smart withdrawals.

Asset Location

We've heard about asset allocation, which specifies how savings is allocated among stocks, bonds, and cash. Its counterpart asset location refers to the accounts where stocks, bonds, and cash are held. The goal of asset location is to make sure investments are placed in the account that offers the greatest tax advantage. In other words, the most tax-efficient assets should be placed in the least-tax-efficient accounts, while the least-tax-efficient assets should be placed in the most-tax-efficient accounts. In practice, interest-paying bonds, dividend-paying stocks, and mutual funds with high turnover are best held in tax-deferred accounts, while municipal bonds that pay tax-free interest and individual stocks that only become taxable when liquidated are best placed in tax-inefficient taxable accounts. For the purpose of locating assets, specific guidelines have been developed.

Taxable brokerage accounts are ideal for:

- Individual stocks you plan to hold for more than one year
- Tax-managed stock funds, index funds, exchange-traded funds (ETFs), low-turnover stock funds
- Stock or mutual funds that pay qualified dividends
- Municipal bonds, I-bonds (savings bonds)

Tax-advantaged accounts are ideal for:

- Individual stocks you plan to hold one year or less
- Actively managed funds that may generate significant short-term capital gains
- Taxable bond funds, zero-coupon bonds, inflation-protected bonds, high-yield bond funds
- Real estate investment trusts
- The Roth IRA is best suited for assets that have a high potential for growth, as the growth of these assets is not generally subject to taxes.

Tax-Smart Withdrawals

Tax planning in retirement is more likely to focus on minimizing taxes on withdrawals rather than on minimizing taxes on growth. Making sure you adhere to tax rules and deadlines, such as early withdrawals and required minimum distributions (RMDs) , is essential. It is also important to sequence withdrawals across all income sources (retirement accounts, Social Security, non-retirement investments, and others) to take advantage of tax rules for each source of income.

Here are the three most common withdrawal strategies from least to most tax efficient.

> *Pro-Rata:* Withdrawals from taxable, tax-deferred, and tax-free accounts are made in no particular order in this distribution strategy.

> *Sequential:* Withdrawals are drawn first from Social Security, annuities, and RMD income, taxable accounts next, then from tax deferred accounts, and finally from tax-free accounts.

> *Sequential w/Roth Conversion:* The most efficient tax distribution strategy combines sequential withdrawals with timely Roth conversions.

By sequentially withdrawing funds from tax-advantaged accounts last, they have a greater opportunity to grow before withdrawals, leading to a higher level of potential after-tax income. Research has demonstrated withdrawing income from taxable, tax-deferred, and tax-exempt sources is superior to a pro-rata strategy.[20]

For most retirees, sequential withdrawals are the best choice. However, Roth conversions or estate considerations can cause exceptions. It may be wise to leave your taxable accounts alone if you plan on leaving money to others after your death (if this is an option for you).

---

20 Benz, Christine, "How to Sequence Withdrawals in Retirement.".

Taxable investment accounts in your estate get their basis reset to the current account value when you pass away, meaning that all unrealized capital gains taxes associated with the portfolio are gone, and the recipients are essentially starting over when the assets are transferred.

This is called "stepping up" the cost basis, and can be a huge deal to heirs, from a tax perspective.

Roth conversions may also be worth considering. A Roth conversion allows you to move money from a traditional IRA (which is a tax-deferred account), incur a lower tax rate now, and then move it into a Roth IRA (which is a tax-exempt account). It results in lower tax payments today and tax-free growth of the assets in the future. In a year with an unusually low-income amount, this can be especially helpful.

A lot goes into optimizing retirement distribution order, but the basics are reasonably straightforward. Your distribution strategy—what you actually take out of your portfolio—and the resulting taxes can contribute significantly to how long your money will last and how much you will be able to spend.

PRIORITIZING TAX-EXEMPT INCOME SOURCES

In retirement, it's less about assets and more about income. Any steps taken to increase post-retirement income will help ensure a smoother retirement. One step you can take to reduce the income subject to federal tax is to identify and prioritize income sources not subject to federal or state income tax.

Common retirement income sources not subject to federal tax, range from the more well-known Social Security benefits and Roth IRA distributions to the lesser-known reverse mortgage payments, cash-value life insurance and municipal bond interest.

Maximizing tax-free income sources is key to managing taxes in retirement, as it can significantly impact your retirement income and overall financial well-being. Increasing tax-free income sources can hedge against future tax increases, lowering adjusted gross and taxable income to save on Medicare tax, Social Security tax, and taxation on other investment income.

Optimizing retirement distribution order involves a number of factors, but the basic principles are straightforward. You should aim for the maximum amount of tax-advantaged growth possible. It will enable you to spend more in retirement and leave behind more after death.

RMD MANAGEMENT

Those who have saved money for retirement via tax-advantaged savings plans like 401(k) or 403(b) or an individual retirement account (IRA) will face withdrawal requirements known as Required Minimum Distributions (RMD) annually after reaching a certain age.

While these distributions are essential to fund spending goals, they will create a tax liability that, if not properly managed, will lower what's available to spend. It will be important to manage distributions in a way that reduces tax liabilities and increases after-tax spending.

Given the limited flexibility to take RMDs, employing ways to efficiently integrate them to maximize their use without burdening the household with increased taxes will be important.

It will be essential to understand the rules as well as how they coordinate with other sources of income to develop a distribution management strategy to manage these distributions efficiently and effectively.

Keep the Rules in Mind

Once you reach age 72 (70 ½ if you were born before July 1, 1949), you must take RMDs from most retirement accounts. Beginning in 2023, the SECURE 2.0 Act raised the age you must begin taking RMDs to 73 or 75 depending on your year of birth. For those with a birth year of 1951 to 1959, RMDs will begin at age 73. For those born in 1960 or later, RMDs will begin at age 75.

Importantly, if you reach age 72 in 2023, the required beginning date for your first RMD is April 1, 2025, for 2024. It will be vital to plan for these distributions to avoid unnecessary penalties and manage tax brackets efficiently. To do this you must identify any RMDs, as there is no discretion around timing and amount, and a 50% penalty on any shortfall is assessed if not taken. The SECURE 2.0 Act drops the excise tax rate to 25%, possibly 10%, if the RMD underpayment is corrected within two years.

Coordinate Social Security and Pension Income

The mandatory nature of RMDs dictates an understanding of how other income sources, such as Social Security and pensions, are taxed. The federal government and most states do not tax Social Security benefits. However, depending on income from sources like RMDs and pensions, up to 85% of those benefits can be taxed. It can be beneficial to find ways to minimize other sources of income to reduce the impact on the taxability of Social Security benefits.

This is notable because if these assets are not spent down, this will create a situation known as the Tax Torpedo, where each dollar coming out of the 401(k)/IRA is taxed, resulting in more Social Security being subject to tax.

Calculate the Appropriate Amounts

A penalty will be assessed if you do not withdraw enough or do not make withdrawals. Knowing when and how much to withdraw will be important. The amount of your RMDs is calculated based on the account balances of your retirement accounts at the end of the previous year and your life expectancy, as determined by IRS tables. If you have multiple retirement accounts, consolidating them may make calculating and taking RMDs easier.

Charitable Giving

If you don't need the income from your RMDs for living expenses and are charitably inclined, consider using it for charitable giving. Think about using Qualified Charitable Distributions (QCDs) to meet your RMDs while fulfilling your philanthropic goals. QCDs are direct transfers from your IRA to a qualified charity, and they count toward your RMDs but aren't included in your taxable income.

Roth Conversions

The RMD amount you withdraw is generally treated as taxable income for the year in which you take the distribution. This can increase your taxable income for that year, potentially pushing you into a higher tax bracket and increasing your overall tax liability. Because RMDs can bump you into a higher tax bracket, it's crucial to consider tax mitigation strategies. Roth conversions earlier in retirement when work income ceases and before other income kicks in can create opportunities to reduce the balance of your tax-deferred accounts later subject to tax. We'll delve deeper into Roth Conversions in the next section.

RMD Withholdings

You may have the option to have federal income tax withheld from your RMD distribution by your retirement account custodian. If you choose not to have withholding or insufficient taxes withheld, you might have to make estimated tax payments or face penalties when you file your tax return.

TAX RATE ARBITRAGE

Tax rate arbitrage refers to the strategic practice of taking advantage of different tax rates or tax treatments in different situations to reduce overall tax liability. This practice is based on the principle of "buy low, sell high," but regarding tax rates. In other words, you aim to earn or realize income when and where tax rates are low and to incur deductions or realize losses when and where tax rates are high.

Utilizing strategies to optimize tax rate arbitrage to minimize taxes and increase tax efficiency will be important. Make the most of tax rate arbitrage by considering these factors.

Roth Conversions

This is the most well-known strategy for implementing tax rate arbitrage. Converting tax-deferred savings (401k and traditional IRA) to tax-exempt savings (Roth IRA) by paying tax at times when rates are lower can reduce future taxes, especially if retirement income is projected to be higher than pre-retirement income. While the conversion will generate taxable income in the year of conversion, Roth IRAs offer tax-free withdrawals in retirement when taxes may be higher than the rate at conversion.

Tax Bracket Management

Individuals might time their income and deductions to take advantage of different tax brackets yearly. For instance, if one expects to be in a lower tax bracket, they might defer income to a later year to pay less tax.

Recharacterizing Income

Investors can reduce taxes by taking advantage of differences between long-term and short-term capital gains rates. An asset is classified as short- or long-term depending on how long it's been owned. A long-term asset is owned for more than one year, and a short-term asset is owned for less than one year. The capital gains tax rates for long-term assets are lower than those for short-term assets when sold. You can reduce your taxes by owning your short-term assets for at least one year, converting them to long-term assets.

Capital Gains Harvesting

In contrast to capital loss harvesting, where decreases in investment value in one asset are leveraged to offset increases in investment value in another asset, capital gains harvesting takes advantage of differences in current and future tax rates by paying taxes on investment gains when tax rates are lower. Paying the tax on the gains when tax rates are lower, generally early in retirement, and before other income sources begin resets the basis, lowering the number of gains subject to tax on a subsequent liquidation.

ESTATE & STATE TAXES

Tax-efficient estate planning should be on the radar if you are concerned about leaving a taxable estate. Consider estate planning strategies, such as gifting assets during your lifetime, to minimize the tax burden on your heirs.

Be mindful of state tax laws as well, which can significantly impact your overall tax burden. Where you retire can have a huge impact on taxes. Retiring to a location that doesn't tax income at the state and local level could be a boon to your retirement. Your income will go further in states that don't tax personal income, like Alaska, Florida, Nevada, South Dakota, Texas, Washington, and Wyoming. Moreover, some states have different tax rules for retirees, including exemptions on certain types of income. Research your state's tax policies and consider the tax implications when choosing your retirement location.

TAX LAW

The tax laws and regulations change constantly, so staying informed about them and how they apply to your situation can greatly benefit your retirement. Taxes can be complex at times in life. The best strategies will vary depending on your unique financial situation. Developing a tax-efficient retirement strategy is one of the most important components of retirement income planning. By being proactive and making informed decisions, you can effectively manage taxes in retirement, potentially maximizing your retirement income and preserving more of your savings for your future needs.

Case Study: How the Banners Mitigate Risks, Maximize Efficiencies, and Manage Taxes

The things that matter greatly to one person might be just an afterthought to another. Each retirement is unique, as are the concerns or risks they will face. It is for this reason alone that the client's concerns should drive the risk conversation. This begins with three questions designed to uncover their concerns regarding retirement. Although these are not the only questions we ask, they raise the most pressing concerns.

> ➢ What do you fear might derail your retirement?
>
> ➢ How do you envision your later years?
>
> ➢ How do you expect to live?

The first question gets at the root of their concerns and fears, while the latter allows us to start a broader conversation about what it means for them to live in retirement. The visioning nature of these questions stimulates thinking about retirement in ways that may not have been considered when answering the first question. This introspection helps us dig deeper and uncover concerns that are not immediately apparent. For example, someone in good health who is active and plans to split time in retirement between the U.S. and overseas and travel extensively will have a very different risk profile compared to someone who plans on retiring in a single location with limited travel and health concerns.

Once I have a sense of their primary concerns about retirement, I add the risks I believe are pertinent to their situation that they may not be aware of. This analysis paints a picture of what they fear most about retirement and what risks they must cope with. This holistic approach to risk management allows us to incorporate strategies to mitigate their risks and manage the retirement-related concerns they and we feel are most relevant to their retirement.

Evaluating and implementing efficiencies in retirement income plans is a much simpler process. While many people are familiar with strategies to reduce risks and save taxes, few people know how to make their retirement more efficient. From their perspective, it is more about the rationale for pursuing a strategy than not pursuing one. The key to getting their buy-in is explaining the costs, benefits, and actions to take. I aim to provide them with the benefits without overwhelming them with the details by focusing on the bottom line. From this, they gain a better understanding and a deeper appreciation of efficiency's impact on their retirement.

Due to the ubiquitous nature of taxes, people don't need as much clarification on the benefits of tax planning. Taxes impact their lives directly. Taxes must be paid by all people, whether they are employed or retired. What is less familiar to most is how taxes change during retirement and how that might affect retirement. Considering taxes from the perspective of retirement can prove highly beneficial.

Let us now turn our attention back to the Banners. They are a late-career couple nearing retirement and are assessing their options for the best ways to convert their financial resources into lifelong income. As we move from the abstract concepts of risk, efficiency, and tax to the practical application of strategies and techniques that mitigate risk, maximize efficiencies, and manage taxes, we will gain an understanding and appreciation for their practical application. Through the Banners' retirement, we can see how this chapter's material is applied in practice.

To illustrate the potential risks to their retirement (vulnerabilities), the efficiencies they can benefit from during retirement (opportunities), and the tax implications they must take into account (consideration), our approach is to identify the risks most important to them, discover the efficiencies that provide the greatest benefit, and incorporate strategies that minimize tax liability.

MITIGATE RISKS

When asked what they fear might derail their retirement, we gained a good understanding of their baseline vulnerabilities. The greatest fear they have is running out of money, which is also the greatest fear of most retirees. It was then a matter of maintaining a sustainable level of spending. Neither of them wanted to spend less at any time due to an extended retirement period. As a final concern, they were anxious about spending shocks that could disrupt financial security and quality of life.

When we asked them how they envisioned their later years and how they expected to live in retirement, both of them had modest retirement goals and expected to keep a similar lifestyle to what they had lived before retirement. They wanted to pursue the things in retirement that weren't possible while raising a family and working, avoid burdening friends and family and ensure the surviving spouse could maintain a similar lifestyle.

Based on a collective understanding of their risks, we can quantify their vulnerabilities and determine the best strategy for mitigating them.

SOLUTION

To address their vulnerabilities, we developed the following mix of solutions.

Longevity

The risk of running out of money before retirement looms large for all but the wealthiest retirees. The Banners have a well-funded retirement, but are not wealthy, and they are aware of the risk of spending over an unknown period. As long as expected spending levels are met, exhausting assets is unlikely because secured income sources like Social Security and pensions exist to cover most essential spending for as long as they live. Allocating a portion of the bond investment portfolio to a simple income annuity (single-premium immediate annuity, deferred income annuity or fixed-income annuity with lifetime income protections) could cover essential spending not covered by other secure income sources. Managing longevity risk in this way is generally much less expensive than the alternatives.

During the asset-liability matching process, it was determined that David and Dawn face a 4.7% ($1,937,000 divided by $2,033,000) lifetime secure income funding deficit. To meet their $96,000 lifetime shortfall, they would need an additional annual income of $2,742 ($96,000 divided by 35). Any deficit is undesirable, and our immediate focus lies in seeking remedies. Our proposed approach entails acquiring a joint life income annuity, priced at $50,000, providing $5,000 in annual benefits to the longest-living spouse upon retirement. Minimum premiums for annuities vary greatly. Typically, an immediate annuity with a single premium requires a minimum $50,000 purchase price. This investment can yield a monthly income of $416, which comfortably covers a $228 monthly secure income shortfall for life.

Alternatively, self-funding $5,000 over 35 years equals $175,000. If life lasts longer, costs will rise. Annuitizing the deficit leads to lifetime savings of

$125,000 ($175,000 self-funded minus $50,000 annuitized). The annuity's advantage grows with longer life, as payments continue for a lifetime. This exemplifies maximizing asset efficiency by choosing the most suitable asset for a specific purpose.

Spending reliability

Spending at desired levels is the next most important goal for David and Dawn after longevity. Structuring reliable funding is vital, as no one wants a diminished lifestyle or to become a financial burden for others in retirement. Only secure sources of income like annuities, pensions, and Social Security can ensure stable and reliable income. Our asset-to-liability matching analysis has confirmed that with the inclusion of the joint life simple income annuity, sufficient resources to address the secure funding gap will be available to produce steady income to meet essential spending needs.

Spending Shocks

<u>Loss of spouse</u>

Losing a spouse can be emotionally devastating, but the financial implications are just as detrimental. It is for this reason that the Banners want to minimize the disruption of the life of the surviving spouse as much as possible.

This risk is best managed by considering the financial and non-financial aspects. Loss of income is the most significant financial impact. Upon the death of one spouse in a two-earner household, income can fall by up to 50%, but living costs will not fall proportionally, due to some expenses being fixed. Viable income replacement strategies include deferring Social Security benefits until age 70 to increase the benefit amount for the surviving spouse, choosing joint-life survivor options on annuities and pensions that payout for the longer of a couple's life, and systematically spending the life insurance death benefit proceeds as well as using them to purchase supplemental income.

We learned that Dawn and David each have $100,000 group term life insurance through their employers that can be converted to individual policies at retirement without medical underwriting. We recommend both convert their individual policies at retirement and increase the death benefit to $500,000 to compensate the surviving spouse and retain the policies until the first spouse dies.

Taking measures to prepare for death while married is not all about money. One spouse often takes on a leadership role in household finances. This may serve them well before retirement, but it can leave the surviving spouse in a position they are ill-prepared to assume if the deceased spouse performs this role. David has taken on the role of household advisor due to his familiarity with finances. We urged Dawn to play a more active role so that should something happen to David, she will be familiar with key aspects of household finances. Moreover, David and Dawn will need to create an estate plan well in advance to handle the things that will happen when either of them passes away.

After losing a spouse, it will be important for us to consider how the budget will evolve. There may be a decrease in some expenses and an increase in others. Planning should always consider this contingency.

Inflation

Increasing living costs can wreak havoc on a fixed-income retirement budget, depleting assets, reducing purchasing power, and requiring higher expenditures than planned. Upon analyzing their income preferences, David and Dawn found that they prefer funding retirement using reliable, fixed-payment income sources that are vulnerable to inflation. Because inflation affects everyone differently, it will be important to know how inflation will personally impact the Banners.

During the Asset & Liability quantification process from Chapter 3, we helped David and Dawn identify the expenses most likely to be impacted by inflation. These were identified as healthcare because they often outpace regular rates of inflation and housing costs due to escalating carrying costs (insurance, taxes, and maintenance). This exercise helped bring these expenses to the forefront so they could be properly mitigated. Next, it will be informative to model various inflation rates to gain insight into when and how it could impact spending. Because we advised them to defer Social Security benefits to age 70 to increase the amount of lifetime inflation-protected income, they are most exposed to inflation early in retirement. Their income is primarily composed of annuities and pensions that are not adjusted for inflation. Since Social Security benefits are inflation-adjusted, cost-of-living increases become less of an issue once benefits begin.

Knowing how and when inflation has the greatest impact on the Banners' retirement gives us insight into where our efforts should be directed. Hedging or outpacing inflation are the primary methods of managing it. We chose to hedge this risk by adding an annual benefit increase rider to approximate the 2-3% long-term inflation average. An annuity benefit increase rider is an additional feature that can be added to an annuity contract to provide a potential increase in the annuity payments over time. This rider is designed to help the annuity payments keep pace with inflation or other specified factors. It typically offers a way for the annuitant to receive periodic increases in their income stream, providing a hedge against the eroding effects of inflation. While this may not always be able to approximate inflation increases, it should hedge a significant portion of the rise in the long run.

When we provide inflation protection to protected income sources, we reduce withdrawals on other assets, allowing them to grow to support greater distributions to keep pace with inflation or to purchase additional annuities to offset cost-of-living increases.

The above strategies will be combined with a multi-asset portfolio with allocations to stocks and treasury inflation-protected securities (TIPS) bonds with built-in inflation protection that are capable of producing returns that outpace inflation. It should be remembered that it is not necessary to have a perfect match between inflation and spending because not all expenditures relevant to retirement are impacted by inflation.

Healthcare Costs

The rising cost of healthcare can strain spending budgets. In addition to increasing costs, healthcare expenditures can be unexpected and costly, making this a serious threat that cannot be ignored. Although Medicare covers most expenses, it does not cover them all, and for many, it only covers a portion. Adding to this, healthcare costs continue to rise faster than general inflation. All of these factors coalesce to pose a formidable threat to a retirement spending budget. None of us knows what our health will be in the future, but it's still imperative to establish baseline estimates for annual healthcare spending. Awareness of what can be spent allows added flexibility to the spending budget to accommodate unexpected expenditures.

We will help the Banners budget for their healthcare expenses by estimating their typical costs, expected deductibles, copayments, and premiums. We need to account for unforeseen healthcare expenses as well. Next, we will confirm that assets are available to fund reasonable healthcare expenses. From there, we will want to optimize coverages to ensure they receive the best care for their money and periodically review coverages and needs to ensure no gaps exist.

Our healthcare cost management planning consists of 1) estimating and budgeting expected needs, 2) planning for unexpected needs, 3) optimizing Medicare coverages, and 4) regularly reviewing and revising.

Estimate and Budget

David and Dawn's personal and family health histories revealed that although they have their share of health issues, they have good family health histories and no current major medical conditions that would require increased costs in the future to manage.

After learning this, we built the healthcare budget based on national averages for lifetime healthcare expenses in retirement. According to Fidelity Investments' 2023 Retiree Health Care Cost Estimate, a 65-year-old retiring this year can expect to spend an average of $157,500, or $315,000 per couple (after taxes), in health care and medical expenses throughout retirement when long-term care is excluded. Their longevity spending goals take into account these costs.

Plan for Unexpected Expenses

Healthcare is one of the most significant expenses people face in retirement, and the cost can be particularly high if you encounter unexpected health issues. The exact cost will depend on your specific health situation, the type of medical care required, and your health insurance coverage. Even though unexpected expenses have finite costs, they are difficult to predict and plan for because you never know when they will occur. David and Dawn know this and want to do what they can to deal with unexpected health issues.

Following several discussions, the Banners felt comfortable adding an additional $50,000 to the healthcare budget to cover unexpected expenses not covered by insurance. Should expenses rise above this amount, growth in the investment portfolio or equity in the home could be accessed to meet the need. Their liquidity spending goals take into account these costs.

Optimize Medicare Coverage

Because David and Dawn want flexibility on doctor choices, low to no deductible or copay, and prefer more predictable costs with an out-of-pocket limit, we've determined that Original Medicare Part A, B, D and Medigap offer the most comprehensive coverage for their needs.

Regularly Review and Revise

Following the development of a healthcare spending budget and selecting appropriate coverage choices, regularly reviewing and adjusting the retirement income plan to account for changing healthcare needs, costs, and insurance coverages will be crucial to reflect the dynamic nature of healthcare costs.

Long-Term Care Costs

It wouldn't be hyperbole to say long-term costs can cripple a retirement budget. For some, this may be their costliest healthcare expense in retirement. According to the U.S. Department of Health and Human Services, someone turning 65 today has almost a 70% chance of needing long-term care services in their remaining years. On average, women need care longer (3.7 years) than men (2.2 years). About one-third of today's 65-year-olds may never need long-term care, but 20% will need it longer than 5 years. The fact that women tend to live longer and marry older partners makes them more vulnerable to long-term care needs, since their financial and physical well-being can be compromised by caring for an ailing partner.

While many people might think of long-term care as primarily nursing home care, the reality is different. According to the National Institute on Aging, most long-term care is home-based. About 80% of older adults receiving long-term care get that help at home. Given these statistics, planning for potential long-term care needs is crucial to retirement planning.

As long-term care costs can strain budgets and compromise quality of life, the Banners want to take measures to manage costs should an event materialize. Our long-term care mitigation planning consists of 1) assessing needs, 2) calculating needs, 3) reviewing funding sources, and 4) evaluating coverage options.

Assess Needs

We begin the conversation around needs by asking several questions to assess the long-term care needs.

How the Banners responded:

> ➤ Do you prefer home, community, or institutional care? *Home initially and then institutional if necessary.*

> ➤ How long would you like care to last, years or a lifetime? *5 years for Dawn and 3 years for David.*

> ➤ Do you want your care to focus on everyday activities (eating, bathing, dressing, transferring, and using the bathroom if you cannot perform independently)? *Yes.*

> ➤ Would you like assistance with other tasks such as meal preparation, shopping, errands, financial management, or housekeeping? *Yes, for the surviving spouse.*

> ➤ Is it important that your coverage keeps pace with inflation? *Yes.*

> ➤ Are you okay with paying out of pocket before coverage begins? *Yes, we prefer to self-fund for 180 days maximum.*

Based on these responses, we can begin to source estimates for the care needed.

Calculate Needs

The Genworth Cost of Care Survey allows us to estimate hourly, daily, monthly, and annual costs across care settings. (see Chapter 4 resources) Inputting their care preferences for their retirement locale (table 4.7) allows us to compare home care costs and institutional care.

Table 4.7 Annual Median Costs for Retirement Bliss, USA (2023)

In-Home Care		Community and Assisted Living		Nursing Home Facility	
Homemaker Services[1]	$59,488	Adult Day Health Care[2]	$20,280	Semi-Private Room[4]	$94,900
2023* Cost	$63,111	2023* Cost	$21,515	2023* Cost	$100,679
Home Health Aide[1]	$61,776	Assisted Living Facility[3]	$54,000	Private Room[4]	$108,405
2023* Cost	$65,538	2023* Cost	$57,289	2023* Cost	$115,007

Source: Genworth, Inc

In-Home Care

Homemaker services allow people to live in their own homes or return to their homes by helping them complete household tasks that they can't manage alone. Homemaker services aides may clean houses, cook meals, or run errands.

Home health aides help those living in their homes instead of residential care facilities. Home health aides may offer care to people who need more extensive personal care than family or friends can or have the time or resources to provide.

These estimates are in today's dollars and reflect a 3% inflation rate. The desire for long-term care coverage is one thing; paying for it is another.

We'll need to review the Banner's financial capacity to determine how to fund the coverage needed. Our first step is determining what assets are designated for long-term care needs to identify funding gaps. Depending on the level of funding needed and the assets designated for long-term care, we will examine other financial resources to fill any gaps if needed.

After speaking with the Banners, I learned that both of them work for organizations that offer group long-term care coverage as a supplemental employee benefit. We later learned the policies can also be converted into individual policies without medical underwriting at the separation of service. We evaluated each policy and recommended they increase the policy benefit period to 5 years for Dawn and 3 years for David, increase the benefit amount to a $200 maximum allowable daily benefit, and increase the elimination period to 180 days to control costs.

Transferring the long-term care risk to an insurer who can manage the risk better by pooling (spreading) it among many individuals is a more efficient method than trying to do it themselves. To replicate this, they would have to set aside substantial assets that could have been used for another purpose. This is another example of how retirement can be made more efficient.

In the above example, the estimated cost of in-home care is $63,000 and $65,000, respectively. Based on 365 days of care and a $200 daily benefit, their long-term care policies will pay up to $73,000 annually. There is sufficient funding in place for homemaker services and home health aide care, but they are still underfunded with respect to care in an institutional setting. A $73,000 annual policy benefit and an estimated $100,000 and $115,000 semi-private and private annual room rates would create a $27,000 and $42,000 funding deficit, respectively.

Review Funding Sources

There is sufficient funding in place for homemaker services and home health aide care, but they are still underfunded with respect to care in an institutional setting. We will need to explore other funding sources to meet this need.

Evaluate Coverage Options

Having heard their share of stories of consumers who had purchased long-term care insurance only to lose coverage, either because their insurer left the market and canceled their policies or because they had to abandon their policies and lose all the premiums due to rising costs, David and Dawn were reluctant to purchase traditional standalone long-term care insurance.

Therefore, we looked for other solutions and recommended either drawing on equity in the home or adding an annuity with a long-term care rider that combines elements of insurance with long-term care coverage. This product is designed to provide financial protection against the potential costs of long-term care while providing income to the insured and a death benefit to beneficiaries.

Following an assessment and estimate of long-term care needs, evaluation of funding sources, and identification of funding gaps, the following long-term care coverage strategy has been developed:

LONG-TERM CARE COVERAGE STRATEGY

Preferred Care Setting

➢ Home then institutional

Estimated Annual Care Costs

➢ Annual In-Home Care Need: $65,000 p/p

➢ Annual Institutional Care Need: $115,000 p/p

Projected Funding Sources

➢ Individual LTC Policy - pensions and Social Security

➢ Home equity

➢ Annuity w/LTC coverage

Funding Options

➢ Individual Long-Term Care Policy Annual Benefit: $73,000

➢ Income Annuity w/Long-Term Care Rider Annual Benefit: $84,000 (2 times $42,000 p/p funding gap) as part of a broader strategy of replacing income lost from deferring Social Security. The mechanics of this will be discussed in the next section, *Maximize Efficiencies*.

Unexpected Expenses

While we try to anticipate all the costs we might face in retirement, some expenses can come as a surprise. Major home repair or upgrade, health-related relocation, or financial assistance to family or friends are often overshadowed by more well-known unexpected expenses like healthcare and long-term care costs, inflation, and taxes. To prepare for these overlooked costs, it's a good idea to include a buffer in the retirement spending plan so that other spending goals are not harmed should unexpected expenses arise.

In discussing various scenarios, the Banners agreed that maintaining a $50,000 cash reserve in case of a major home repair or upgrade, relocation due to health reasons, or financial assistance to the family would be sufficient. As a last resort, money could be withdrawn from the investment portfolio to meet any needs above and beyond this amount.

Spending Variations

For households with annual incomes of less than $150,000, overall spending volatility was largely due to changes in nondiscretionary or essential spending. David and Dawn's income is projected to fall under this amount, and one of their greatest concerns is having reliable income to meet their basic needs. When Dawn and David learned that retirement expenditures can fluctuate greatly at any time, and increases may persist, they agreed that it would be beneficial to have adequate allocations to liquid assets to reduce financial stress during times of increased spending. They felt comfortable maintaining a $50,000 cash reserve and exposure to growth assets to supplement additional income needs beyond guaranteed income sources.

MAXIMIZE EFFICIENCIES

Many retirees know that unmanaged risks can seriously threaten retirement and that mismanagement of taxes can result in higher costs and lower spending. What many do not realize is that planning for retirement income with efficiency in mind can reduce risk, lower costs, and increase spending.

It is often overlooked that efficiency plays a vital role in retirement income planning, but as we've seen, implementing a few strategies can boost income by nearly 37 percent.

The combination of increasing inflation-protected income by delaying Social Security, managing longevity risk more affordably with annuities, and strategically using home equity to sustain the portfolio provides retirees with opportunities to create a more efficient retirement.

We will examine the Banners' retirement to determine which efficiencies are suitable and select the best applications to demonstrate how we applied them to their retirement income plan. This will hopefully provide you with some ideas you might find useful.

Opportunity

> - Delaying Social Security to Increase Lifetime Inflation-Protected Income
>
> - Managing Longevity & Long-Term Care Risks With Secured Income
>
> - Enhance Spending Potential Through Total Wealth Asset Location, Efficient Asset Location, and Liability Relative Optimization

SOLUTION

To leverage their opportunities, we developed the following mix of solutions.

Delaying Social Security to Increase Lifetime Inflation-Protected Income

Many factors make delaying Social Security benefits an effective strategy for maximizing retirement income.

- ➤ It can result in higher monthly benefits of up to 32% and increase the amount of inflation-protected income.

- ➤ It can serve as longevity insurance against the risk of running out of money because it pays lifetime benefits.

- ➤ A higher benefit amount can extend the life of other retirement assets by preserving and allowing them to grow longer.

- ➤ It can increase survivor benefits if the higher-earning spouse dies first.

- ➤ It provides an opportunity to strategically draw down tax-deferred retirement accounts earlier in retirement during lower tax periods to reduce required minimum distributions when taxes may be higher and potentially eliminate Social Security taxes, Medicare premiums, and Net Investment Income taxes.

Exhibit 4.8

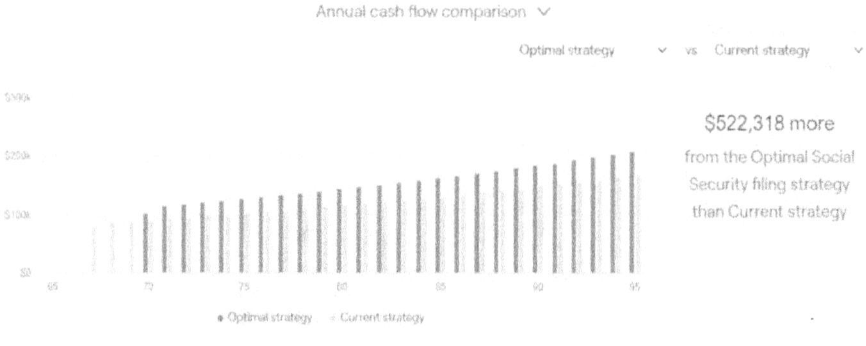

Source: *Right Capital, Inc*

Based on an analysis of over 700 Social Security claiming strategies, we determined that delaying benefits to age 70 is the most advantageous strategy for the Banners. According to Exhibit 4.8, delaying Social Security will result in $522,318 more benefits based on a total of $4,039,308 lifetime benefit if they claim at 70 versus a $3,516,990 lifetime benefit claimed at full retirement age in Exhibit 4.9.

Exhibit 4.9

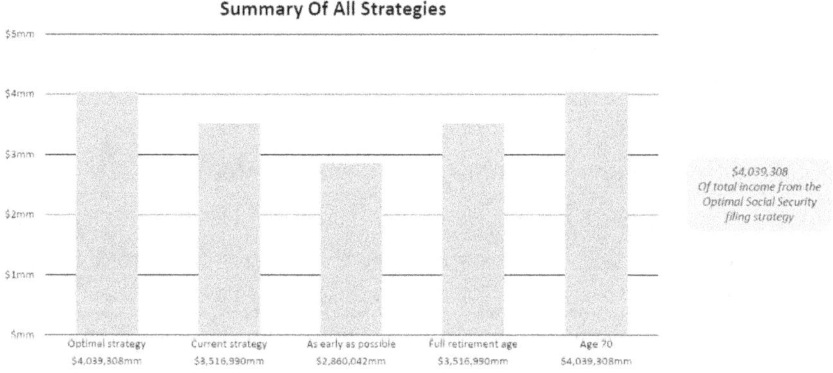

Source: Right Capital, Inc

To reap long-term rewards, it is often necessary to incur an upfront short-term cost for efficiency. The upfront cost is the income lost by delaying Social Security benefits. Consider this a deductible that you'll have to pay to receive higher benefits.

While the Banners benefit from pensions, they cannot rely on them solely to meet all their income needs. Generating additional income is necessary to replace lost Social Security benefits and supplement pension income to sustain their spending.

During the transition from work to the start of benefits, they require a bridge of income to cover any spending shortfall. Delaying Social Security benefits from retirement to their start is estimated to result in a $7,000 annual income gap. This gap is calculated as follows: $60,000 annual spending need minus the $5,000 joint life simple income annuity to address the secure funding spending gap, subtracting Dawn's $1,250/month pension, David's $1,750/month deferred compensation, and $1,000/month rental income.

Annuities offer an effective way to bridge Social Security income gaps. The Banners will purchase a 5-year period certain annuity for $25,091, providing a $7,000 annual benefit starting at retirement until Social Security benefits begin funded with a portion of their portfolio bonds. Alternatively, to bridge the $35,000 ($7,000 multiplied by 5) Social Security income gap, they could withdraw this amount from the investment portfolio. However, this would cost an additional $9,909 ($35,000 - $25,091) compared to the annuity. Here we re-purpose one stable asset for a more reliable one, allowing assets with the greatest growth prospects (stocks) to reach their true potential at a low cost compared to other solutions.

Sourced from ImmediateAnnuities.com, the estimated cost for a 58-year-old male non-smoker in Oregon purchasing a 5-year period certain annuity to begin payout of $7,000 annually at age 65 is $25,091. This serves as the "deductible" for obtaining the increased Social Security benefits of $522,318. A 5-year period certain annuity pays income for 5 years starting at a specified future date but does not cover a lifetime. If the individual passes away before the start date, beneficiaries receive a premium refund. If death occurs during the "Period Certain" term, beneficiaries continue to receive income for the remaining term.

Leveraging an annuity to supplement spending lost due to delayed Social Security benefits demonstrates a more efficient use of assets for retirement income plans. The annuity creates a secure income stream at a lower cost than income sourced directly from their portfolio. With an upfront cost of $25,091 from the portfolio, it's less than the $35,000 needed to offset the 5-year funding deficit resulting from delaying Social Security when self-funding. By leaving $9,909 of the portfolio untouched to grow alongside the creation of a stable income, the annuity offers a more efficient asset utilization, unlike investments. Since assets are fungible, how they are used matters more than what they are used for. By delaying Social Security and using an annuity to supplement income, we have helped the Banners increase lifetime income potential, hedged the inflation risk by increasing the amount of inflation-protected income, and mitigated sequence of returns risk by supplementing spending with an annuity rather than income from the portfolio. Delaying Social Security is another strategy to improve efficiency in the long run that outweighs the short-term costs. Since assets are fungible, how they are used matters more than what they are used for. By delaying Social Security and using an annuity to supplement income, we have helped the Banners increase lifetime income potential, hedged the inflation risk by increasing the amount of inflation-protected income, and mitigated sequence of returns risk by supplementing spending with an annuity rather than income from the portfolio. Delaying Social Security is another strategy to improve efficiency in the long run that outweighs the short-term costs.

Managing Longevity & Long-Term Care Risks With Secured Income

Social Security and pensions are often assumed to mitigate the risk of a long life because they come with lifetime income protections. While that may be true for those dependent on Social Security and fortunate to have pensions, it may not be a sensible strategy for those relying on income sources without lifetime income protections, such as an investment portfolio or real estate. With pensions becoming less common, retirement income security is more dependent on Social Security benefits and other assets that do not pay lifetime benefits, putting many at risk of depleting their assets should life last longer than expected.

When left to their own means, many try to manage this risk by either spending conservatively early to maintain the capacity to spend longer later or setting aside a cash cushion as a safety net to spend from in the event that life goes beyond expectations. One backloads spending, and the other creates a reserve to support spending. While the risk is minimized in both cases, it's not eliminated. Keeping assets in reserve or cutting spending to extend spending over an unknown lifespan is not an efficient or effective method of managing the risk of a long life. Fortunately, there are more practical and efficient alternatives.

Longevity risk is best treated by transferring it to a third party such as an insurance company that can better manage it by spreading the risk of a long life among many people in a "pool" at a lower cost than a retiree could hope to do themselves. By pooling risks, individuals in the pool benefit from lower costs and greater benefits than they could achieve on their own. Long-lived individuals benefit from subsidies (mortality credits) because those who live shorter lives subsidize those who live longer lives.

Risk pooling is fundamental to all insurance products, from life insurance to annuities, and it can be used effectively in retirement income planning to efficiently manage a long-life expectancy.

We have chosen to incorporate risk pooling through an income annuity with a lifetime income guarantee to the longest-living spouse for David and Dawn's plan. An immediate annuity with a single premium turned on at the beginning of retirement is cost-effective to treat the risk. And because the Banners are underfunded regarding their long-term care spending needs, a long-term care rider will be added to the annuity to supplement long-term care benefits from their individual long-term care policies.

A portion of bonds from the taxable and tax-deferred savings will fund the annuity. Bonds are a better use of assets than stocks (or assets with growth expectations) for filling gaps in secure income. This is an excellent example of how assets can be utilized to their best potential. The withdrawals should be made in a tax-efficient manner since distributions may be taxed. While withdrawals from either account could trigger taxes, our analysis confirms that the annuity's long-term benefits are significantly greater than its short-term costs (investment principal and taxes).

The annuity strategy is more efficient than self-funding because the costs to fund an unknown life are much higher if self-funding than the cost to purchase an annuity that will pay a benefit for as long as the survivor spouse lives. How much should be set aside if life expectancy is unknown? Guessing is expensive and risky. Underestimate and risk financial insecurity or overestimate and diminish the quality of life. Neither outcome is desirable, and both are avoided easily. Efficiencies like these aren't anecdotal, as research into portfolio optimization reveals that allocating at least 10% of a retirement portfolio to a single-premium immediate annuity helps reduce market and longevity risks.[21]

Enhance Spending Potential Through Total Wealth Asset Location, Efficient Asset Location, and Liability Relative Optimization

We'll close out David and Dawn's efficiency overhaul by implementing a few tweaks to make their retirement income plan even more efficient.

We'll begin with Total Wealth Asset Location since it is the least understood and utilized. Structuring assets from a total wealth perspective is an incredibly powerful concept. The failure to take a broad view of assets and their interactions can erode their advantages and magnify their disadvantages, creating inefficiencies that are difficult to overcome.

The inefficiency is locating assets from a narrow perspective rather than more broadly to maximize their value. Efficiencies are about making the most of what you have, and actions that obstruct this can be counterproductive to retirement. To counteract this, you must understand the composition and characteristics of your assets so you can determine how

---

21 Murguia, Pfau, "Selecting a Personalized Retirement Income Strategy," Retirement Management Journal, November 2021, Selecting a Personalized Retirement Income Strategy.

to use and structure them most effectively. This understanding is necessary to make strategic decisions likely to lead to superior outcomes.

Understanding the interactions between assets is as important as understanding the assets themselves. In other words, decisions about asset structure should consider ALL assets and not be made in isolation. For instance, someone with more income from secure sources may allocate other assets differently from someone with more income from less secure sources. In practice, someone with greater amounts of secure income can be more aggressive with other assets than those with little or no such income. To a large extent, secure income sources (e.g., Social Security or pension benefits, or an annuity) are similar to bonds in growth and stability.

Not considering these characteristics when arranging assets results in under- or mis-allocation of other assets. The Banners' Income Protection income style, which emphasizes using secure sources of income to fund retirement, serves as a guide for deploying the other assets they have. Looking at Exhibit 4.10 reveals that investments comprise the bulk of the Banners' assets.

Exhibit 4.10

Asset Composition Before Total Wealth Asset Location

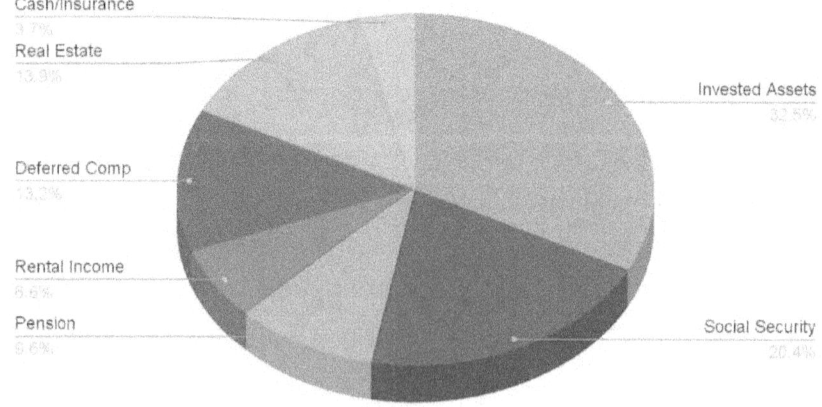

Due to their preference for using protected income sources to pay for their essential retirement expenses, some of their invested assets are available to acquire additional sources of protected income. This allows us to direct assets to their highest needs while reimagining other uses for the remaining assets.

Because their essential living expenses are covered by protected income sources, there are opportunities for them to pursue increased growth prospects with the remaining invested assets, since no matter what the market does, they will always be able to cover their essential spending needs with protected income sources.

This perspective helped them understand the value of taking less risk in one area to take more risk in another. A person with a less holistic perspective would naively allocate assets more conservatively, not realizing how secure assets impact the total allocation equation.

The circumstances of each individual differ, and risk tolerance plays an important role. However, having greater access to secure income allows increased opportunities to pursue growth with other assets than otherwise possible.

To address the $5,000 annual shortfall in secure lifetime income and fund the $7,000 5-year joint life income bridge, we propose purchasing a joint-life income annuity and a 5-year period certain annuity. The life income annuity would cost $50,000, and the 5-year period certain annuity would cost $25,091, totaling $75,091 from low-payment-reliable assets.

Due to the wide range of variables influencing annuity rider costs, including insurance provider, specific features, age, health, and coverage amount, we are unable to provide cost estimates for either the annual benefit increase rider or the long-term rider for the joint life income annuity. Nevertheless, funding is available, and the benefits would outweigh the costs.

Exhibit 4.11

Asset Composition After Total Wealth Asset Location

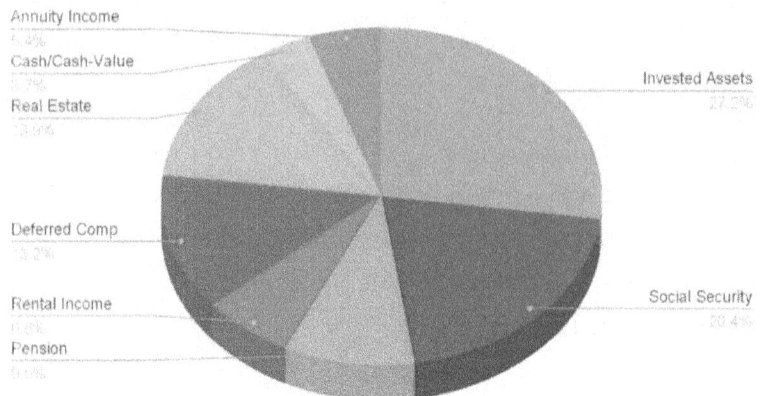

As illustrated in Exhibit 4.11, using a Total Wealth Asset Location perspective, we have created an additional 5.4% of high payment assets through the annuities using $75,091 of low payment reliable assets (investments) to $25,091 of secure funding for essential spending due to the $50,000 secure income funding deficit and income bridge needed to delay Social Security, while addressing the long-term care funding deficit and expanding options to better utilize the remaining investments.

Efficient Asset Location

Locating assets efficiently has many benefits that are often overlooked. This is due to a focus on asset allocation that determines the composition of asset classes (stocks, bonds, and cash) that best balance risk and reward based on investment goals and risk tolerance. In contrast, asset location is about deciding which accounts to hold the various asset classes.

It is important to take note of this because accounts are taxed differently, which impacts investment returns. It is therefore necessary to understand the tax treatment of the various accounts and assets placed in them to minimize taxes and maximize after-tax returns. An increase in net returns results in increased savings and greater spending potential.

A well-designed asset location strategy would see you typically put investments producing taxable income (bonds or REITs) in tax-advantaged accounts like traditional IRAs or 401(k)s that shield assets from taxes until withdrawal. Investments that qualify for more favorable tax rates (stocks or stock funds) are better suited in taxable accounts that are taxed annually. Investments you expect to appreciate greatly over time (thus generating larger capital gains and higher taxes) are candidates for tax-exempt accounts that will never be taxed.

The Banners' investment portfolio was reviewed to ensure that the least efficient assets were positioned in the most efficient accounts, and the most efficient assets were positioned in the least efficient accounts.

Liability Relative Optimization

There is no retirement income strategy immune to the ravages of inflation. Where possible, income sources need to account for and mitigate inflation. A crucial part of preserving their purchasing power will be identifying their inflation risks and utilizing strategies to protect them from inflation. Unchecked inflation can lead to unsustainable spending levels that exhaust assets, threaten living standards, and compromise financial security.

Our review of David and Dawn's inflation exposure reveals they are most susceptible to inflation early in retirement with regard to health care and housing. To alleviate this risk, we advise them to acquire annual income benefit increase riders for both the joint life income annuity and the 5-year period-certain annuity. Once Social Security begins, the amount of inflation-protected income will increase, and the annuity will no longer be needed.

An alternative would be to use the investment portfolio to finance inflation-related spending. However, having a preference to source income from protected sources of income, the Banners wish not to rely on unpredictable market returns to fund essential spending needs.

It would be preferable for them to pay the cost upfront to fund an annuity to ensure essential spending levels are maintained to keep pace with inflation.

With the help of Total Wealth Asset Location, which involves analyzing the entire portfolio of assets to optimize the use of assets, and Efficient Asset Allocation, which identifies how assets should be efficiently structured across a variety of investment accounts, the Banners are now able to enjoy increased opportunities to capture greater market returns, reduced taxes, and increased after-tax spending. We were also able to move toward stabilizing spending goals most impacted by rising costs of living by incorporating liability relative optimization.

MANAGE TAXES

Taxes are always a concern, whether you're working or retired. Many retirees are surprised at the impact taxes can have on their retirement. Taxes impact everything from asset preservation to spending potential and overall living costs. Fortunately, taxes are one of the few retirement planning areas that you have some amount of control over. Tax planning is a vital part of retirement income planning and can enhance retirement outcomes when done properly.

To illustrate how tax planning can enhance spending potential, preserve assets, and reduce taxes, we will discuss common strategies used and how they were applied to the Banners' tax situation. By examining the considerations and associated solutions, we will demonstrate how tax planning benefited their retirement.

Considerations

- ➤ Tax-Advantaged Accounts
- ➤ Tax-Rate Risk
- ➤ Tax-Exempt Income Sources
- ➤ Tax Rate Arbitrage
- ➤ RMD Management
- ➤ Portfolio Efficiency

SOLUTION

Tax-Advantaged Accounts

Financial security requires most people to save for retirement. Some individuals have access to various tax-qualified savings plans that allow them to save for retirement tax-efficiently during their careers.

Individuals can also save on their own with tax-advantaged traditional or Roth IRAs. Your choice of retirement savings plan can seriously affect your financial security after you have retired.

David's nonqualified deferred compensation and Dawn's 403(b) are tax-qualified savings plans. Contributions to these plans are tax-deferred, which means they're not taxed when made, but at withdrawal, both they and their earnings are taxed.

While there is a tax benefit at contribution, withdrawal can often result in a large tax liability, to the dismay of many retirees.

Roth IRAs differ from employer-sponsored retirement plans in a few ways. Taxes are paid before contributions are deposited into the account and generally, contributions and earnings are withdrawn tax-free. These are tax-exempt accounts that do not incur tax liability in retirement.

It will be crucial to determine whether David and Dawn have sufficient savings and are saving at a rate that will sustain future spending goals, as well as whether their assets are structured to reduce investment costs, preserve savings, and reduce taxes.

The Banners have a variety of account types. We have compiled a listing of their assets in Exhibit 4.12 below.

Exhibit 4.12

Assets Used to Generate Retirement Income				
Asset	Value	Timing	Reliability	Payout
Dawn				
403(b)	$500,000	As early as 59 ½ or retirement, whichever is the earliest	Market performance	lump sum or annuity
Roth IRA	$250,000	As early as 59 ½ or retirement, whichever is earliest	Market performance	Lump sum
David				
401(k)	$500,000	As early as 59 ½ or retirement, whichever is earliest	Market performance	Lump sum or annuity
Roth IRA	$250,000	As early as 59 ½ or retirement, whichever is earliest	Market performance	Lump sum
Joint				
Brokerage account	$250,000	Anytime	Market performance	Lump sum
Rental Equity	$100,000	Buyer availability	Secure	Lump sum
Cash value life insurance	$50,000	Assuming cash value anytime	Secure	Lump sum loan
Home Equity	$500,000	Buyer availability	Secure	Lump sum
Cash Savings	$50,000	Anytime	Secure	Lump sum

David and Dawn are appropriately allocated with regard to taxes across the various account types (Exhibit 4.13). Our analysis reveals savings are equitably diversified across tax-advantage savings accounts. There are $1,000,000 of tax-deferred savings from David's 401(k) and Dawn's 403(b) plans, and $500,000 tax-exempt savings with each spouse owning a Roth IRA for $250,000 each. The remaining $250,000 in retirement savings are held in the taxable account.

Exhibit 4.13 Tax Allocation Summary

Source: *Right Capital, Inc*

Investing in tax-deferred accounts is a smart way to save for retirement because it allows assets that haven't been taxed to grow tax-free as long as they remain in the account. Tax-exempt accounts are also good savings accounts, but they don't offer an immediate tax break like tax-deferred accounts.

Although tax-deferred accounts offer many benefits, it will be helpful to remember that contributions and their earnings are subject to federal and possibly state income taxes, since they have never been taxed. Account balances do not reflect the actual value of the account since state and federal taxes are due when withdrawals are made. It's helpful to think of a tax-deferred account as a partnership between you and the federal and state governments, where your tax rate reflects the state and federal ownership of the account value. In the Banners' case, their tax-deferred savings amount to $1,000,000. Assuming federal and state taxes of 22% and 8%, respectively, their share of the "partnership" is *only* $700,000 once the $300,000 ($1,000,000 times 30%) of the tax bill is paid to the federal and state taxing authorities.

It was disconcerting to tell them this, but they expressed gratitude for having a realistic view of their savings. Moreover, we warned that higher future tax rates may lead to an even higher government partnership percentage than currently forecast. Keeping their savings from being eroded by higher taxes is something we must address to protect them from tax rate increases.

Tax Rate Risk

It is often said that predicting tax rates is as easy as predicting the weather. However, like weather forecasts, tax rate predictions are subject to numerous factors and can be influenced by unexpected events, making them inherently challenging and uncertain. Although the Banners have diligently saved, the substantial amounts held in their tax-deferred accounts subject them to considerable tax rate risk if rates remain the same or increase. As Exhibit 4.14 shows, tax projections through retirement show tax rates remain at pre-retirement levels through most of retirement with a dip in taxes beginning at age 89.

Exhibit 4.14

Source: Right Capital, Inc

It is a common misconception among retirees that taxes in retirement will be lower than they were while working because work income has stopped. There is certainly a decrease in paid income. But most people fail to realize that the tax-deferred accounts that offered a nice tax break while working have taxable mandatory withdrawals in the form of required minimum distributions that can push them into higher tax brackets, resulting in high tax liabilities in retirement, rather than the low tax liabilities they expected.

We will take a two-pronged approach to managing this risk exposure. First, redirect future contributions from their tax-deferred accounts to the tax-exempt Roth accounts of their employer savings accounts (David's Roth 401(k) and Dawn's Roth 403(b) option) to increase tax-exempt savings rather than tax-deferred savings. Second, move money from tax-deferred to tax-exempt accounts through strategic Roth conversions. We'll discuss the latter in more depth in Tax-Rate Arbitrage.

Prioritizing Tax-Exempt Income Sources

Roth IRAs and Health Savings Accounts (HSAs) are examples of tax-exempt accounts where contributions and earnings can be withdrawn tax-free. It would be advisable for David and Dawn to prioritize savings in tax-exempt savings accounts because they face a looming tax rate risk. Our strategy going forward will be to help them protect more of their savings from future taxes by ramping up contributions to tax-exempt accounts.

Tax Rate Arbitrage

Tax rate arbitrage refers to the practice of exploiting variations in tax rates between the various tax brackets. It involves taking advantage of disparities between current and forecasted tax rates to prioritize paying tax on income when tax rates are at their lowest.

All things considered, paying taxes at a lower rate versus a higher rate lowers tax liabilities and results in greater spending potential. Tax rate arbitrage occurs through Roth conversions that create opportunities to pay tax on income and earnings when tax rates are lower, with the goal of reducing taxes, lowering tax liabilities, and minimizing exposure to tax rate risk.

Roth conversions are worth considering when future tax rates are expected to be higher than current rates.

A particular focus should be placed on this topic because the current tax provisions of the Tax Cuts & Jobs Act (TCJA) signed into law in 2017 that lowered the tax rate and widened tax brackets will expire in 2025. It will be replaced by the pre-TCJA tax provisions, which raised tax rates and narrowed tax brackets (unless action is taken to extend them). Assuming future taxes will be higher is a prudent and conservative approach. Should taxes trend lower, great. If not, then we have done our best to prepare the Banners for a worst-case scenario.

Exhibit 4.15 illustrates that even as the Banners' income steadily increases over retirement, it never exceeds the 24% tax bracket.

Exhibit 4.15

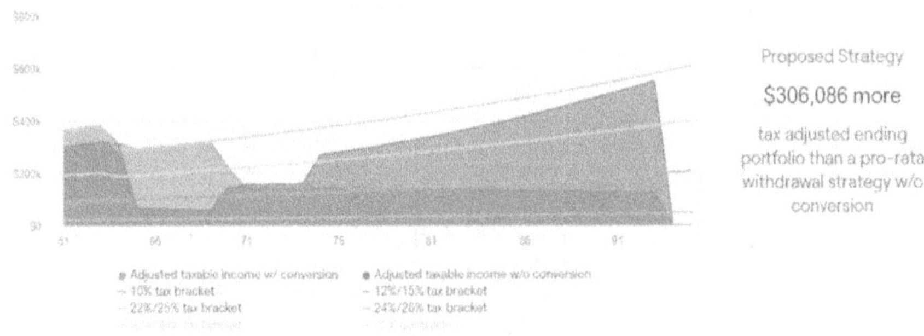

Source: Right Capital, Inc

According to Exhibits 4.16 and 4.17, our proposed tax planning strategy of paying taxes at the 24%/28% tax bracket versus not doing so increases the Banners' tax-exempt assets by 59% (from 41% to 100%) and tax-adjusted ending wealth (the final amount of assets remaining at plan end after taking into account the impact of taxes) by $306,086 ($13,985,243 - $13,679,157) while reducing the federal income tax by $1,101,834 ($2,279,561 - $1,177,727) (Exhibit 4.17).

Exhibit 4.16 Tax-exempt Assets and Tax-adjusted Ending Wealth

Source: Right Capital, Inc

Exhibit 4.17 Federal Taxes Paid

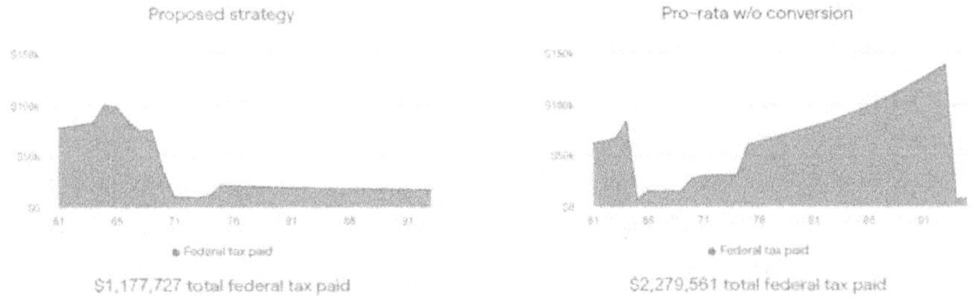

Source: Right Capital, Inc

This projection does not consider the possibility that future tax rates will be higher than current tax rates. The benefits of our tax strategy truly shine when viewed through the lens of required minimum distributions and increased tax-exempt account values. Tax rate arbitrage aims to reduce taxes *and* mitigate the impact of future tax rate increases. An important part of any retiree's tax plan is reducing the amount of income that will be subject to unknown future tax rates.

Exhibit 4.18 illustrates how strategic conversion of tax-deferred assets into tax-exempt assets reduces the former's account balances and required minimum distributions (RMDs) to zero. Notably this means that future withdrawals from the tax-exempt will never be taxed or subject to tax rate risk (an increase in tax rates).

Exhibit 4.18 Required Minimum Distributions

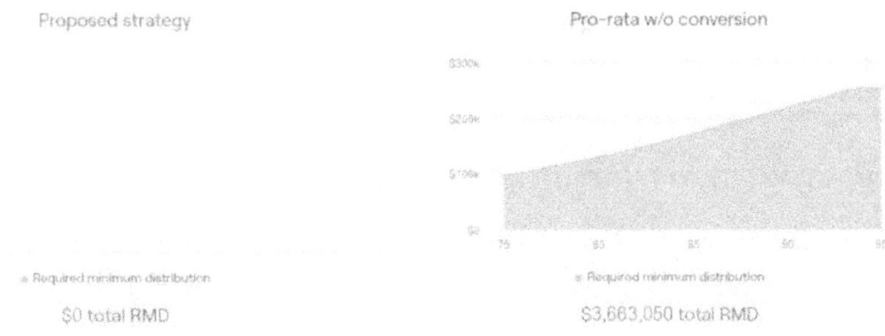

Source: Right Capital, Inc

We're assuming tax rates will revert to 2017 levels that were higher than what they are currently. At that point, Congress can take one of several actions. They can extend them, revert to the 2017 tax rates, or institute higher rates.

An additional benefit of executing the Roth Conversions is that a greater portion of assets will be recharacterized from taxable to tax-free. According to Exhibit 4.16 tax-exempt assets would increase from 41% to 100% with a 24%/28% Roth conversion strategy that can provide unique benefits and opportunities for individuals looking to pass on their assets to heirs and beneficiaries. Roth IRAs can be used strategically in conjunction with other estate planning tools like trusts to help control the distribution of assets, protect assets from creditors, and manage complex family situations.

RMD Management

A plan for effectively managing RMDs is essential for anyone who has accumulated retirement savings in a tax-deferred account. Because the Banners have a substantial share of their savings in accounts subject to required minimum distributions, a policy is needed to effectively manage these distributions.

As shown in Exhibit 4.18, strategic Roth conversions result in the elimination of required minimum distributions when compared to not doing them. The benefit of Roth conversions would dramatically increase if tax rates exceeded 2017 levels as there would be no required minimum distributions to pay taxes on.

Implications to Other Benefits, Income, and Taxes

Considering the nonlinearities in the tax code resulting from annuities and pension income, we must examine their effect on the Banners' health insurance costs, taxes on other income sources, and additional taxes. Let's explore how each of these could impact the Banners.

Medicare is a federal health insurance program in the United States for people aged 65 and older and is funded through two primary sources: payroll taxes and premiums paid by beneficiaries. Premiums are based on income, and premiums increase with income. Anything that increases income, such as annuity and pension income, can raise premiums.

Premium increases are determined by the IRMAA which stands for Income-Related Monthly Adjustment Amount. It's a surcharge that high-income retirees in the United States pay in addition to their regular premiums for Medicare Parts B and D.

The IRMAA is determined by the federal government based on the Modified Adjusted Gross Income (MAGI) reported on the tax return from two years prior. The MAGI include adjusted gross income plus any tax-exempt interest income. As of 2024, the IRMAA affects individuals with a MAGI above $103,000 or couples filing jointly with a MAGI above $206,000. The higher your income, the higher your IRMAA surcharge will be.

If you're affected by the IRMAA, you'll receive a notice from Social Security. It's also worth noting the IRMAA is not a once-and-done calculation. It's recalculated each year based on your latest tax return, so it may change each year.

Our analysis shows that even though David and Dawn's income is forecast to increase, it is expected to remain well below the levels that would trigger an increase in their IRMAA. Roth conversions and diverting savings to tax-exempt accounts before retirement are contributing factors to this reduction.

Taxation to Other Sources

As you can see, collecting annuity and pension income isn't as simple as it seems, paying the tax, and spending the money. It is vital to consider the potential negative consequences of that income on other areas of retirement income.

The tax torpedo is one such area that often goes unnoticed until tax filing time when the additional tax liability is felt. It refers to the way Social Security benefits become taxable when income exceeds certain thresholds. As retirees generate additional income from sources other than Social Security, they not only pay tax on that income but potentially push themselves closer to the threshold where a portion of their Social Security benefits becomes taxable.

The tax torpedo is an important concept for retirees to know because, with careful planning, it can often be minimized or avoided.

The term "tax torpedo" is used because, in some cases, this combination of factors can lead to a sudden increase in the effective tax rate for retirees as they enter a range where their Social Security benefits are subject to taxation and result in paying higher taxes on Social Security benefits that were intended to provide a source of income during retirement.

Because of their wealth and spending goals, the tax torpedo is the Achilles' heel of the Banners' tax plan. Projections indicate retirement income will exceed levels that will make a portion of Social Security benefits taxable.

Among the main strategies we will employ to alleviate the impact on their Social Security are:

1. Start contributing post-tax to employer retirement savings plans rather than pre-tax, as post-tax withdrawals come out tax free.

2. Convert tax-deferred savings into tax-exempt savings before Social Security benefits start to recharacterize taxable into tax-free income.

3. Delay the start of Social Security benefits to reduce the number of years their benefits are subject to taxation. By waiting until age 70 we will reduce the exposure of their SS benefits to taxation.

4. Plan the timing of withdrawals from retirement accounts strategically to minimize the impact on Social Security benefits. This may involve withdrawing from tax-free accounts first.

5. Itemize deductions when applicable to reduce taxable income.

6. Fund a health savings account (HSA) to reduce taxable income in retirement because contributions are tax deductible, and withdrawals are tax-free.

Additional Taxation

In addition to increases to Medicare costs and taxation of Social Security benefits, annuity and pension income may also result in additional taxation through the Net Investment Income Tax (NIIT).

The NIIT is a 3.8% tax on the lesser of (1) your net investment income or (2) the amount by which your modified adjusted gross income (MAGI) exceeds certain threshold amounts ($200,000 for single filers, and $250,000 for married couples filing jointly).

While annuity and pension income aren't considered net investment income, they are included in your MAGI for NIIT purposes. Therefore, receiving them can increase your MAGI and, if your income is near the threshold levels, could push you over the limit where the NIIT applies. As a result, you might end up paying NIIT on some or all your net investment income, even though the annuity and pension itself is not subject to the NIIT.

For example, let's say you're single, and your only source of income in a given year is $50,000 in dividends and a $170,000 annuity and pension income from your retirement account. The dividends are net investment income, and the annuity and pension income are part of your MAGI. In this case, your MAGI would be $220,000, which is $20,000 over the NIIT threshold for single filers. As a result, you would owe the NIIT for the $20,000 of your dividends, even though the annuity and pension income itself is not subject to the NIIT.

Our review of the Banners' projected MAGI during retirement shows it remains well below the limits where NIIT would apply. Our efforts to reduce their MAGI through Roth conversions and beefing up tax-exempt accounts played a significant role. Their exposure is also limited because they have little investment income outside tax-sheltered savings accounts.

Portfolio Efficiency

Investment efficiency in retirement is all about ensuring retirees get the most out of their investments without taking undue risk. Given the complexities associated with investing, taxes, and market returns, maximizing portfolio efficiency is essential, especially since a large percentage of retirees will rely on their portfolios for their income over an uncertain period of time.

Having most of their retirement income derived from sources unaffected by financial markets makes portfolio efficiency less of a concern for the Banners. But for those income needs that are not funded by these sources and are funded from their investment portfolio, optimizing for efficiency is key. We must take measures to ensure the portfolio is constructed in an efficient manner. It is likely that focusing on aspects of their portfolio such as asset location, tax-smart withdrawals, tax-aware transitions, and tax deductions will have the greatest impact. Let's go through them one by one.

<u>Asset Location</u>

Exhibit 4.19 illustrates the Banners have a good representation of account types. The goal is to allocate assets across the three account types, with the majority held in tax-free accounts impervious to tax rate risk, required minimum distributions, and impact on other income sources like Social Security. One of the biggest risks for them is the majority of their assets reside in tax-deferred accounts that are subject to all the risks mentioned above. David and Dawn should prioritize making all future contributions to their employer retirement savings plans as an after-tax contribution and begin converting assets from their tax-deferred accounts to tax-exempt Roth IRA accounts when appropriate.

Exhibit 4.19 Tax Allocation Summary

Source: Right Capital, Inc

Along with these steps, they will also want to do the following:

> Prioritize placing dividends, interest, and capital gains-generating assets in tax-deferred and tax-exempt accounts to shield them from ongoing taxes.

> Prioritize placing assets that produce the least dividends, interest, or capital gains in taxable accounts because assets in this account are taxed whether or not they are withdrawn.

> Prioritize investing in tax-exempt accounts for dividends, interest, and capital gains assets with the greatest growth prospects because withdrawals are always tax-free regardless of account growth.

Tax-Smart Withdrawals

The combination of proper tax allocation and tax-smart withdrawals is a powerful one-two punch for efficiency. It's all about order here. Research has demonstrated that withdrawing income from taxable, tax-deferred, and tax-exempt sources, in this order, is superior to a pro-rata strategy that withdraws income in no specific order.[22] Inefficient asset withdrawals can lead to increased taxes, reduced spending, and decreased portfolio sustainability.

Pro-Rata is the default and least tax-efficient retirement distribution strategy where withdrawals are taken from all accounts (taxable, tax-deferred, and tax-free) in no specific order.

Sequential is a more tax-efficient distribution strategy where withdrawals are taken from taxable accounts first, tax-deferred second, and tax-free last.

Sequential w/Roth Conversion is a distribution strategy that pairs sequential withdrawals with timely Roth conversions to produce the most efficient tax distribution strategy.

Our analysis reveals the Banners are best served by using a Sequential w/Roth Conversion strategy early in retirement, and later, when Roth Conversions ceases, to employ a Sequential withdrawal strategy.

Tax-Aware Transitions

Tax-aware transitions are the final element of portfolio efficiency. They refer to strategies employed during portfolio reallocations or restructuring, especially during large shifts like consolidating accounts, distributing required minimums, or changing one's investment strategy.

Using tax-aware transitions allows retirees to reduce the risk in their portfolios while minimizing taxes to meet their financial goals. The primary goal is to make these transitions in a way that is cognizant of the tax implications to ensure taxes don't unduly erode the portfolio's value.

---

22 Morningstar, May 2023, How to Sequence Withdrawals in Retirement.

We do not anticipate major changes in the portfolio as a result of account consolidations or distributions since it is a secondary source of retirement funding. However, as income is drawn from the taxable account to fund discretionary spending and pay the Roth conversion tax that they will withdraw from first, tax-aware transitions will have an impact. Tax-deferred and tax-exempt accounts are less likely to require tax-aware transitions.

Our tax-aware transition strategies for the Banners include the following:

> ➢ ***Capital Gains Management*** to guide them to selectively sell positions or stagger liquidations over multiple tax years to manage the capital gains impact.

> ➢ ***Tax Loss Harvesting*** to help them identify and sell securities at a loss to offset capital gains from securities sold at a profit in other parts of the portfolio.

> ➢ ***Tax Gain Harvesting*** to help them identify highly appreciated assets to liquidate in low-tax rate environments to reduce tax liabilities and increase after-tax income.

> ➢ ***Holding Periods*** to help them identify assets held for more than one year to qualify for lower long-term capital gains rates.

Maximize Deductions

Maximizing tax deductions during retirement is essential for retirees who want to reduce their tax liability and retain more of their income. While retirees might not have the same deductions available as they did during their working years, there are still several strategies and deductions they can utilize. For taxpayers with deductible medical expenses, charitable contributions, and loss claims, it may be better to lump them together and itemize deductions rather than take the standard deduction.

Savings over the course of retirement are often hard to quantify at the beginning of retirement. It is due in part to the uncertain nature of public policy and personal circumstances. However, taking these limitations into account, our projections show the combination of efficiency-enhancing and tax reduction strategies has netted the Banners an additional $2,347,228 (Exhibit 4.20) ($939,308 of increased efficiency and $1,407,920 from reduced taxes respectively) of lifetime income resulting from the following:

- $1,101,834 in tax savings resulting from tax-efficient withdrawals and Roth Conversions.

- $306,086 increase in tax-adjusted ending wealth resulting from tax-efficient withdrawals and Roth Conversions.

- $351,732 additional savings from the growth of the $125,000 difference between the $175,000 cost to self-fund and the $50,000 cost to annuitize, which would have otherwise been spent to self-insure against a long life left in the portfolio to grow at 3% over 35 years.

- Delaying Social Security benefits results in a $497,227 increase in lifetime spending, calculated as the $522,318 increased lifetime Social Security benefit minus the $25,091 cost of the income bridge annuity to delay SS benefits.

- $27,882 in additional savings are generated from the growth of the $9,909 difference between the $35,000 cost to self-fund and the $25,091 cost to annuitize, which would have otherwise been spent to delay Social Security. This amount remains in the portfolio, growing at a rate of 3% over 35 years.

- Implementing the six efficiencies results in $62,467 in additional lifetime income. This is calculated by assuming a conservative $22,000, based on 37% of the $60,000 annual income, left in the portfolio to grow at 3% over 35 years.

- The income not spent through the risk mitigation strategy is difficult to quantify. But it would be more than reasonable to assume that spending potential would be reduced significantly if the risks went untreated.

Exhibit 4.20 Savings on Taxes and Efficiency

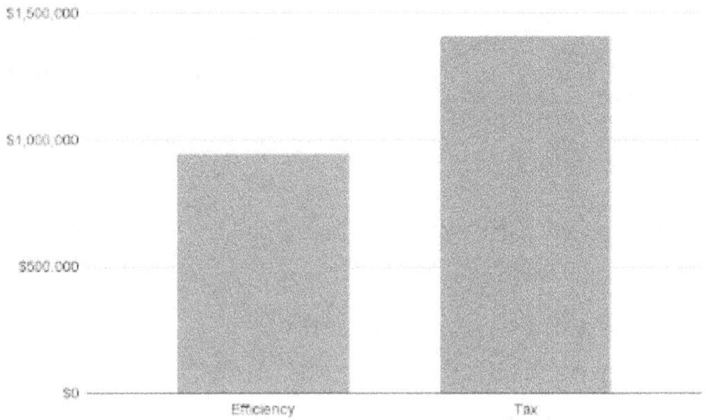

Tax planning has netted total savings of $1,407,920

> Tax-efficient withdrawals and Roth conversions resulted in $1,101,834 less taxes.
> Tax-efficient withdrawals and Roth conversions resulted in $306,086 in increased wealth after tax.

Efficiency optimizations have netted total of $939,308

> An annuity generated $351,732 more savings compared to self-funding against longevity.
> Benefits increased by $497,227 due to the decision to delay Social Security.
> Compared to self-funding the Social Security income bridge, utilizing an annuity and allowing the funds to grow in the portfolio resulted in additional savings of $27,882.
> Implementing a subset of efficiencies creates additional savings of $62,467.

Not only are the dollar savings significant, but when viewed from the perspective of investment returns, the full impact of efficiency optimizations and tax-reduction strategies becomes evident. By calculating the Internal Rate of Return (a financial metric used to assess the profitability of an investment) and in this case the profitability of each optimization and strategy, we can estimate the investment return between electing and not electing the optimization or strategy. It is from here that various efficiency optimizations and tax reduction strategies can be shown to be highly beneficial to retirement.

- ➤ Social Security Optimization: 3.0%
- ➤ Social Security Income Bridge Optimization: 3.0%
- ➤ Longevity Protection Optimization: 3.0%
- ➤ Miscellaneous Optimizations: 3.0%
- ➤ Tax Reductions: 7.6%
- ➤ Total Investment Return: 19.6%

These results demonstrate how a few tax reduction strategies and efficiency optimizations provide benefits similar to a 19.6% before-tax investment return. To make this even more realistic, let's calculate the net return for efficiency optimizations that, unlike the 7.6% return attributable to the tax reductions, are before tax returns. Assuming a combined 30% tax rate (22% federal and 8% state) and using the formula for *after-tax yield = (1 - tax rate) × (before-tax yield)* where (1 - .30) x (12%) nets an 8.4% after-tax return, that when combined with the 7.6% tax reduction efficiency return yields a total net return of 16%. It's undeniable that tax strategies and efficiency optimizations can have a positive impact on the bottom line. And unlike unpredictable investment returns with no guarantees, various strategies and optimizations that offer greater chances of success are available for retirees that result in savings that mimic strong market returns.

MARK'S KEY TAKEAWAYS

➢ Assess your retirement risks and develop a plan to mitigate them.

➢ Create more efficient resource usage by maximizing synergies.

➢ Manage tax liabilities to preserve assets to increase after-tax spending by integrating tax planning into retirement income planning.

CHAPTER 5

Turn Your Assets into Income to Fund Your Liabilities

"Never look back unless you are planning to go that way."

— HENRY DAVID THOREAU

Learning Objectives

- ➤ Traditional Methods May Not Tell You How to Turn Assets into Income

- ➤ How Income Preferences Allow Assets to Be Effectively Turned into Income

- ➤ Case Study: How the Banners Used Their Income Preferences to Determine How to Turn Their Assets into Income

Retirement was once largely paid for by your employer. As long as you met your employer's age and service requirements, you knew exactly how much you would earn at retirement. All you had to do was cash the check every month, sit back, and enjoy retirement.

It is a different world now. Pensions are increasingly rare; fewer companies have pensions today than in past decades. According to the Bureau of Labor Statistics, the percentage of private employers that offered pensions fell from 35% in the early 1990s to 18% in 2011 and to 15% in 2022. As employers have shifted away from saving for retirement and turning those savings into income for their employee's retirements, employees are increasingly left to do these things on their own. Unfortunately, most are ill-equipped to do this effectively, often resulting in detrimental consequences for their retirement.

This means that at retirement, a soon-to-retire or newly retired is sitting on a pot of money that requires yet one more retirement decision: how to draw down this capital to finance retirement. They must avoid taking too much or too little to ensure they won't run out of income before running out of life or have to live a substandard life. They must structure and manage both a withdrawal and investment strategy while trying to grow the remaining balance. That's a lot to ask of someone in their golden years.

Determining an appropriate strategy for converting assets into lifetime income is a crucial piece of any retirement plan. Providing a regular income stream and doing it efficiently for as long as needed are important aspects of an income strategy. A successful retirement plan requires thorough analysis to determine the best strategy to maintain spending power. No one strategy is right for everyone, and no one strategy is better than another. Each strategy should be tailored to the needs and challenges of the individual. For example, converting a 401(k) account into a life annuity can be an excellent solution for someone with little other guaranteed lifetime income but less appealing to someone with a significant pension benefit.

A starting point for achieving this begins with choosing the appropriate way to frame the issue. For some, it's more helpful to think about creating a floor of income for essential expenses, while for others, it starts with the question, "How much can I afford to withdraw from the portfolio each year and still make my money last?" It's essential to understand the different approaches to framing the problem and be able to pick appropriate solutions. By framing the strategy, you can outline how it will meet your income goals while managing the risks.

The task can be as difficult as you want or as easy as you need. Having seen how assessing income preferences can definitively help identify the income strategy most appropriate for retirement, it should be the first step.

The retirement income proposition is straightforward: accumulate enough assets to cover expenses over an indeterminate period while managing the risks that undermine the ability to do so. It will be important for you to do two things reasonably well to achieve this.

1. You must identify an income strategy for turning your financial resources into income in a manner that is most meaningful to you.

2. You must implement an income strategy that combines and uses your financial resources in such a way as to optimize the balance between meeting spending goals and protecting those goals from the unique risks of retirement.

Traditional Methods May Not Tell You How to Turn Assets into Income

Your retirement will rarely be healthier than your income strategy. Determining a strategy to turn your assets into income during retirement is the single most important decision that you must make that has the greatest impact on the outcome of your retirement. How you choose to go about doing this takes precedence over everything else.

Despite its simplicity, this task is riddled with challenges, none of which are your own doing. The difficulty lies squarely with an inadequate decision-making framework that doesn't support making the right decision. An ineffective decision-making system often leads to poor decisions because it limits choice, introduces bias, adheres to outdated practices, and distances the stakeholders from the decision-making process.

Making choices based on what has worked for others can limit your choices. Solutions may be skewed by biases that may subvert your interests to those of others. Methods that are proven to be effective in other areas can do more harm than good in this case. Processes heavily weigh other factors but neglect the most important one: you.

A closer look at the framework people use to make this decision will be helpful. Observing how they succeed or fail using it will help to see the need for a different approach. New interest is sparked by alternatives that enhance these advantages while overcoming their disadvantages, paving the way for reintroducing a more effective method of assessing one's beliefs, concerns, and values about spending in retirement that identify appropriate solutions to turn assets into income.

The traditional framework rests on a risk tolerance questionnaire (RTQ) , advice from professionals and laypersons, and mass media. Each of these, in its own way, can do more harm than good.

Let's briefly review each before moving on to the alternative.

RISK TOLERANCE QUESTIONNAIRE

An investment risk tolerance questionnaire (RTQ) is used in the financial service industry to gauge someone's willingness and ability to take on investment risk. The goal is to align the investment strategy with the investor's risk tolerance and financial objectives. The focus is all on investments rather than income.

It can tell you how to invest, but it cannot poll the sensitivities needed to determine how to spend down your retirement investments, where the income from the investments matters more than the investment itself.

Your retirement will rarely be healthier than your income strategy. Determining a means to turn your assets into income during retirement is the single most important decision you must make.

Risk surveys have their place and are very helpful when used appropriately. I can think of two scenarios where they might be useful. They can be useful to assess the alignment of investment goals with time horizons, emotional, and financial capacities for someone saving for retirement and to maintain regulatory compliance for financial professionals by providing investment recommendations that are appropriate for the individual's risk profile. Apart from these cases, they have limited use. It's a helpful tool, just not the one you will need to determine how to source income in retirement.

What they can tell you...

1. The level of risk you are comfortable with at a particular time

2. Insights into your investment preferences (i.e., ability, capacity, and willingness to take on investment risk)

3. How to invest according to your investment preferences

What they won't tell you...

1. How you want to source retirement income

2. The most appropriate way to turn assets into retirement income

3. How you feel about the risks to your retirement income

ADVICE FROM PROFESSIONALS AND LAYPERSONS

Financial professionals can be extremely valuable in retirement income planning when they possess the competence, objectivity, and right skills.

The problem lies there. There are a few things you need to keep in mind if you decide to go this route to determine your retirement income strategy.

First, retirement savings planning is the area of financial planning focused on determining retirement savings goals and the actions and decisions necessary to achieve those goals. It involves identifying various income sources, estimating expenses, implementing a savings program, and managing assets and risks to achieve spending goals.

Retirement income planning is an area of financial planning focused on managing spending, investments, risks, and taxes to meet daily expenditures for as long as possible, maintain a desired standard of living, provide a legacy for the family or community, and preserve liquidity for unexpected expenses and contingencies during retirement.

These are two separate knowledge domains that require different abilities, competencies, and skill sets that should not be mistaken for one another.

Second, when providing financial advice, it is often determined by what one is comfortable with and knowledgeable about. You can only say so much about what you don't know. If your only solution is a hammer, every problem appears to be a nail. Using a hammer when a drill or saw would be more appropriate won't give good results. Even if someone is familiar with retirement income planning, they may only use preferred strategies they are familiar with rather than strategies that might be more appropriate for your situation. This can result in a misalignment between their solutions and your needs and should be avoided at all costs. In the next section, we'll discuss how to avoid it.

Third, conflicts of interest are at play whenever human involvement is introduced into the planning process. In some cases, your best interests can be sacrificed for the sake of others. Someone who is financially motivated to favor certain solutions over those better suited to your situation can lead you to unintended consequences.

There is no one-size-fits-all solution to spending in retirement. Choosing how to draw income from your financial resources to support yourself in retirement is highly individualized and requires a thorough understanding of your financial resources, goals, risks, and other intangibles not easily perceived. The increased risk associated with professionals or laypersons occurs because they are often biased, uninformed, or inexperienced.

What they can tell you…

1. How to assess and plan for retirement goals
2. Considerations for retirement savings and the optimal allocation of funds
3. Biased solutions for converting your financial resources into income

What they cannot or won't tell you…

1. How their plan for evaluating and selecting an appropriate income strategy prioritizes impartiality, informed decision-making, experience, and freedom from competing interests
2. That alternative solutions may better meet your needs
3. There may be more cost-effective alternatives

MASS MEDIA

This includes various media outlets, financial services publications, and the financial services industry.

There is a saying: the squeaky wheel gets the grease. Mass media can be that squeaky wheel, promoting the idea that saving and investing in a diversified investment portfolio is the only means to fund retirement. This leads to internalization of the message, which then subverts other promising and effective approaches. The alternatives are overshadowed by the dominant message to the detriment of many a retirement.

Financial incentives drive this investment-first approach to retirement income planning. Specific financial products and strategies are more lucrative for the financial services industry than others. It is common for these to be heavily marketed over alternatives that are just as effective, if not more so. The public will have limited choice if viable alternatives are drowned out.

Many of the challenges associated with relying on financial professionals for retirement income planning apply to mass media as well. A symbiotic relationship exists here where similar efforts lead to similar outcomes. You are more likely to receive biased and self-serving advice filled with preconceived notions about what is right for you. You are again sold a solution rather than picking one that best fits your needs.

What they can tell you…

1. What's worked for others in a similar situation
2. The popular and prevailing ways to fund retirement income needs
3. Financially incentivized ways to fund retirement income

What they cannot tell you…

1. How they will assess and identify an appropriate income strategy free from competing interests
2. Their unwillingness to promote alternatives due to their biases and self-interest
3. Crafting, implementing, and overseeing a retirement income solution that aligns best with your needs and preference

How Income Preferences Allow Assets to Be Effectively Turned into Income

There are many things an income profiling tool such as the RISA does very well, but what sets it apart from other options for determining retirement income strategies is the fact that it emphasizes the most important thing: you.

Compared to how things are currently done, this is quite a change. The quest for an appropriate strategy for converting assets into income does not have to be based on subjective and limited recommendations or preconceived notions about what is best. It is now possible to determine the most appropriate income strategy for doing this simply by assessing your income beliefs and preferences.

The key to achieving favorable retirement outcomes is determining how your assets can be turned into income best for you. This starts and ends with understanding your income beliefs and preferences.

A new era is ushered in where clarity and confidence replace uncertainty and skepticism. For the first time, choosing how to generate income in retirement from your assets is entirely up to you. By removing outside distractions and engaging you in meaningful ways, you can discover your preferences for income in retirement to choose the income strategy that matches them best.

It's a simple premise. Create an intuitive and approachable framework to help individuals approaching retirement understand their retirement income style preferences and explore how they translate to certain income solutions. Basing this decision on your income preferences can improve the chances for retirement success and personal fulfillment. Furthermore, choosing your own strategy over one chosen by others engenders commitment.

It's a novel concept but one that has long been needed.

Is there anyone better equipped to determine how you want to source income in retirement than you? Did someone make decisions for you when it came to your career, your life partner, or your place of residence? Most likely not. Your decisions were based on your preferences, not someone else's. Choosing life decisions based on how you feel and not what someone else feels increases your chances of fulfilling your potential. Whatever the skill level of your advisor, they don't know you as you do. Assessments of risk miss the point entirely.

The consequences of seeking advice from well-intended but biased sources are well-known.

Let's turn our attention to profiling your income preferences, overcoming the disadvantages, and building on the advantages of current methods.

How Income Preference Profiling (IPP) Builds On The Advantages Of Traditional Income Strategy Determination Methods (TISDM)

TISDM ADVANTAGES	IPP EXTENDING EFFECTS
Individualized and nuanced solutions	A methodical approach to tailoring retirement income solutions
Explore the possibility of evaluating your income preferences and the corresponding aligned strategies	Income preference-driven income strategies
Determining the required amount for retirement savings and deciding on the optimal asset allocation	Prioritizes spending savings and assessing spending thresholds
What to invest in if you plan to fund your retirement with a diversified portfolio	Reimagining how resources can be best utilized to support spending

TISDM ADVANTAGES	IPP EXTENDING EFFECTS
Investing risk you are comfortable with at a particular time	Evaluates the full spectrum of retirement risks
The extent to which you are willing and capable of taking on investment risk, an indication of your investment preferences	Emphasis on income preferences instead of investment risk, as income, not wealth, matters in retirement
An investment risk profile-based approach to investing	Provides insight into how you prefer to receive retirement income from savings, not how to invest them

How Income Preference Profiling (IPP) Overcomes The Disadvantages Of Traditional Income Strategy Determination Methods (TISDM))

TISDM DISADVANTAGES	IPP MITIGATING EFFECTS
Disproportionate focus on investment solutions, neglecting potentially more suitable alternatives	Solutions prioritizing client needs, devoid of bias towards any particular income strategy
Financially incentivized solutions laden with conflicts of interest and external influences	Impartial, software-driven solutions unaffected by external influences
A prevailing assumption that a diversified investment portfolio acts as the primary source of retirement funding	Explores a wider array of options that could offer superior outcomes compared to relying exclusively on a diversified investment portfolio for retirement funding

TISDM DISADVANTAGES	IPP MITIGATING EFFECTS
Constrained set of solutions, vulnerable to subjectivity, conflicts of interest, and preconceived biases	Client-centric solutions that prioritize objectivity, neutrality regarding strategies, and freedom from conflicts of interest, restrictions, and preconceived notions
Solutions are sold, not bought	The solution you implement is the one you actively choose
Limited insight into your income preferences, income personality, income style, and income strategy	Reveals the correlation between income preferences, income personality, income style, and income strategy
Costly, inaccurate, and time consuming	Affordable, precise, and quickly accomplished

Favorable outcomes in retirement are not random. They are predicated on good judgment, prompt action, and a bit of luck. Keeping an eye on what you can control and planning for what you cannot is essential. Luck can strike at any time, but you can take the right actions at the right time to improve your chances. Here is where deciding to engage in a discovery of the things important to you, your income beliefs and preferences, and choosing your preferred income strategy at the onset of the retirement income planning process can make all the difference.

Case Study: How the Banners Used Their Income Preferences to Determine How to Turn Their Assets into Income

A comprehensive income preference analysis revealed the Banners' preferred income strategy for funding their retirement is Protected Income. People who want a lifetime income floor to fund essential expenses backed by contractually protected income sources like annuities with lifetime income protections, government bonds held to maturity, defined-benefit pensions, and Social Security prefer this income strategy.

By assessing their income preferences, we help them to identify their retirement income personality (style) to select and implement a retirement income strategy in a manner that was most meaningful to them. This consists of questions designed to translate an individual's preferences and style markers into appropriate and practical retirement income strategies free from outside influences and subjective interpretations characteristic of traditional financial planning assessment tools.

Following standard practice, we walk clients through each key element of their income profile report to interpret the results and how they will be used to turn their assets into secure, safe, and sustainable income. We introduce clients to these elements through the Retirement Income Style Awareness Overview report, as viewing them has a greater impact than simply discussing them. By sharing this real-life example, it is hoped you will grasp the practicality and the significance of how we can assess their beliefs and preferences to identify how to generate income in retirement.

We'll walk through the key elements of the Banners' report to understand how we used it to identify appropriate income strategies for their retirement.

When discussing the results, it is best to begin with the two main factors that best reflect an individual's preferences for how they desire to source retirement income. These are Probability-Based vs. Safety-First and Optionality vs. Commitment. Research has identified these as the most influential factors describing income preferences.[23]

The Probability-Based factor is predicated on the potential for market growth from traditional diversified investment portfolios to provide a

---

23   Murguia, Pfau, "How Retirement Income Preferences Inform Retirement Income Styles," Retirement Income Institute, November 2022, How Retirement Income Preferences Inform Retirement Income Styles.

continuous and sustainable retirement income stream. This construct appeals to those willing to endure market losses in exchange for gains.

On the other hand, the Safety-First factor does not believe a continuous and sustainable income can be generated from income sources based on the probability of positive outcomes that may or may not occur and instead incorporates income sources with contractual obligations to ensure a more reliable income. It will most appeal to those who want to fund essential expenses with protected income sources and some degree of income safety.

The next construct is Optionality vs. Commitment. Optionality implies a preference to maintain flexibility to respond to economic developments and changes in personal circumstances. It aligns with income strategies that do not have predetermined holding periods and can be easily adjusted. In contrast, Commitment reflects a preference to resolve a life-long need in a relatively simple manner and without the complication of future reassessment.

Exhibits 5.0 and 5.1 from the Banner's Retirement Income Style Awareness Overview shows their affinity with the Safety-First & Commitment income style.

Exhibit 5.0

Source: RISA, LLC

Exhibit 5.1

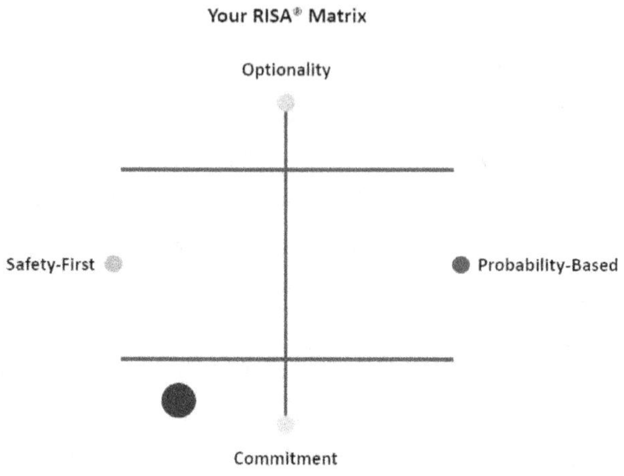

Source: RISA, LLC

Exhibit 5.2 shows how their Safety-First & Commitment income style maps to a Protected Income strategy that favors using more secure funding sources to support retirement income needs when contrasted with alternative, less secure retirement income sources.

Exhibit 5.2

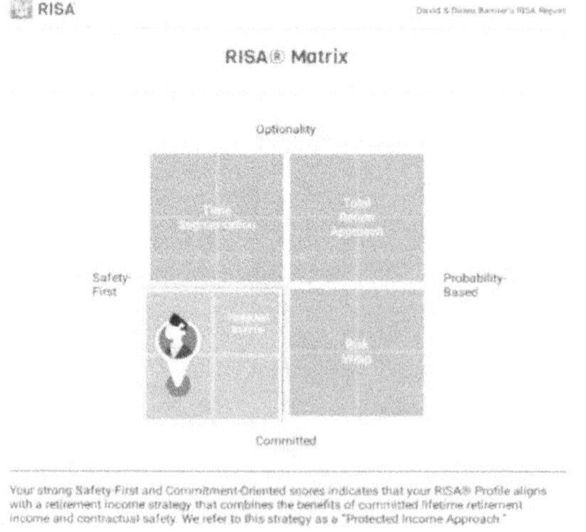

Source: RISA, LLC

In the following charts, we share deeper insights into how their answers to key questions reveal how their income preferences align with the Safety-First vs. Probability and Commitment vs. Optionality income factors.

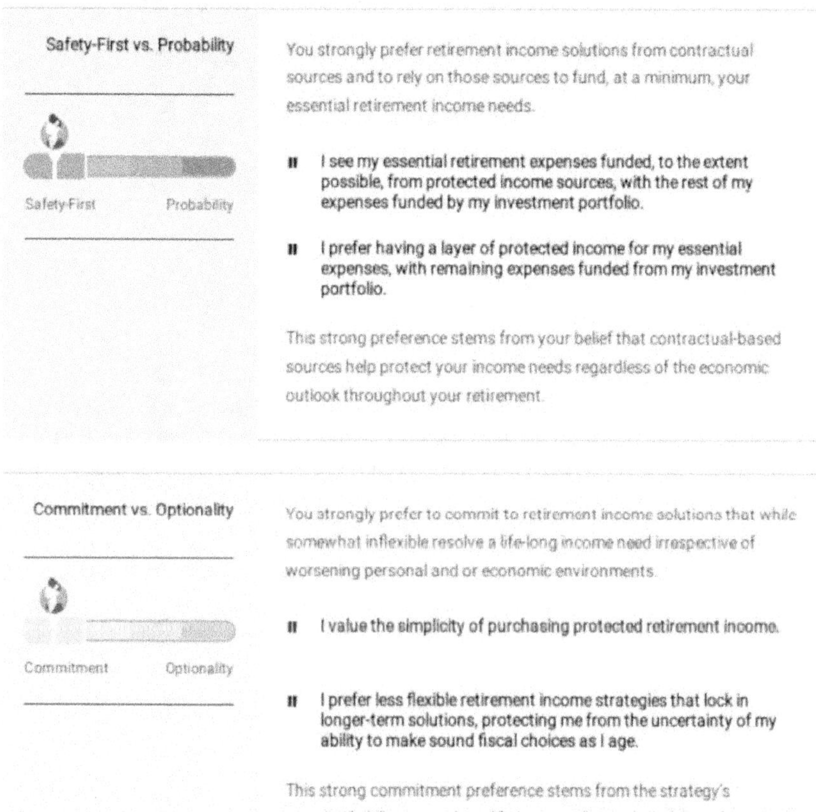

Source: **RISA, LLC**

These income preferences reflect a Protected Income strategy that typically calls for immediate and deferred annuitization to support greater downside spending protection through contractually guaranteed lifetime income accompanied by a willingness to commit fully to a strategy that provides the utmost safety protection for retirement income.

We must understand that Probability-Based vs. Safety-First and Optionality vs. Commitment factors do not represent the entire spectrum of someone's income preferences. Though to a lesser extent, other factors are at play here. As shown in Exhibits 5.3 and 5.4, secondary factors like Technical Liquidity vs. True Liquidity, Front vs. Back-Loading, Time Based vs. Perpetuity, and Accumulation vs. Distribution Gauge are worth reviewing.

Exhibit 5.3

David & Dawn Banner's RISA Report

Secondary RISA® Factors

Technical Liquidity vs. True Liquidity

Technical   True

You have a strong liquidity preference for having assets set aside and earmarked for unexpected emergencies.

❚ I would rather set aside assets or cash for unplanned emergencies so as not to potentially disrupt future retirement spending needs.

These set aside accounts may include a combination of cash reserves, insurance coverage, home equity, and investments.

You strongly prefer not to co-mingle assets and you separately track assets meant for retirement income and those meant for emergencies. This helps ensure you can come up with cash for any spending shocks without causing an undue burden on your retirement income needs.

Front vs. Back-Loading

Front   Back

You have a strong preference for spending less early in retirement to avoid significant spending cuts as you age.

❚ I prefer to spend more during my later retirement years rather than having to make future spending reductions because I've overspent early in my retirement.

A more conservative lifestyle early in retirement leads to greater satisfaction because you can protect yourself from potential spending reductions later.

You prefer maintaining a lower standard of living early in retirement and are willing to increase it as you age if your assets increase.

You also don't want to be a potential burden to anyone because you overspent early in retirement.

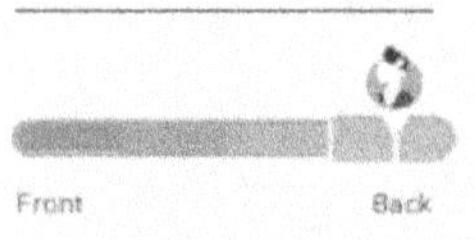

Source: RISA, LLC

Exhibit 5.4

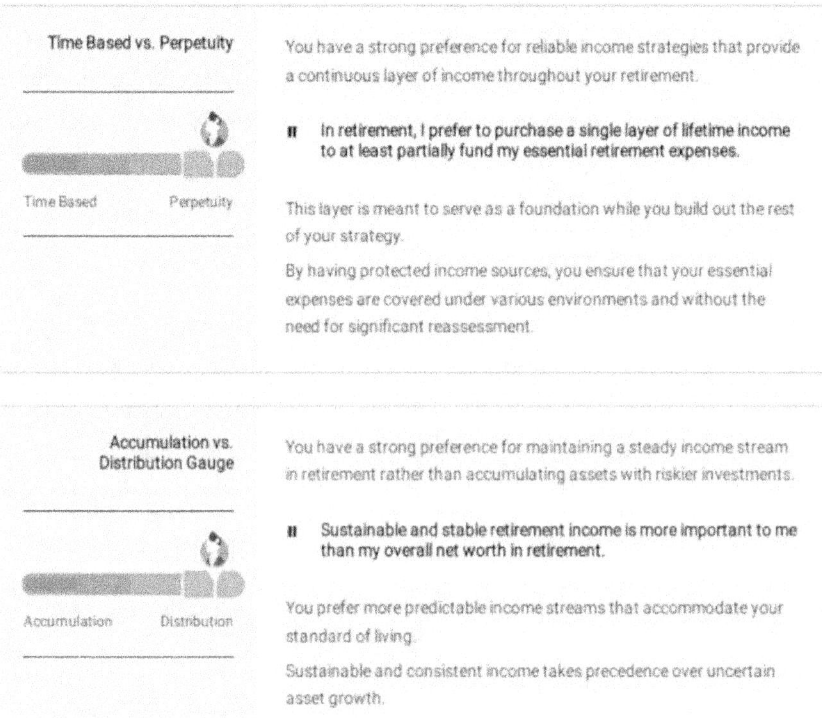

Source: RISA, LLC

These results illustrate the Banners' Safety-First & Commitment income style and a preference for maintaining **True Liquidity** by dedicating funding for emergency spending so as not to divert funds away from other spending needs.

Moreover, they are willing to reduce spending early in retirement by **Back-Loading** consumption to have more money to spend later to avoid having to make spending cutbacks. Additionally, they stressed a desire for an income strategy emphasizing the **Perpetuity** of income that provides a continuous layer of income throughout retirement.

Finally, they wish to focus on **Distribution** (sustainable and consistent) income over **Accumulation** (uncertain asset growth).

Besides identifying someone's retirement income preferences and corresponding retirement strategies tailored to their preferences, it will be important to consider their retirement concerns. People are most concerned about running out of money before running out of life. The longevity concern is particularly relevant in retirement since it can be largely ignored while working.

Planning for retirement while working is essential to reaching retirement savings milestones. The main determinant of a successful investment experience during accumulation is the asset allocation decision, and the investment discipline to seek steady returns that grow wealth without needing ongoing distributions because human capital (earnings), not investment capital, sustains spending.

It's only when human capital can no longer support living expenses that investment capital must be consumed. Longevity concerns become prominent and begin to influence retirement investment choices.

Having sufficient reserves to cover spending shocks without compromising longevity spending goals is also top of mind. A liquidity concern is the fear that unexpected expenses will materialize and cause funds to be diverted from their original purpose, undermining the ability to fund other spending goals. It's like robbing Peter to pay Paul. Again, this isn't a concern before retirement, as human capital can be used to cover unexpected expenses. But retirement changes the spending calculus since spending is constrained due to the loss of earned income. Savings may not be replenished because there are fewer funds to go around, and spending cutbacks may not be desirable.

In my experience working with many retirees, most are more concerned about running out of money (longevity) and maintaining reserves for unexpected expenses (liquidity) than funding non-essential spending (lifestyle) and passing assets to future generations (legacy).

In Exhibits 5.5 and 5.6, the Banners exhibit similar sentiments. Our planning will account for these concerns by ensuring that protected income sources cover their essential expenses and that sufficient reserves are established to finance the most probable spending shocks.

Exhibit 5.5

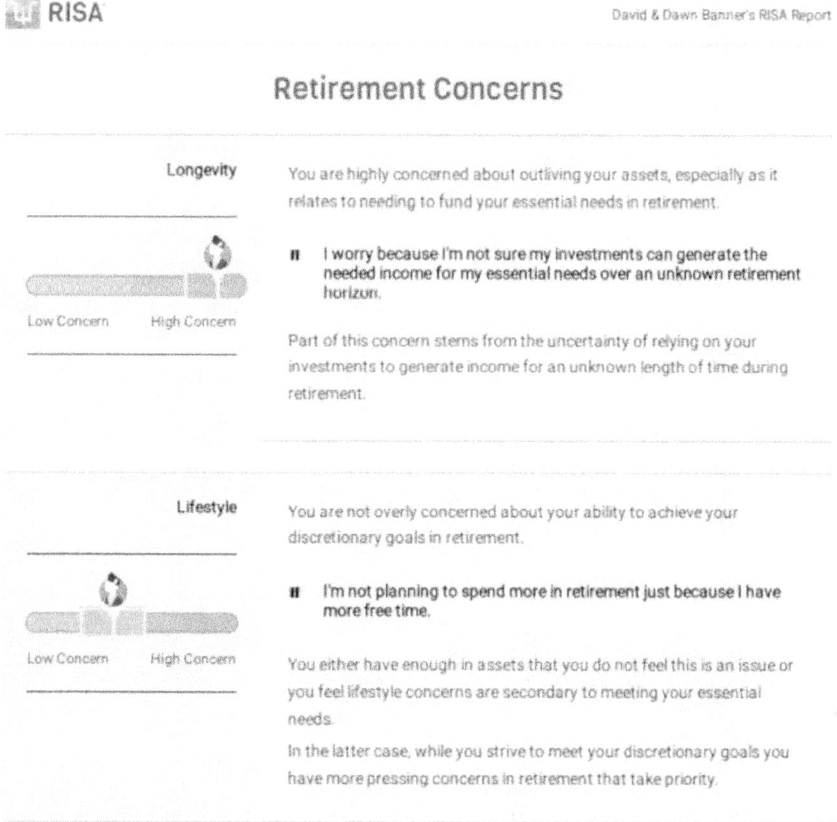

Source: RISA, LLC

Exhibit 5.6

Retirement Concerns (Continued)

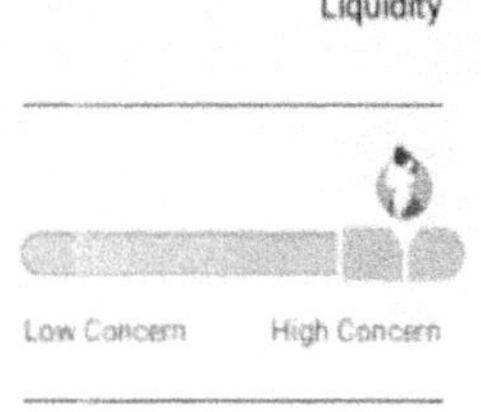

You are highly concerned about your ability to fund unexpected needs.

I need to have an emergency reserve throughout retirement to address unexpected spending shocks.

You want to be able to address unexpected spending shocks and healthcare needs without overly taxing your retirement income needs.

This greater concern also centers on a general uncertainty about impending unknown events.

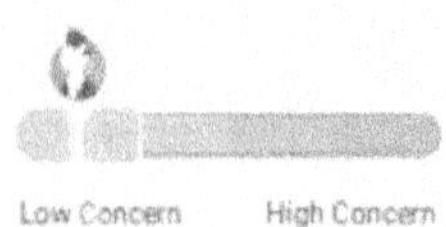

While nice if it happens, leaving behind a financial legacy for loved ones is not a concern.

Leaving something behind for my loved ones is something I would like, but it is not something I will actively try to do.

Besides assessing income preferences, the RISA informs decisions about income tools (income sources) necessary to implement the resulting income strategy (Exhibit 5.7). These recommendations will guide our selection of products to ensure David and Dawn's assets are utilized according to their income strategy. Because of their Safety-First & Commitment income style, we'll supplement existing protected income sources like their pension and Social Security with low-cost commercial income annuities to build secure income to support essential spending goals and address gaps in risk coverage.

Exhibit 5.7

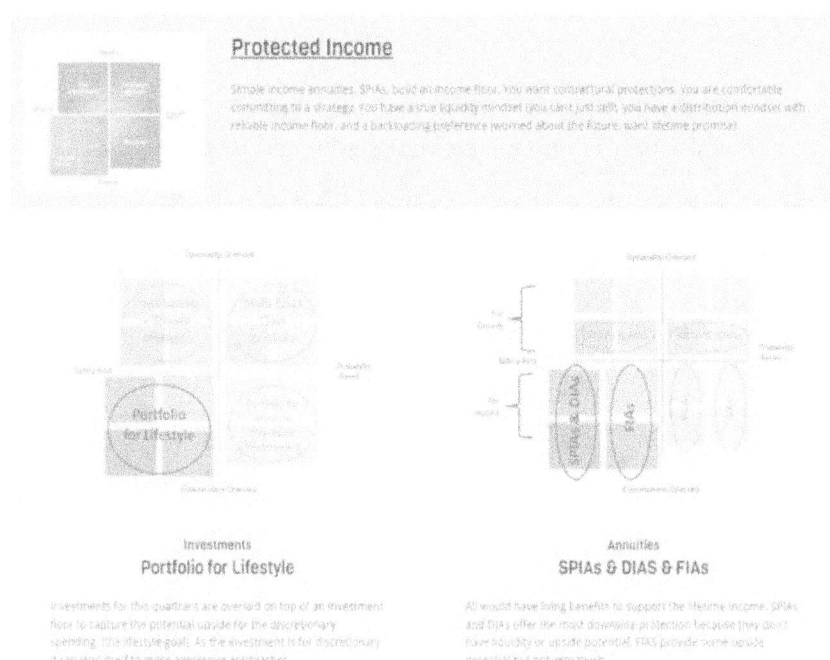

Source: RISA, LLC

WHAT THE BANNERS' RESULTS REVEAL

➢ A Protected Income Style best reflects their retirement income personality.

➢ Their income preferences inform a *Safety-First* orientation that aligns with an income strategy based on income sources with lifetime income guarantees.

➢ Their income preferences inform a *Commitment* orientation that aligns with an income strategy that solves for a lifetime income need.

➢ There is a preference for setting aside assets earmarked for unexpected expenses indicative of a preference for *True Liquidity*.

➢ There is a preference for spending less early in retirement to avoid making spending cutbacks later in retirement, indicative of a *Back-Loading* preference.

➢ There is a strong preference for maintaining a continuous income layer during retirement, reflecting a *Perpetuity* preference.

➢ They have a *Distribution* preference for stable retirement income over investment upside.

➢ Their most common retirement concerns are *Longevity* and *Liquidity*.

MARK'S KEY TAKEAWAYS

➢ Income preferences are extremely important for favorable retirement income outcomes.

➢ Personalized retirement income strategies rely on income preferences.

➢ Secondary income factors and considerations are equally important.

CHAPTER 6

Putting it All Together

"You do not rise to the level of your goals. You fall to the level of your systems."

— JAMES CLEAR

It's difficult to save poor early decisions with good late decisions. It's difficult to create reliable income with the wrong income strategy. It's difficult to create a resilient retirement without considering risks. It's difficult to spend if you haven't saved enough at the beginning. Certainly, things can be improved by making good decisions, but the effects of poor early decisions tend to linger. Better choices made later cannot save poor early decisions about income strategy, coping with risks, optimizing efficiencies, and managing taxes. Making good decisions early about the choices covered in chapters 1-5 can have a profound and lasting impact on your retirement.

The previous five chapters have illustrated how retirement income planning can be applied in a real-world situation. We have used it to help the Banners navigate the difficult transition from work life to retirement by finding answers to important questions of whether, when, and how to retire.

Because they were unsure how to find answers and much was at stake, they contacted us for help. We understood their dilemma and assured them we would help them find answers to the questions most impactful to their retirement. We assured them that these questions would be answered, along with others they had not considered, through our comprehensive retirement income planning process. This resonated with them, and they agreed to come on board for the journey.

Here's a recap of how we helped them move from retirement uncertainty to clarity using our 6-step retirement income planning process.

Assess Income Beliefs to Identify Income Preferences to Determine Income Strategy

Here's where it all begins. Knowing how you will draw income from your assets in retirement is the most important decision a soon-to-retire or newly retired must make. It's important because income matters more than wealth in retirement, and determining how to turn wealth into income according to one's personal preferences cannot be overlooked.

By exploring their beliefs and concerns through profiling their income beliefs, the Banners were able to gain a deeper understanding of their income preferences and the most appropriate income strategy to turn their assets into income to fund their retirement in a manner that was most meaningful to them. The Banners found the answer to one of their biggest questions: the how of retirement. After sorting out the "how" of retirement, we worked to help them determine the "if" and the "when" of retirement.

Quantify and Match Assets With Liabilities

Without knowing how much is available, it's difficult to estimate how much can be spent. For David and Dawn to know how much retirement will cost and what's available to pay for it, we must quantify their assets and liabilities. Assets are financial resources that can be used to pay for liabilities (spending goals).

By assessing their assets and estimating their liabilities, we helped the Banners identify the mix of resources available to cover anticipated retirement costs. We helped them see that even though retirement is fully funded, they were still underfunded with enough secure income to fund essential income needs. Our asset-liability matching analysis identified and found solutions to address gaps between secure income and essential spending needs.

The six-step retirement income planning process can help to lay the foundation for financial security in retirement.

Assess Retirement Preparedness

Those soon-to-retire or newly retired must determine if and when retirement is feasible. Understanding if retirement is possible and when it might occur will require evaluating costs relative to what's available to pay for those costs.

To help the Banners know if and when they could retire, we employed the Funded Ratio. This financial metric is used to gauge how well-prepared someone is for retirement based on their assets and liabilities today. Simply put, it calculates current assets by liabilities (or projected obligations). Using the funded ratio, it can be determined how well-prepared (the level of assets they have) someone is to meet their future spending obligations. A ratio of 100% means they have enough assets to cover all projected liabilities. Ratios under 100% indicate deficits and difficulty meeting liabilities, while a ratio greater than 100% indicates a surplus of assets over liabilities.

With a Funded Ratio above 100%, the Banners can cover all their projected liabilities with their assets. They have a surplus of assets relative to liabilities that offer a cushion should spending needs increase. It was a relief for Dawn and David to learn their saving and investment discipline had put them on track to retire comfortably on time. They now have the assurance that retirement is a reality and just need to decide how they want to spend their time!

Mitigate Risks, Maximize Efficiencies, and Manage Taxes

Almost all heavy lifting has been done. Having a clear idea of the ifs, whens, and hows of retirement makes the remaining tasks more manageable. While this is true, there are numerous challenges that hold the potential to undermine retirement security worth considering. The burden of taxes must be managed whether working or retired. Furthermore, it's more important than ever to make the best use of available resources now that earned income from work is less likely to be available to supplement spending.

Our assessment identified the risks most relevant to the Banners. It enabled us to develop strategies to avoid them altogether or mitigate them and save them untold heartache and additional costs. Reviewing their retirement plan revealed opportunities to optimize efficiency, resulting in an additional $939,308 in lifetime savings. And as part of our efforts to ensure that they were not paying more taxes than they were legally required to, we reviewed their financial situation and employed strategies that reduced their lifetime tax liabilities by $1,407,920. Spendable assets increased by nearly $2.5 million, ensuring a comfortable retirement lifestyle for all but those with the heftiest spending budgets.

Implementation

Now that we have laid the groundwork, we can begin developing a retirement income plan. This phase of the retirement income planning process centers on 1) implementing the identified income strategy and 2) putting in place risk mitigation, tax management, and efficiency optimization strategies.

We will circle back to the results from David and Dawn's Retirement Income Style Awareness Overview report, as it not only determines which strategy is appropriate but also identifies the appropriate products to implement the strategy. After selecting the appropriate products, we'll incorporate them into the retirement income plan and analyze them to ensure they meet expectations.

We will then layer on various strategies to tackle the risks that threaten spending goals, the tax liabilities that can erode assets, and the efficiencies that enhance spending potential and legacy value.

Review & Revise

The process of planning out your financial moves over a multi-decade retirement is not a one-time event. Over time you'll need to update your plan, make course corrections, and recalibrate your expectations based on what life throws your way. Sadly, this process is never going to be easy. The good news is it's okay if you don't have it all figured out just yet. No one else does either.

Our comprehensive planning efforts have enabled us to build a retirement income plan using strategies, solutions, and techniques to ensure David and Dawn have a successful transition into and through retirement. But we'll need to regularly monitor their retirement plan to ensure it continues to reflect the realities of their current situation and the broader economic climate. To accomplish this, we will use our Retirement Prosperity Index (Exhibit 6.0) to quantify key metrics of retirement that have the greatest impact on the outcome of David and Dawn's retirement. Only through vigilant monitoring of these metrics, where higher scores indicate greater strength and lower scores indicate greater weakness, and swift proactive action can we ensure they are in the best position possible to achieve desirable retirement outcomes.

Exhibit 6.0 Retirement Prosperity Index

INDICES	SATISFACTORY	DEFICIENT	HIGH	MODERATE	LOW
ASSET PROTECTION	✓				
DEBT					✓
EFFICIENCY			✓		
ESTATE			✓		
GOALS	✓				
SPENDING	✓				
LIQUIDITY				✓	
RESILENCY			✓		
TAX					✓
THREATS				✓	

That's a brief overview of the retirement income planning process we use with clients. It was our aim to illustrate how the retirement income planning process can help:

1. Assess income beliefs, identify income preferences, discern income style, and determine an appropriate income strategy.

2. Establish spending goals and gather data.

3. Determine whether retirement is on track based on the income needed to support the desired lifestyle.

4. If retirement is not on track, embrace modification to make it realistic.

5. Address retirement risks, manage taxes, and maximize efficiencies.

6. Implement a strategy for converting assets into income and incorporate strategies from item 5.

7. Put all the pieces together to build a plan that considers alternatives that address the most important concerns.

8. Review and revise over time to ensure planning remains effective and responsive to changing circumstances.

9. Demonstrate how assessing and accounting for income preferences is an effective way to ensure alignment with income preferences and strategy.

The chart in Exhibit 6.1 is a breakdown of the 6 steps in our retirement income planning process:

Exhibit 6.1

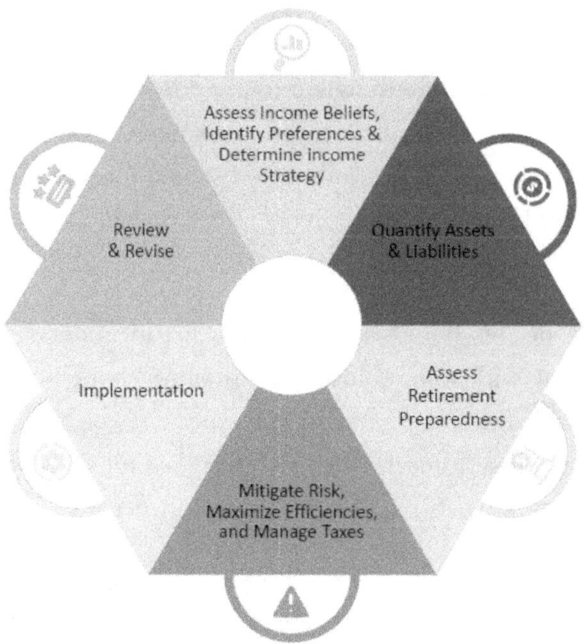

To achieve a desired retirement outcome, you must plan for it purposefully. In the lead-up to retirement, you can't drift aimlessly and then see what kind of retirement you'll enjoy later. To achieve the retirement you want, you must decide early on. Putting your retirement within reach requires deep reflection, intentional action, reasonable expectations, and higher thinking.

You must plan, execute, and follow through on each to reach a fulfilling and satisfying retirement. If you're not periodically reviewing your retirement income plan, retirement will quickly morph into something you don't want.

Don't worry about getting it right all the time—just fix the fundamentals, like knowing how you want to source income for retirement, spending within your budget, paying for unexpected expenses, and managing taxes, since focusing on these things will be your passport to a better retirement.

Next Steps

The previous chapters were designed to provide readers with knowledge, information, and insight on how to use their financial resources to fund retirement spending. No one would believe me if I said doing this would be easy. It's not. Learning and applying all you need to know takes much more than can be contained in this brief work.

However, I hope this book will give you a broad understanding of the challenges, along with some solutions, without overwhelming you. It will be more difficult for some and less for others. If you feel you have an excellent handle on accomplishing this, great! But for those less confident in their ability to move forward, we can certainly help.

If you're looking for a financial services partner to help you transition from work to retirement, these three questions will help you determine whether we would be a good fit for you.

ARE WE RIGHT FOR EACH OTHER?

Our proposition is simple: help those who are 5 years on either side of retirement to determine how to use their financial resources accumulated before retirement to fund spending in retirement. If you are someone looking for the best means to turn your assets into income while mitigating risks, managing taxes, and maximizing efficiencies to do more with what's available, a partnership with us may be right for you.

We view retirement success as different from investment success. Having the income to spend in retirement when you need or want to spend it is our definition of a successful venture with you. It is less important to get the best investment return than it is to get the return you need to ensure predictable and reliable income to fund your spending.

It is the achievement of this goal by which we measure your success, and by extension ours. Because of this emphasis on stable income over net worth, investments are not the focus, and as a result, the size of your portfolio matters less than the stability of your retirement paycheck.

We offer our services on a flat fee annual retainer, where every client, depending on partnership status, pays the same price regardless of the size of their assets. If you are interested in partnering with a financial service firm that helps you generate steady and reliable income regardless of the size of your portfolio, we may be a good fit.

WHAT SERVICES DO YOU PROVIDE?

Our services are centered on three core competencies to help clients

1. Transition from accumulating assets to decumulating assets

2. Bridge the gap between your financial resources and your retirement

3. Create the highest after-tax income from all income sources

WHAT TYPES OF CLIENTS WOULD BENEFIT MOST FROM OUR SERVICES?

We serve middle- and upper-income households across the country and even abroad, if willing to work on a virtual basis. Each year, we'll conduct 3-4 meetings where we meet online to implement the 6-step planning process outlined in Exhibit 6.1.

If you're looking to generate predictable and reliable income from your assets in a tax-efficient manner and are comfortable doing so virtually, our services could be a good fit.

WHAT CAN PROSPECTS EXPECT IF THEY CALL OR EMAIL?

Everybody loves to buy, but nobody loves to be sold. Perhaps you're afraid of getting trapped in a sales funnel that you'll never escape by giving up your email or phone number. You may be worried that you will receive repeated calls or emails from a high-pressure salesperson. I get it. No one dislikes pushy and intrusive sales calls or emails more than me. Let me instead share with you what you can expect if you decide to contact us.

First, I will conduct a 20-minute intake interview with you by phone. If it seems like an ideal fit, we will schedule a Zoom meeting to decide whether we are a suitable match. It's that simple. If we're not a good match, we'll thank you for your time and let you get back to your life. If we are a good match, we'll get the ball rolling right away.

MARK'S KEY TAKEAWAYS

➢ An income planning framework such as the 6-step retirement income planning process makes retirement income planning easier.

➢ Know your abilities and seek assistance when you need it.

Parting Thoughts

A hearty congratulations. You have done the all-important work of learning how to develop a successful retirement income plan. This book is written to help you understand and appreciate the value of comprehensive retirement income planning and the transformation needed from an individual decision framework to the comprehensive planning mindset you must adopt when planning retirement income. I offer you the following items I think are important to consider as you embark on this journey, framed as my professional manifesto.

Big and Small Things Matter

What's more important and doable for most is to make sure you nail the big stuff, make course corrections as necessary, plan for the worst, and hope for the best. When working with clients and prospective clients, I'm constantly reminded how many fall short here.

The big stuff is ultimately deciding how you will draw income from your assets in retirement, the amount and duration of your spending, keeping taxes in check, protecting yourself from potential risks, and making the most of what you have.

You don't need to read the tea leaves or look into a crystal ball to predict what will happen if you don't properly prepare for how to spend in retirement. The wrong income strategy can reduce spending potential, diminish assets, increase stress, and lower quality of life. Decisions have consequences.

Because your income, not your wealth, matters in retirement, it is critical to determine what you have to spend and what you have available to spend. You must also be aware of the risks you're likely to face and devise a management plan so that they won't compromise your retirement security and lifestyle. We must give taxes the respect they deserve since they follow us from the cradle to the grave. The finite nature of resources forces us to make the most of what we have.

Taking care of the little things is as important as the big ones. It is so important to consider retirement from a big-picture perspective. But that doesn't mean putting aside the little things, like deciding when the best time to retire, where is the best place to live, and what is the best way to integrate your retirement income plan with your estate planning goals. Small things matter when they accumulate. This is one of the main lessons of my work—and one of the principles I try to follow in my life. When finely polished and carefully combined, small actions compound over time to big achievements. It is better to have 50% of twenty dollars than 100% of one dollar.

Success is Not Linear

Imagining what life would be like at 60 was probably difficult when you were still in high school. It is just as challenging to anticipate what life will hold for us in the last decades of our lives as we prepare for retirement in our 60s.

One of our greatest traits is our ability to adapt. Our innate ability to adjust to changing circumstances, to make changes, and to flex and flow with the inevitable things life will throw our way is just as important in retirement as it was before. Things like estimating how long we will live, predicting what the markets will do, anticipating inflation, dealing with geopolitical events, navigating climate change, managing pandemics, and all the other things lurking around the corner will require an adaption mindset. Put yourself in the right position from a direction standpoint and adjust accordingly.

It Takes Commitment

An ongoing commitment is needed. Your retirement income plan will only be as strong as your resolve to maintain it. No matter how many books or blog posts you read, how many people you talk with, or what videos you watch, you will not get it all right with retirement. Most things will work most of the time, but some just won't. Some expectations will be met, others will not. There is just too much to plan for, around something we have little to no first-hand experience doing, over a potentially lengthy and unknown period of time for us just to ignore it.

The road to retirement is full of ups and downs. You will make mistakes, but no one mistake will sink retirement. The first mistake is never the one that ruins things. It's the spiral of repeated mistakes that follows. These, on a cumulative basis, like inaction, investment behavior, neglected risks, excessive taxes, using assets inefficiently, underestimated income needs, following the wrong income strategy, and obscure goals, will largely determine the outcome of your retirement more than any single one alone.

Having a successful retirement is a choice. You have to decide you want it, not let it happen to you. It is not a result but a choice you make. You can only achieve that by taking intentional and concerted action. Security and happiness depend partly on having sufficient income and replacing work with activities and roles that bring meaning and fulfillment.

Cultivation is Required

Your retirement progress depends on how productive you are in preparing for retirement. Taking the right steps is crucial. Whether doing the wrong thing correctly or the right thing incorrectly, both result in undesirable outcomes.

Being intentional in preparation and striving for meaningful productivity is paramount to creating a retirement that matches expectations. Examining your preparation carefully is the key to discovering and eliminating bad habits before they become internalized and detrimental to retirement. No one stumbles into a fulfilling retirement. Developing a plan, reflecting upon it, and reviewing it are essential. It must be nurtured.

Trust in the Process

When there is no process in place, or the process is wrong, it becomes immeasurably more difficult. Planning retirement is not something to be attempted in a piecemeal manner. Decisions that, on the surface, appear unrelated are inextricably linked. Taxes impact every retirement planning action. Every retirement planning action impacts taxes. Investments, no matter the retirement income strategy, are impacted by taxes. There is very little that is not interconnected in retirement income planning. Everything impacts just about everything else. Don't miss the forest for the trees.

A methodical approach to retirement income planning can be invaluable here since 1) it can identify the right income strategy to ensure you understand how you will pay yourself in retirement, to reassure you how it will achieve spending goals, and to help you stay the course when things don't go as planned, 2) strike a balance between meeting retirement goals while managing the risks confronting those goals, 3) leverage synergies to sustain assets and increase spending potential, and 4) tailor a solution to meet your needs.

Avoid Compounding Mistakes

Mistakes are inevitable, but they don't have to compound. You lose twice if you follow up an error with a foolish reaction. While a wise response may not erase a foolish mistake, it can redeem it.

Turn Weaknesses into Strengths

Work on what's the most challenging for you. A retirement plan is only as strong as its weakest components. Fortifying your weaknesses will serve you better than refining your strengths.

Run Your Own Race

You already know that retirement income plans are as individual as people themselves. The right retirement income plan is the one that optimizes the balance between meeting spending goals and the risks confronting those goals in a manner that is suited to your personality and financial situation. You cannot base your planning on what has or hasn't worked for others. Depending on your circumstances and financial situation, solutions inappropriate for someone else may suit you, while those suitable for others should be avoided. Spend time understanding your situation from top to bottom, identifying your retirement goals, focusing on what makes your situation unique, and ignoring the noise.

Don't be Intimidated by the Task

We all know planning for retirement isn't easy, but let's face it: you aren't trying to land on the Moon. The process of moving from accumulating assets to successfully drawing them down does not happen overnight, but it is absolutely possible. It will take time and be made immeasurably easier if you apply the things discussed in this book. For some it will be enough to use the information here, while others may need to seek outside assistance. Help is often sought least by those who need it the most. It's in your best interests and that of your retirement to seek help when you realize you're in over your head. For the Do-It-Yourself (DIY) types, we invite you to join our Facebook user group How To Pay Yourself In Retirement, for weekly thought leadership, helpful resources, and the chance to engage with other like-minded individuals. For those in need of more hands-on assistance, we offer a complete range of services.

It's More Than Numbers

Retirees need to consider all the financial aspects of retirement, but retirement planning goes beyond the numbers.

Retirement has changed. It's no longer about getting your gold watch and passing afternoons at the country club sipping margaritas, although if that's in the cards for you, do enjoy it! Retirement is a frame of mind. A time when you can do what you want. It doesn't necessarily have anything to do with whether you are drawing a paycheck. Retirement is the freedom to decide what you want to do. At the same time, retirement has also gotten longer. You could be looking at a retirement that lasts 30 years or more, making retirement planning more complex than it used to be.

You must sit down and spend some time deciding what retirement means. What would you like to do if you didn't need to worry about anything? For some, it's leaving work as soon as possible, taking vacations, and spending time with those important to them. For others, it's a continuation of what they are already doing. Most are somewhere in the middle. There is no platonic ideal of "Retirement"; it's whatever you want to make it.

Don't forget to consider what your partner wants, especially if they have not had a career outside the home. When a partner stays home, they often have different ideas of what retirement means, so ensure you're on the same page.

Your retirement will change over time. Most people reading this book are probably considering 30 years of retirement at a minimum, so your definition of retirement will likely change. You'll find new interests and lose old ones, and your health will change. You weren't the same person at 50 as you were at 20, so why would you be the same person at the beginning of retirement as at the end?

Retirement is complicated. There is no one-size-fits-all plan; everyone wants something different, and your retirement income plan needs to support that. Figure out where you stand today and where you want to be, and then put in a retirement income plan to ensure you get there.

Don't Lose Perspective

Retirement is at once a finish line and a starting point. It isn't like crossing some magical threshold that makes all the challenges, issues, and problems of the past disappear. The transition will bring difficulties, obstacles, and struggles that you haven't faced before. I believe most retirees will face two major challenges.

First, a constrained income because they can no longer rely on employment income and must draw income from other assets to cover living expenses over an unknown time. Some will find this a monumental shift. The task will be challenging. Make sure you're prepared for it.

Second, there will be a dramatic change in risks when you retire. New ones will emerge, and old ones will take on greater meaning. Investing risk will change as the preservation of assets becomes more important than the growth of assets. Market declines before retirement could be weathered by riding them out, increasing savings, or taking on greater risks. Now, riding it out isn't an option since you'll need to spend those assets instead of your paycheck. You are unable to increase your savings because you no longer work. Taking on greater risk could create more problems than it solves.

When retired, there is no longer the opportunity to offset inflation through measures like pay increases. In addition, the employer's burden of funding healthcare shifts to you when you stop working.

The key to maintaining perspective is not losing sight of what matters. When the market is bouncing around, should it concern you if your spending is coming from assets that are immune to market turmoil? How important is it if inflation spikes but the goods and services you use are unaffected? Are tax increases something to worry about if your income is structured in a way that minimizes tax liabilities? The answer, in most cases, is no. Injecting realism into and maintaining an objective view about retirement is important.

It's a long game in which the journey—how you experience it— matters more than the destination. Just because you've retired, the rules of life won't radically change in your favor. Things that were out of your control before you retired will continue in retirement. It's important to accept things as they come and to be realistic about expectations. You won't always get what you strive for, but you will definitely get what you settle for. You won't magically outperform your standards.

Ultimately, it is about staying focused, having a clear vision, trusting in the process, embracing change, being realistic, staying positive, and persevering.

It's a Daily Practice

Retirement Income Planning is not a one-time event, but an ongoing process of reevaluation in response to changing circumstances.

Retirement is About Faith and Numbers

We prove constantly, over and over again, that we cannot predict the future accurately. Neither I nor anyone else can tell you what the future holds. Still, I will say this: if you make the effort to learn your income strategy, determine the costs of retirement and what you have to pay for them, maximize efficiency, mitigate the risks, and manage taxes, you will be well on your way to achieving a retirement that your future self with thank you for.

You Must Let Go at Some Point

Retirement brings a multitude of obligations, expectations, desires, and worries that will always be ready to insert themselves between you and the feeling of peace. You will never have enough if you never let them go and allow things to unfold as they inevitably must.

May you and your retirement be well, happy and peaceful.

~ MARK

Index

References

Chapter 1

Pfau, Murguia, "Retirement Income Beliefs And How They Impact Investment Behavior and Retirement Outcomes", Vienna, VA: Retirement Researcher, 2021, <u>Retirement Income Beliefs And How They Impact Investment Behavior and Retirement Outcomes</u>

Pfau, Murguia, "A Model Approach to Selecting a Personalized Retirement Income Strategy.", Vienna, VA: Retirement Researcher, 2021, <u>A Model Approach to Selecting a Personalized Retirement Income Strategy</u>

Kitces.com, Pfau, Murguia, "The RISA Framework: A Systematized Approach To Personalizing Retirement Income Strategies For Clients.", Vienna, VA: Retirement Researcher, 2022 <u>The RISA Framework: A Systematized Approach To Personalizing Retirement Income Strategies For Clients</u>

Chapter 2

Pfau, Murguia, "How to Identify Your Retirement Income Beliefs." Vienna, VA: Retirement Researcher, 2022, <u>How to Identify Your Retirement Income Beliefs</u>

Branningon, Grubbs, "Crafting Retirement Income That Is Stable, Secure, and Sustainable.", Journal of Financial Planning, 2017, <u>Crafting Retirement Income That Is Stable, Secure, and Sustainable</u>

Pfau, Murguia, "How the Retirement Income Style Awareness (RISA®) Informs Retirement Income Recommendations.", Vienna, VA: Retirement Researcher, 2022, <u>How the Retirement Income Style Awareness (RISA®) Informs Retirement Income Recommendations</u>

Chapter 3

McCleod, Saul, "Maslow's Hierarchy Of Needs." Simply Psychology, 2023, <u>Maslow's Hierarchy Of Needs</u>

French, Robert, "How Much Income Do I Need in Retirement?", Vienna, VA: Retirement Researcher, 2010, <u>How Much Income Do I Need in Retirement?</u>

Blanchett, David (2015). "Estimating the True Cost of Retirement?", Vienna, VA: Retirement Researcher, 2015, Estimating the True Cost of Retirement?

Hebner, Mark, "<u>The Funded Ratio: An Actuarial Approach to Retirement Spending</u>."

Index Fund Advisors, 2019, <u>The Funded Ratio: An Actuarial Approach to Retirement Spending</u>

Sharp, Mark, "How to Make a Retirement Budget." MarkSharpRetirement.com, 2022, <u>How to Make a Retirement Budget</u>

Chapter 4

Littell, Hopkins, Pfau, "Retirement Income Process, Strategies, and Solutions" Bryn Mawr, PA: The American College Press, 2018.

Pfau, Wade, "Retirement Planning Guidebook", McLean, VA: Retirement Researcher Media, 2021.

Pfau, Wade, "Reverse Mortgages: How to Use Reverse Mortgages to Secure Retirement Income", McLean, VA: Retirement Researcher Media, 2018.

Pfau, Wade, "How Much Can I Spend in Retirement?", McLean, VA: Retirement Researcher Media, 2017.

Sacks, Sacks, "Reversing the Conventional Wisdom: Using Home Equity to Supplement Retirement Income" Financial Planning Association, 2022, Reversing the Conventional Wisdom: Using Home Equity to Supplement Retirement Income

Munnell, Wettstein, and Hou. 2019. "How Best to Annuitize Defined Contribution Assets?" Working Paper 2019-13. Chestnut Hill, MA: Center for Retirement Research at Boston College. How Best to Annuitize Defined Contribution Assets?

Sanzenbacher, Rutledge, 2019. "What Financial Risks Do Retirees Face In Late Life?" Chestnut Hill, MA: Center for Retirement Research at Boston College. What Financial Risks Do Retirees Face In Late Life?

Ballenger, Branden, "12 Types of Retirement Income That Are Not Taxable" Financial Planning Association, 2023, 12 Types of Retirement Income That Are Not Taxable

Chapter 5

Pfau, Murguia (2021). "How to Select a Retirement Income Strategy that is Right For You.", Vienna, VA: Retirement Researcher, 2022, How to Select a Retirement Income Strategy that is Right For You

Resources

A number of resources are presented in this book's chapters that can help retirees better prepare for retirement. Below is a complete list by chapter.

Chapter 2

- ➤ RISA Profile tool at this link RISA Profile tool (without cost)

Chapter 3

- ➤ American Academy of Actuaries and the Society of Actuaries Longevity Illustrator available at www.longevityillustrator.org

- ➤ Retirement Hierarchy of Needs income worksheets available at Mark Sharp Retirement

- ➤ Calculate retirement income needs online at Alliance for Lifetime Income

- ➤ Multi-year funded ratio calculator available at Oblivious Investor

Chapter 4

- ➤ Living to 100 longevity calculator available at Livingto100.com

- ➤ The Social Security Life Expectancy available at Social Security Administration

> Inflation calculator available at Kitces.com

> The Cost of Long-Term Care Survey available at Genworth
> Immediate Annuity Pricing available at ImmediateAnnuities.com

> Nuveen Bond Ladder calculator available at Nuveen.com

> Facebook User Group How to Pay Yourself In Retirement

Meet Mark Sharp

Mark Sharp is passionate about helping people achieve their retirement goals and enjoy their post-work lives. In pursuit of that passion, he is a certified financial planner, retirement income strategist, and author. He is the founder and owner of Mark Sharp Retirement, a fee-only financial service firm that helps soon-to-retire and newly retired individuals make the best use of their resources in retirement. Mark has extensive experience and credentials in retirement income planning, tax advisory, and wealth management.

Mark lives in the Pacific Northwest. He loves traveling the world, learning new languages, playing the flamenco guitar, and cooking international cuisine. As a fitness enthusiast, he also enjoys amateur piloting, as well as eating healthy foods. Mark firmly believes retirement is not the end of a journey but the beginning of a new one. He wants to inspire his readers to plan for retirement income comprehensively and confidently. He hopes his book will provide readers with the tools and insights they need to make informed choices about how to draw income from their resources to fund spending goals that make sense to them.

Connect with Mark Sharp Retirement:
www.marksharpretirement.com
info@marksharpretirement.com
800.622.1045